IMAGES
of America

Iowa's WHO Radio
The Voice of the Middle West

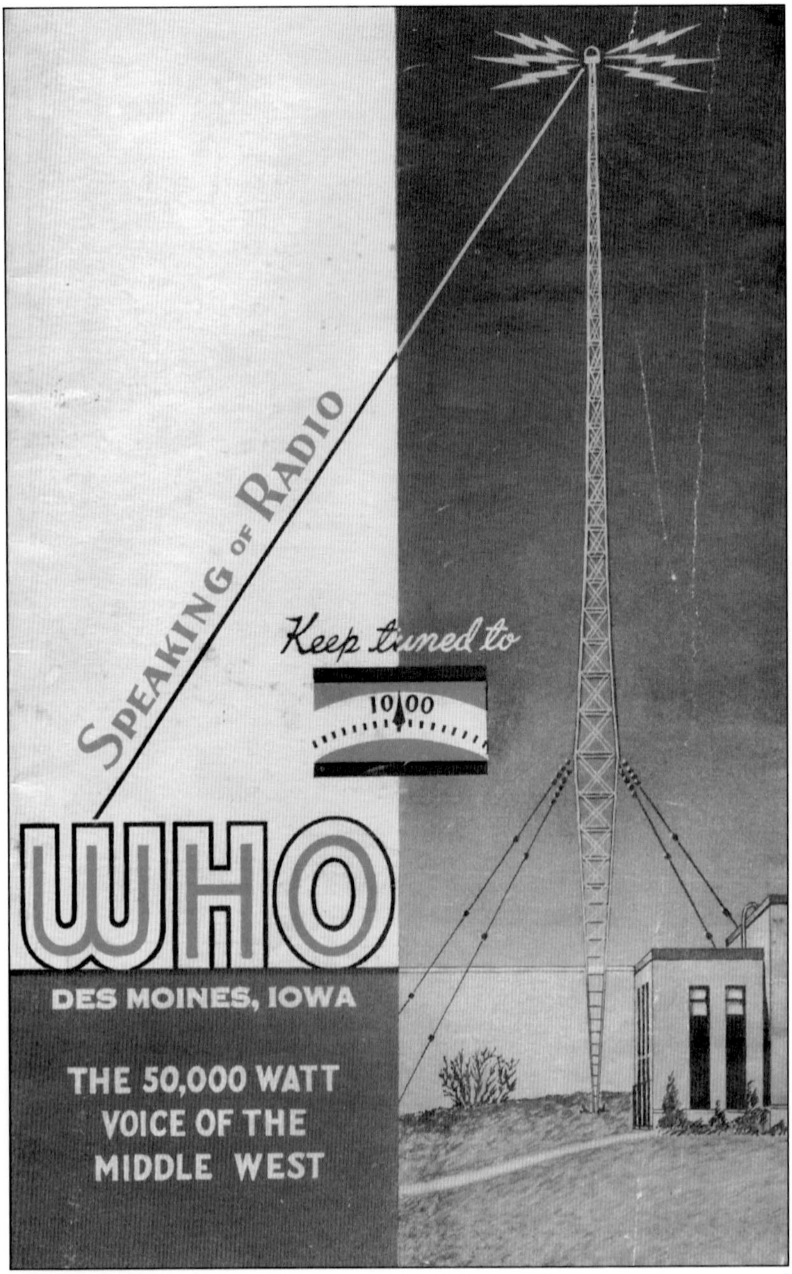

This 1939 brochure for WHO Radio promotes the station's large signal to potential advertisers by featuring the station's tower and transmitter site near Mitchellville on the cover. The slogan, "Voice of the Middle West," has been used by the station consistently through virtually all of its history since it was upgraded to the maximum power allowed by the federal government in 1933. (Archives of Iowa Broadcasting.)

On the Cover: The unique lighted neon sign on the front of the building at 914 Walnut Street marked the home of WHO Radio from 1932 to 1954, when the addition of television led to the creation of a new combined radio and television facility two blocks away in downtown Des Moines. (Archives of Iowa Broadcasting.)

IMAGES
of America

Iowa's WHO Radio

The Voice of the Middle West

Jeff Stein

ARCADIA
PUBLISHING

ISBN 978-0-7385-7630-5

Published by Arcadia Publishing
Charleston, South Carolina

Printed in the United States of America

Library of Congress Control Number: 2011924506

For all general information, please contact Arcadia Publishing:
Telephone 843-853-2070
Fax 843-853-0044
E-mail sales@arcadiapublishing.com
For customer service and orders:
Toll-Free 1-888-313-2665

Visit us on the Internet at www.arcadiapublishing.com

To the memory of Jack Shelley (1912–2010), whose work informed thousands of residents and whose example continues to inspire generations of journalists.

To the devotion of Jim Zabel (1922–), whose spirit infected thousands of Iowa sports fans and whose work on-air continues to make us hug and kiss our radios.

Contents

FOREWORD

"There's just something special about Iowa." I suppose people all over the country say something similar about their state, but I've never heard it more frequently and passionately than from Iowans. They can just "feel it," as do I. One of the very special things found in Iowa is WHO Radio. There are hundreds of radio stations across the nation, yet as Jeff Stein so artfully demonstrates in this book, the entity known as WHO Radio is far beyond transmitters, microphones, music, and the rest of the things people think of when they think of a radio station.

As a little boy growing up in Adel, Iowa, I listened to WHO Radio, and in all honesty it was not by choice, at least at first. WHO was the lifeline of news, weather, and companionship for my parents. Like so many others, I learned there were certain times I needed to remain silent because of my parents' scheduled listening to WHO. I now remember thinking to myself as I listened, "Why are they [WHO] doing that? Why aren't they doing this?" I never dreamed some day I'd be making some of those decisions.

Before I knew it, WHO Radio had captured me, as it has so many others. Don Warren and his 6:45 a.m. playing of "Reveille" became an important part of my life, as did Roy Fox with his *Fox's Den* in the afternoon and *Clear Channel Conversation* in the evening. We all felt as though we knew these people. They were our friends, and they gave me a dream of wanting to be a broadcaster too.

Today, many—perhaps most—local radio stations have abandoned community. Many have dumped local news staffs, gone to all-music formats, or decided to carry programs originating in other states to cut costs. That's not radio; that's filling airtime. WHO Radio had a commitment to community nearly 90 years ago, and we still do today. It is a true breath of fresh air to work for a station with such a commitment. What a tremendous service Jeff Stein does for us in this amazing book, giving us not only memories, but reminding us that the local news and companionship continues to flow from the 50,000-watt clear channel voice of the Middle West, WHO, Des Moines!

—Van Harden
program director and morning cohost, WHO Radio

ACKNOWLEDGMENTS

The author thanks all those at WHO Radio for their cooperation in providing support and many of the materials used in the preparation of this book. Particular thanks go to Joel McCrea, Van Harden, and Steve Parrott for their cooperation on this project and so many others like it—and for preserving the spirit of public service that has been a hallmark of WHO Radio for nearly 90 years.

Many thanks also go to those who have supported the Archives of Iowa Broadcasting—including the members of our national advisory board, Wartburg College, the Iowa Broadcasters Association, and the R.J. McElroy Trust—since my mentor, the late Grant Price, and I cofounded the entity more than a decade ago.

Great appreciation is expressed to the staff of Arcadia Publishing, not only for supporting this project but for production of the entire Images of America series as an important contribution to preserving history in our country. Special thanks to my editors—first, Ted Gerstle for receiving the project, and then Winnie Rodgers for her helpful advice and patience—and to publisher Joe Walker. Arcadia has generously agreed to donate a portion of the proceeds from this book to preserving Iowa broadcasting history, for which I am personally grateful.

Most significantly, to my wife, Carole Lackey, for her unfailing support, and tireless efforts connected with the broadcasting archives.

All photographs came from the WHO Radio collection, via the Archives of Iowa Broadcasting, and are protected by appropriate copyright laws. Permission for their use was granted to the author by WHO Radio.

Introduction

WHO Radio is synonymous with Iowa itself. Despite a powerhouse signal that literally reaches "from coast to coast, border to border, and then some," the station still preserves the sound and feel of daily life in our unique Midwestern state.

On a typical day, a WHO listener might hear a discussion of the latest political topics, learn about current agricultural practices, call in and pose parenting and lifestyle questions, follow play-by-play action of Iowa Hawkeye athletics, and be roundly entertained by familiar on-air personalities who talk about their daily lives in the large city where they work and the small town where they live.

In short, a typical day in the life of an Iowan.

As a boy growing up in a small town in central Iowa, like thousands of others, our kitchen radio was tuned each morning to WHO for the proper balance of news, information, and laughter to guide us into our day. When you needed to know something, whether it was a school cancellation, the high school football scores, or severe weather warnings, you simply tuned in to WHO Radio as *the* trusted source.

It was the case then and is still the case today.

Many Iowa stations still provide a great local community service, but WHO Radio is unique in that its signal blankets Iowa and surrounding states and brings a touch of home to native Iowans who move away. In the days before the Internet and cable television, a friend who moved to North Carolina told me he stood outside his home with a transistor radio late on Saturday nights to hear the replay of Jim Zabel's broadcast of Hawkeye football games because it made him less homesick. Others who drive back for a visit reach for their car radio dials while still hundreds of miles away, as soon as they can pick up the station's powerful signal clearly.

Few people can hear a set of call letters and know where the station is from, but 1040 WHO is one such station.

No book can convey the full story of such an important part of our lives, and I apologize for not including everyone you may remember hearing on the radio. My hope, however, is that this will bring back wonderful memories and put context to one of our state's great cultural resources. It is a privilege to share the story of WHO with you.

—Jeff Stein
administrator, Archives of Iowa Broadcasting

One

The Promise of Radio

It may surprise people to learn that one of the most powerful and influential radio stations in America was actually founded by an insurance company as a way to get its name out to the public.

It was somewhat common for a company to start a radio station as a way to help sell its products. Many local electric companies operated radio stations to hasten the spread of electricity into rural areas. The famous seed men, Earl May and Henry Field, used their respective radio stations in the small town of Shenandoah, Iowa, as promotional vehicles for their garden products. And of course, nationally, the Radio Corporation of America (RCA) founded NBC as yet another programming source to justify a customer's purchase of the radios RCA produced.

So when the Bankers Life Insurance Company founded a Des Moines radio station in April 1924, it was another way for the company to reach out to customers. The station-break announcement, "This is W-H-O. Who? Bankers Life, Des Moines," was a not-so-subtle reference to the station owner.

But Bankers Life president George Kuhns was also interested in public service. A popular proposal to help farmers in the 1930s was to promote the use of corn sugar rather than cane sugar. Kuhns once offered a pound of corn sugar to each listener of the *Little Jack Little* program; more than 100,000 listeners responded, giving testimony to the power of radio.

One print article at the time of the station's maiden broadcast described the studios in great detail for an audience still not accustomed to this new invention called radio:

> The reception room and studio of the new station are luxuriously appointed, the latter room being as near sound-proof as it is possible to make it. The walls are deadened with heavy velour curtains of old rose shade, the entrance being curtained with the same material. Heavily padded carpet eliminates vibration of footsteps. . . . Colored lights flash "all ready," "quiet," and other operating conditions.

But by the end of the 1920s, Bankers Life had lost $600,000 operating WHO and opted to sell to the Central Broadcasting Company, controlled by Col. B.J. Palmer, who operated WOC Radio in Davenport. It was then that the fortunes of WHO Radio would forever change.

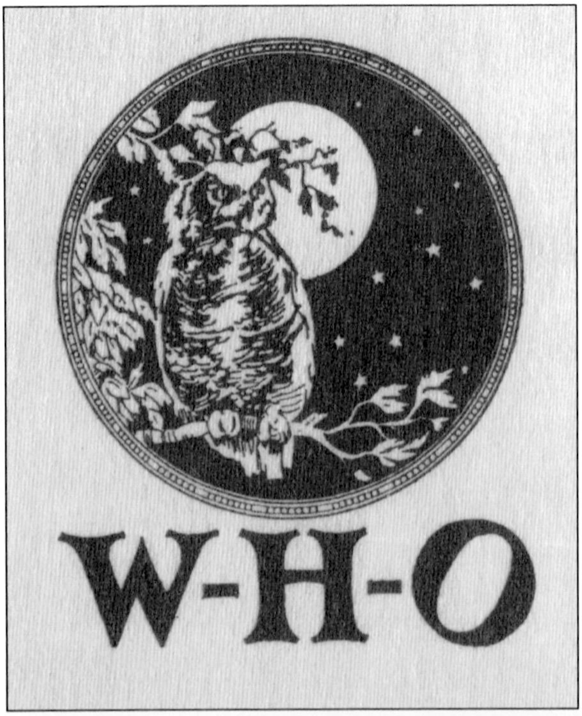

The first logo representing the new radio station came within a few weeks of its first broadcast on April 10, 1924. This owl logo was trademarked with the federal government on July 1, 1924. A variation of an owl has represented WHO Radio virtually ever since.

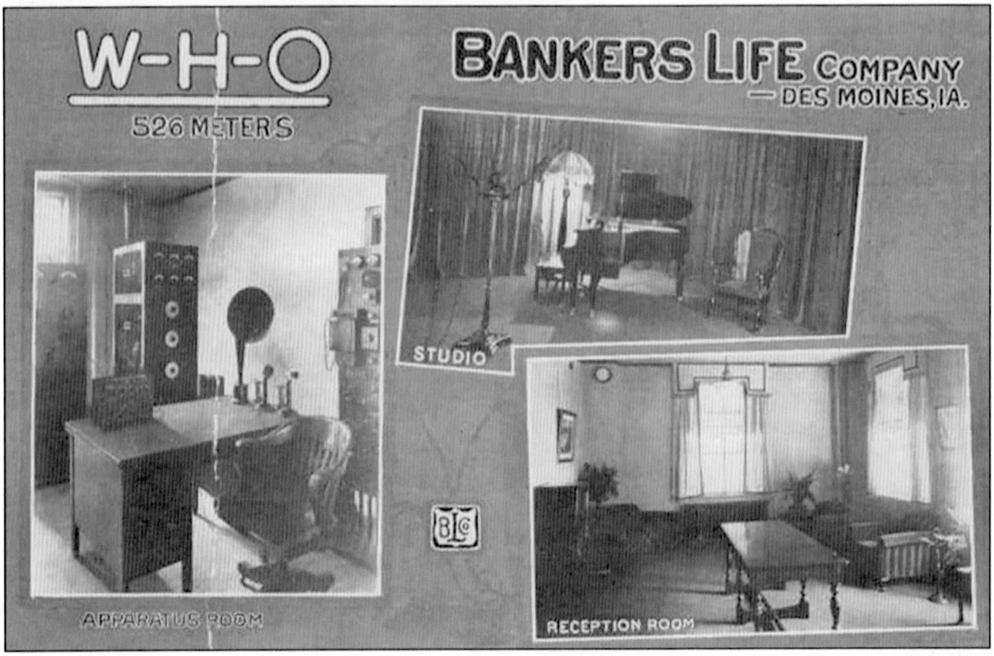

This postcard, printed by the Bankers Life to promote WHO Radio, dates from the late 1920s and depicts scenes from the studios located on the 11th floor of the Liberty Building. (The Bankers Life headquarters were on the 6th through 10th floors.) Given the newness of radio, these postcards and similar promotional items provided insight to an audience still unaccustomed to "sounds flying through the air." The original station equipment and installation cost $35,000—no small amount in 1924.

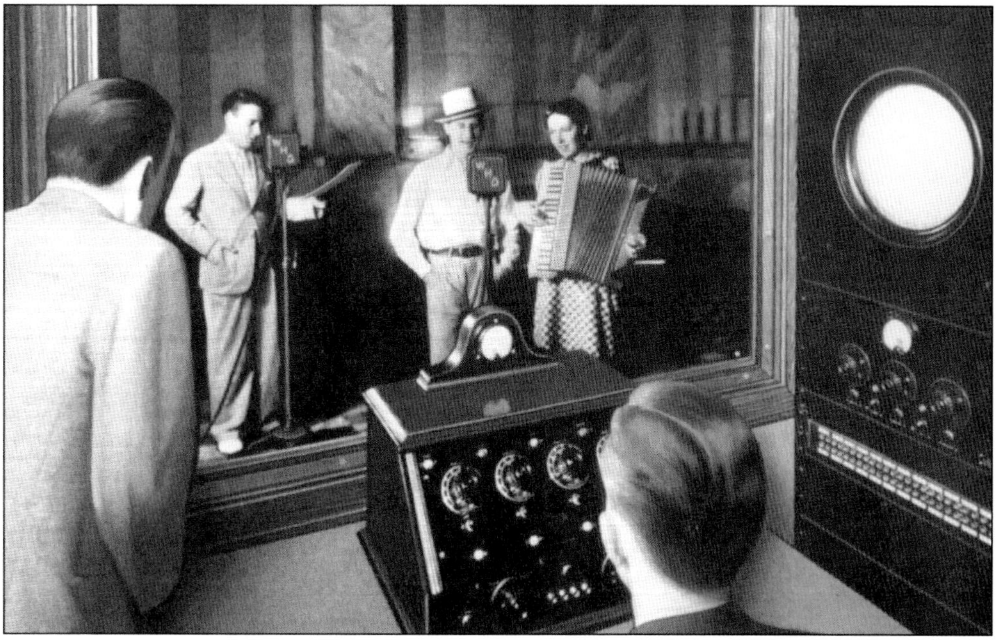

Live musical performances, like this one from 1937, were frequently broadcast from the station's longtime home at 914 Walnut Street. WHO Radio has not always been found at its well-known 1040 frequency. The first listeners found the station at 570, then at 560; it was moved to 1000 in 1928, when WHO began a unique time-share agreement with Davenport's WOC Radio. To enjoy the benefits of a clear channel frequency, the stations had to share the dial position, with one broadcasting during the daytime and the other in the evening, then switching time slots the next day. WHO assumed its familiar 1040 frequency as part of a national reassignment in 1941.

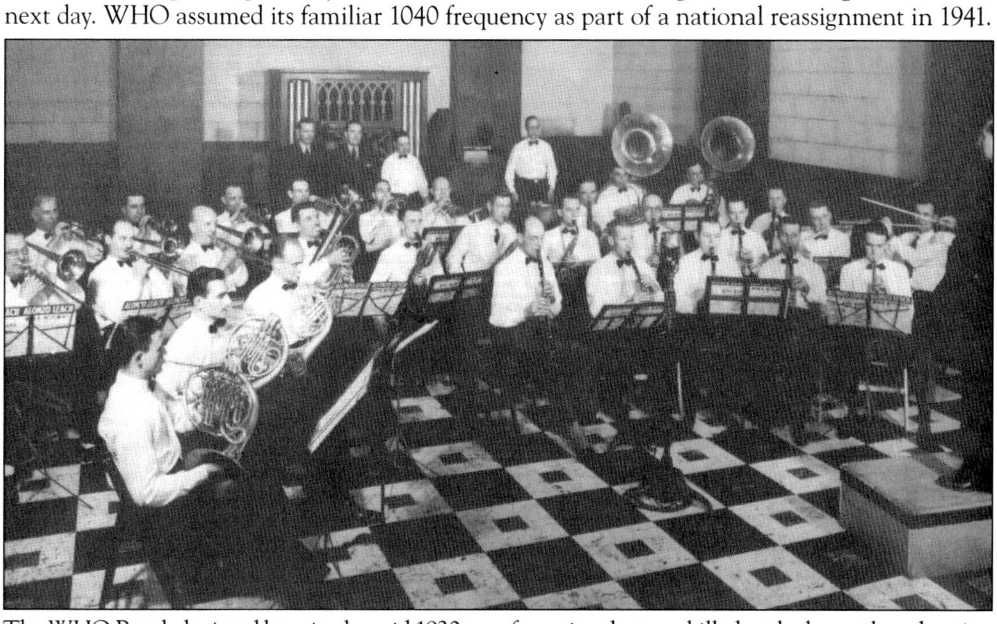

The WHO Band, depicted here in the mid-1930s, performs in what was billed as the largest broadcasting studio between Chicago and the West Coast. Originally, WHO broadcast a daily schedule from 7:30 a.m. to 9:00 p.m. Soon, three short broadcast periods—one to five minutes each—were added for farm market reports and weather information at mid-morning, noon, and mid-afternoon.

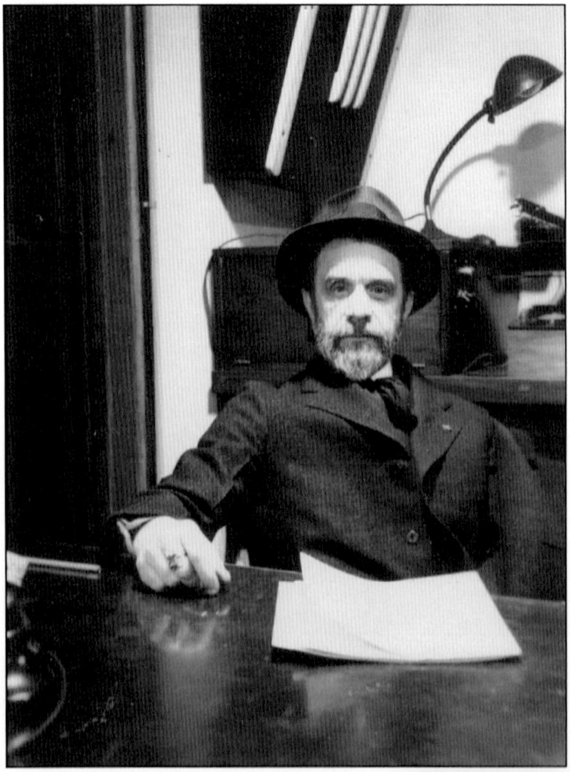

He was referred to as a "scientist, businessman, author, lecturer, humanitarian—a public figure whose host of friends hail him affectionately as B.J." He was Col. B.J. Palmer, a pioneer of chiropractic, and the man who saw the power of radio as a means to reach large numbers of people—not only to inform and entertain, but to promote as well. As the guiding force behind the Palmer School of Chiropractic in Davenport, Palmer—pictured in a rare candid photograph behind his desk at WHO Radio in Des Moines in the 1930s—purchased a fledgling Quad Cities radio station and moved it across the border into Iowa, where WOC would be the original station in a set of Palmer Broadcasting Company holdings that would extend across America.

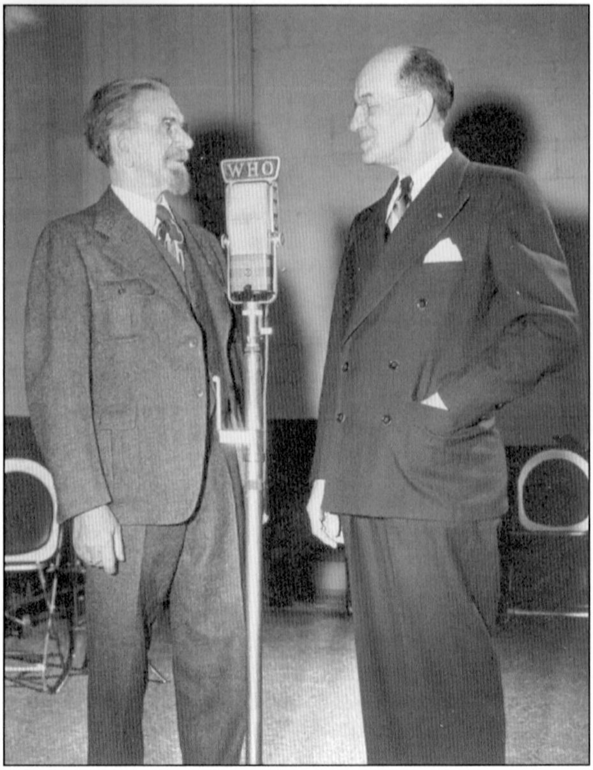

Palmer, seen at left in this 1940s photograph at the WHO studios, used marketing to its fullest potential. He claimed that the call letters of the stations he owned were handpicked to fit his chiropractic school: WOC stood for "Wonders of Chiropractic," while WHO stood for "With Hands Only." The story is a good one—except at that point call letters were randomly assigned by the federal government (WOC, for example, came sequentially after the licenses granted to WOA and WOB), and WHO went on the air before Palmer formed the Central Broadcasting Company and bought the station from the Bankers Life Company. He was the author of several books on a variety of topics, including *Radio Salesmanship*, the first edition of which was published in 1943.

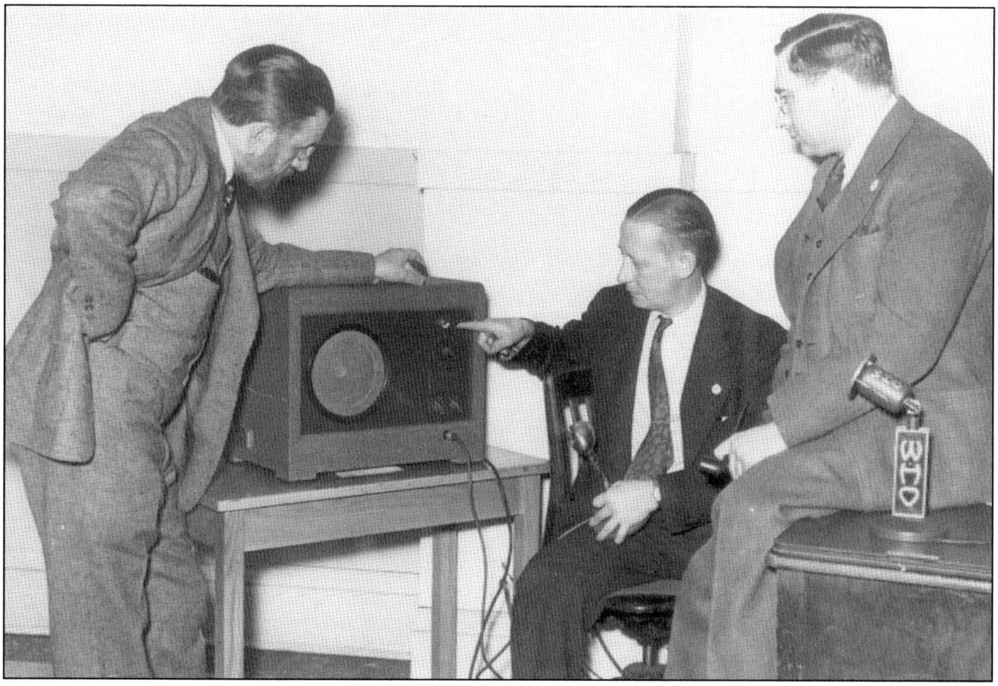

At the dedication of the new transmitter building that integrated WHO and WOC on a single 50,000-watt clear channel transmitter in 1933, Palmer pledged to serve Iowa through this unique resource. "As long as we have served Iowa, it has been our desire to have this Iowa station known as one that served Iowa for community good," he said. "Although privately owned, from the beginning, this company has always taken the position that it belongs to Iowa; that it is to be used for Iowa's good, to better serve Iowa interests." Bartlett Joshua Palmer died in 1961 of intestinal cancer at the age of 78.

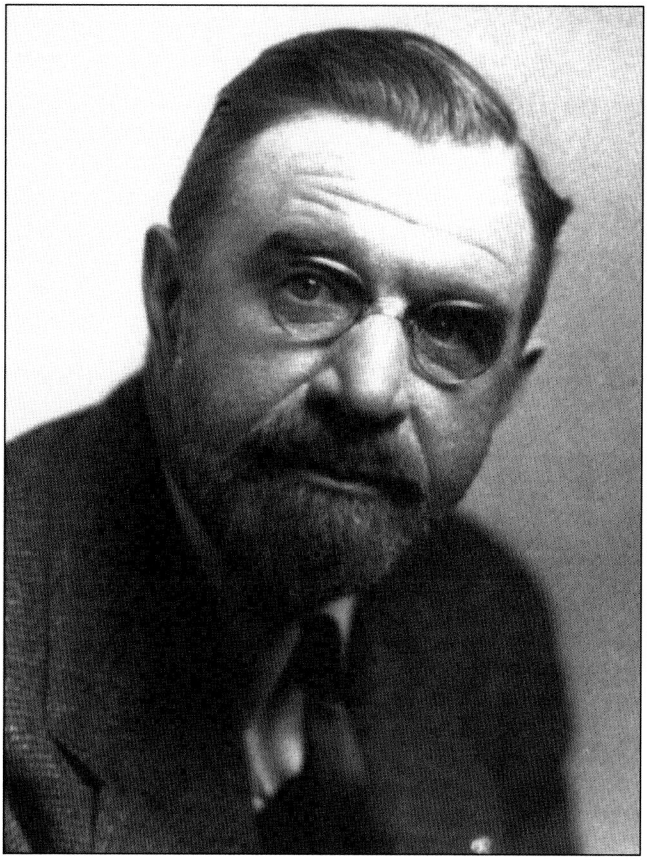

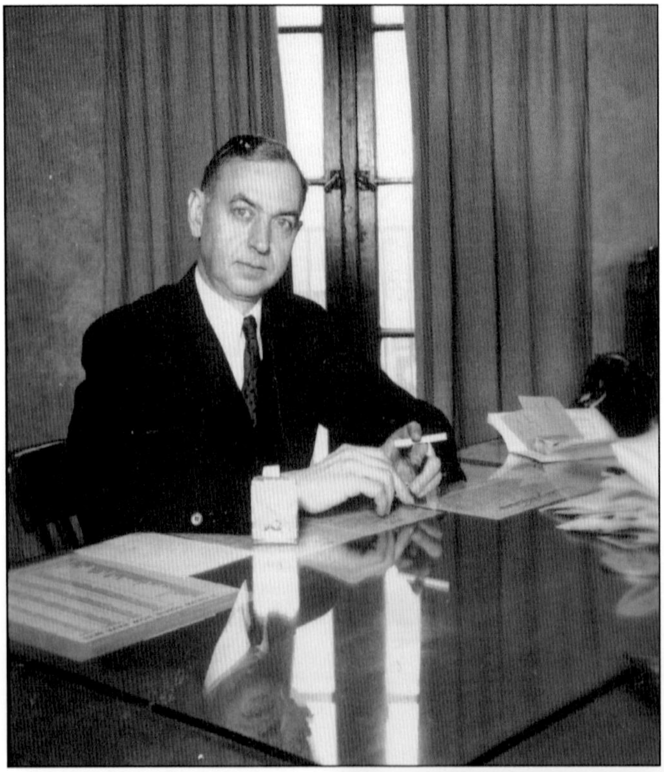

J.O. "Joe" Maland was vice president of the Central Broadcasting Company and manager of WHO Radio. He started in radio in 1922, first with what became WCCO in Minneapolis and then WLS in Chicago. He worked for the Columbia Broadcasting System before coming to WHO in 1931. While at WLS, he produced the nation's first commercialized barn dance broadcast in 1928, gaining sponsorship so the costly program could remain on the air. The practice was well utilized at WHO Radio, as several different businesses sponsored separate quarter-hour segments of WHO's legendary *Barn Dance Frolic* broadcast.

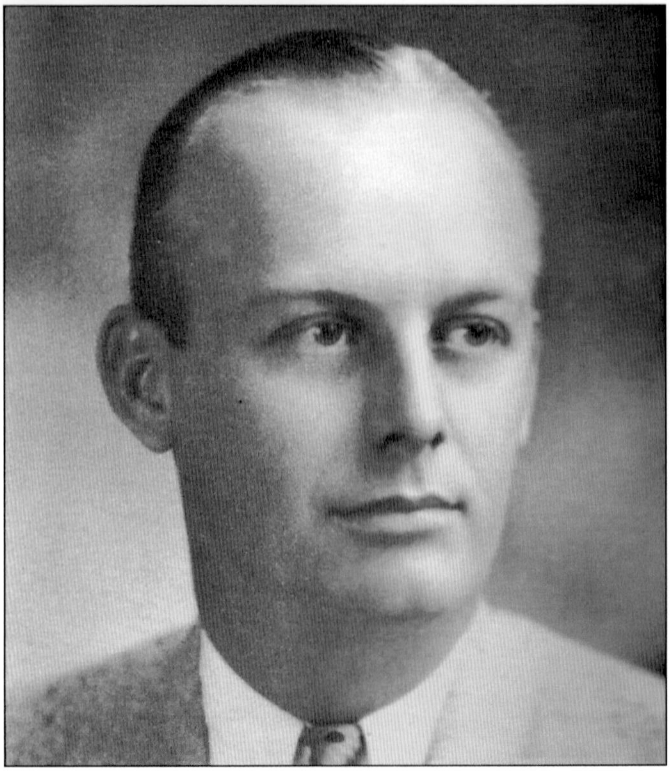

Longtime WHO employee Paul Loyet is pictured in 1938, when he served as the station's technical director. A station biography of the time credits Loyet with a "brilliant record of pioneering in synchronization, wireless re-broadcasting, improvement of transmitting, and speech input equipment and facsimile." He would conclude his career with the Palmer Broadcasting Company as vice president and general manager of WHO-AM/FM and television.

Dr. David D. Palmer ("Dr. Dave") is seen in a 1937 photograph when he served his father's radio company as vice president and treasurer. He was then described as a "versatile and youthful executive" who was in charge of other Palmer interests as well. He would succeed his father as head of the family broadcasting interests, which became known as Palmer Broadcasting Company and included stations in other states. At the time of WHO Radio's 50th anniversary in 1974, station alumnus Ronald Reagan, then governor of California, returned to Des Moines as the keynote luncheon speaker and paused for a photograph next to a portrait of Dr. Dave, who died in 1978.

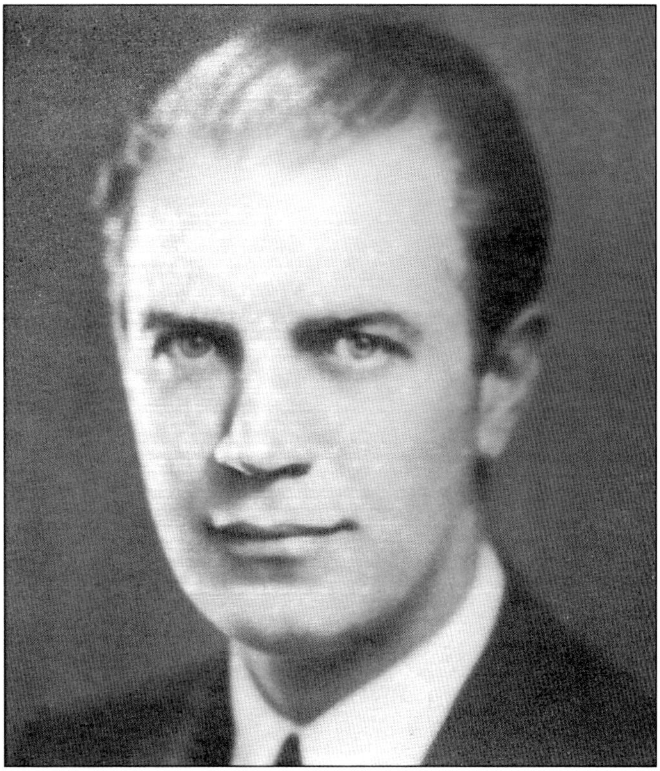

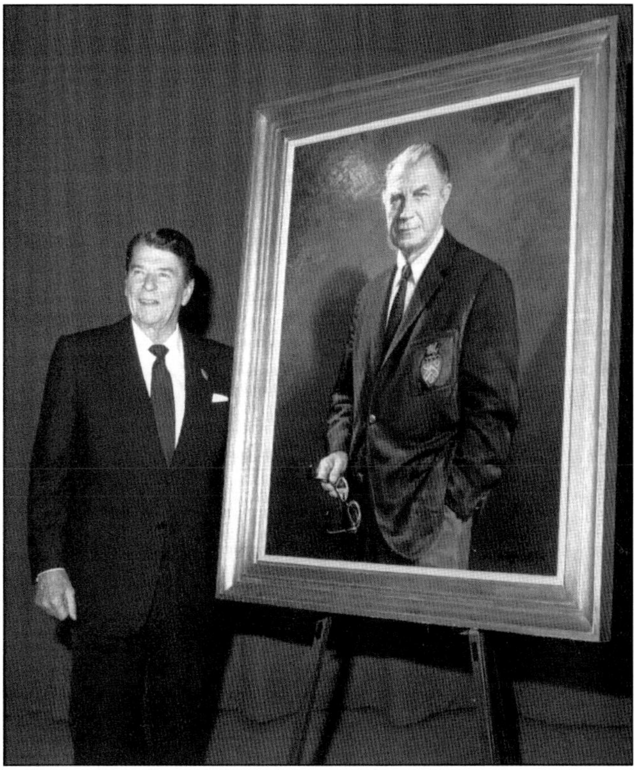

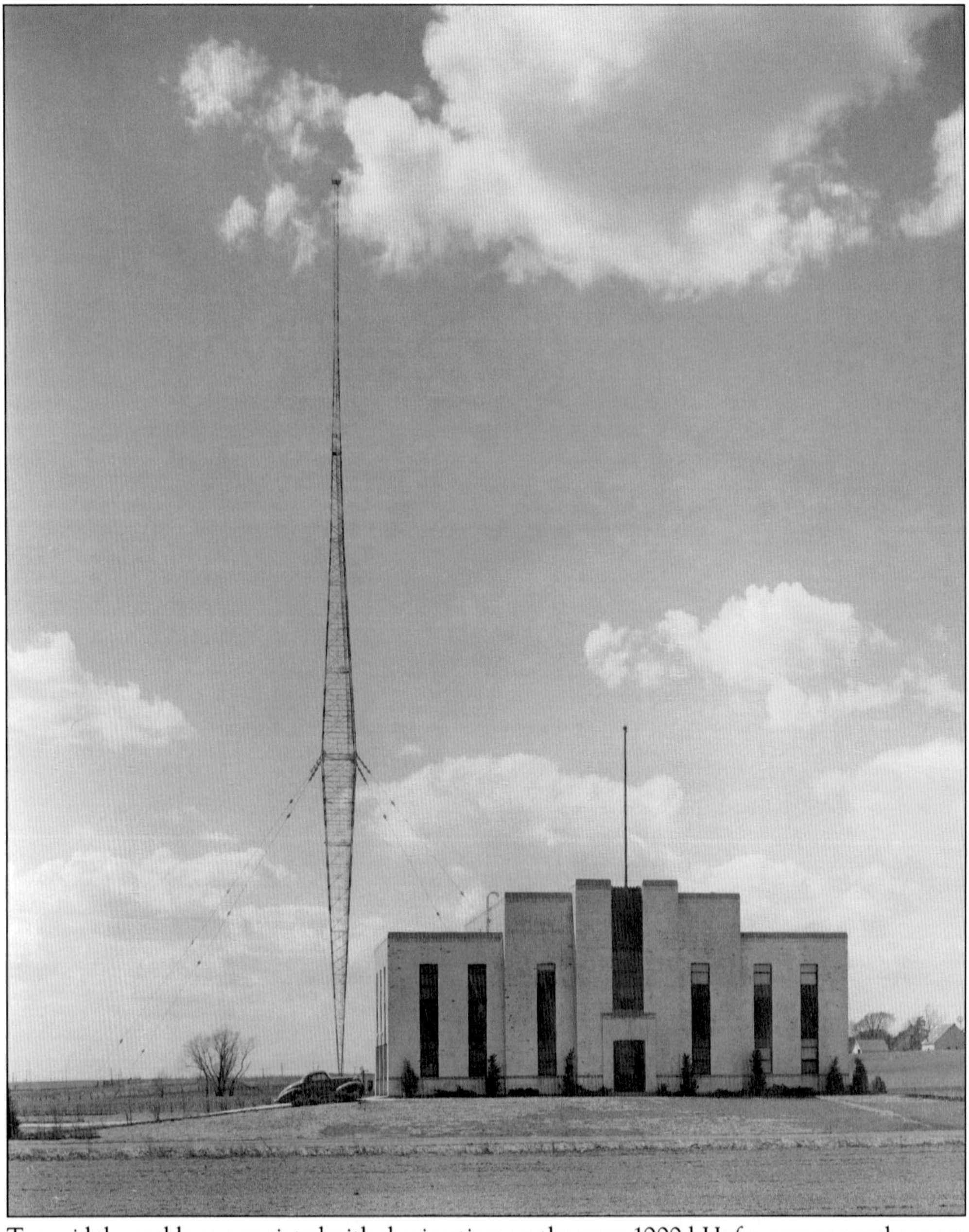

To avoid the problems associated with sharing time on the same 1000-kHz frequency, synchronous operation—airing the same signal over the transmitters for both WOC and WHO—began in the summer of 1930, likely the first stations in America to operate continuously with synchronized transmitters. Landlines were used between Davenport and Des Moines at a cost of $40,000 per year so that programs originated from both cities. But the real solution was to combine the operations, and in early 1933 the staffs were merged in Des Moines under the dual call letters WOC-WHO. The merger of operations in Des Moines coincided with "the inaugural of another giant of the ether," as the company termed it. On April 22, 1933, the separate transmitters of the two stations were turned off in favor of a single, 50,000-watt transmitter. The 532-foot, 213,000-pound steel tower that held the antenna was Iowa's tallest structure for a time.

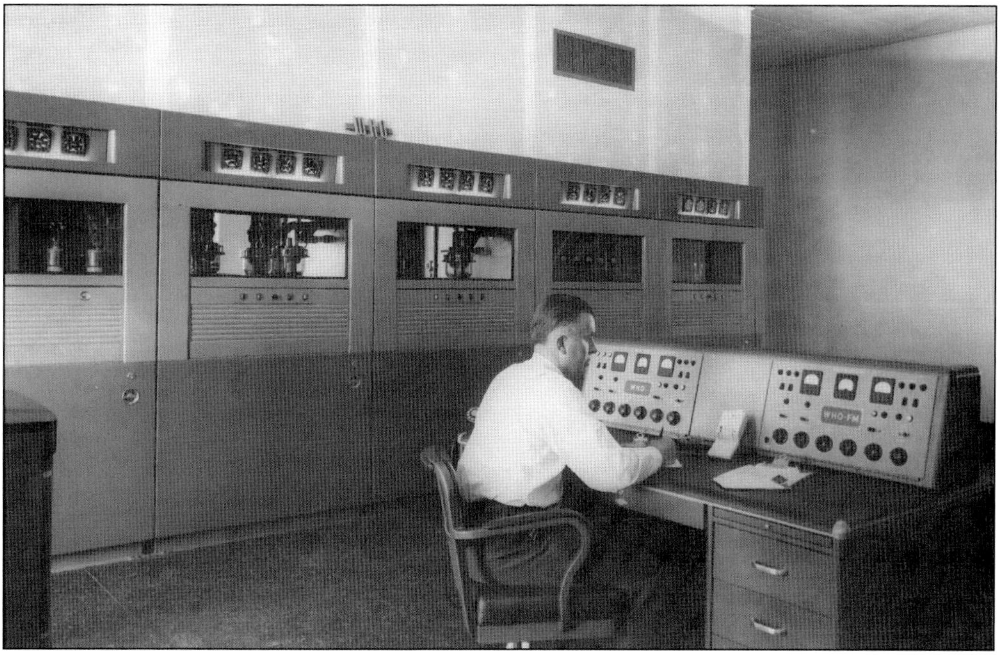

"WHO is big, but friendly," claimed a mid-1930s promotional brochure. The new facility near Mitchellville housed the station's first 50,000-watt transmitter—the maximum power allowed by the Federal Communications Commission. After initially running the single transmitter under the dual WOC-WHO call letters, in November 1934 the WOC call letters were retired, and the station was simply called WHO. (Another station under the WOC name would soon be founded in Davenport.) The increase in power meant that by 1938 WHO had eight times the evening power of all other Iowa commercial radio stations combined. Later renovations to equipment, including the advent of FM broadcasting in 1948, led to the control panels and equipment depicted in these photographs of the Mitchellville facility, which were taken about 1950.

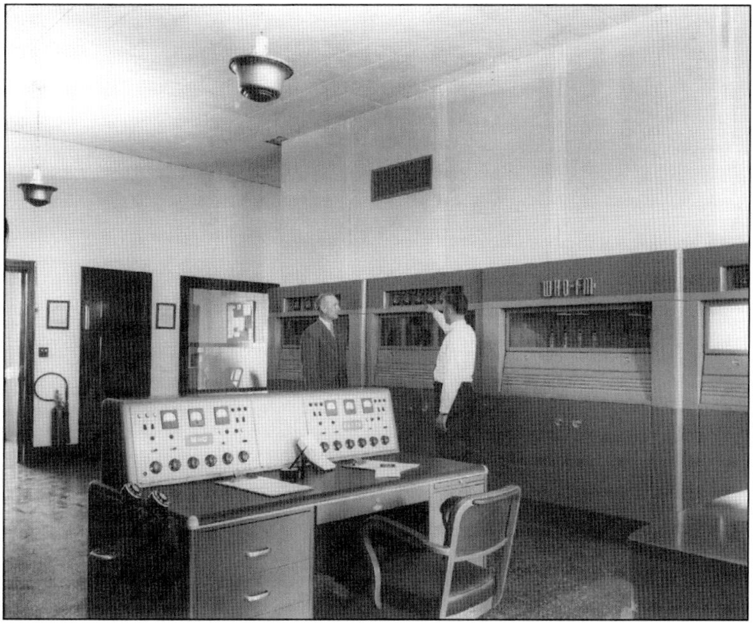

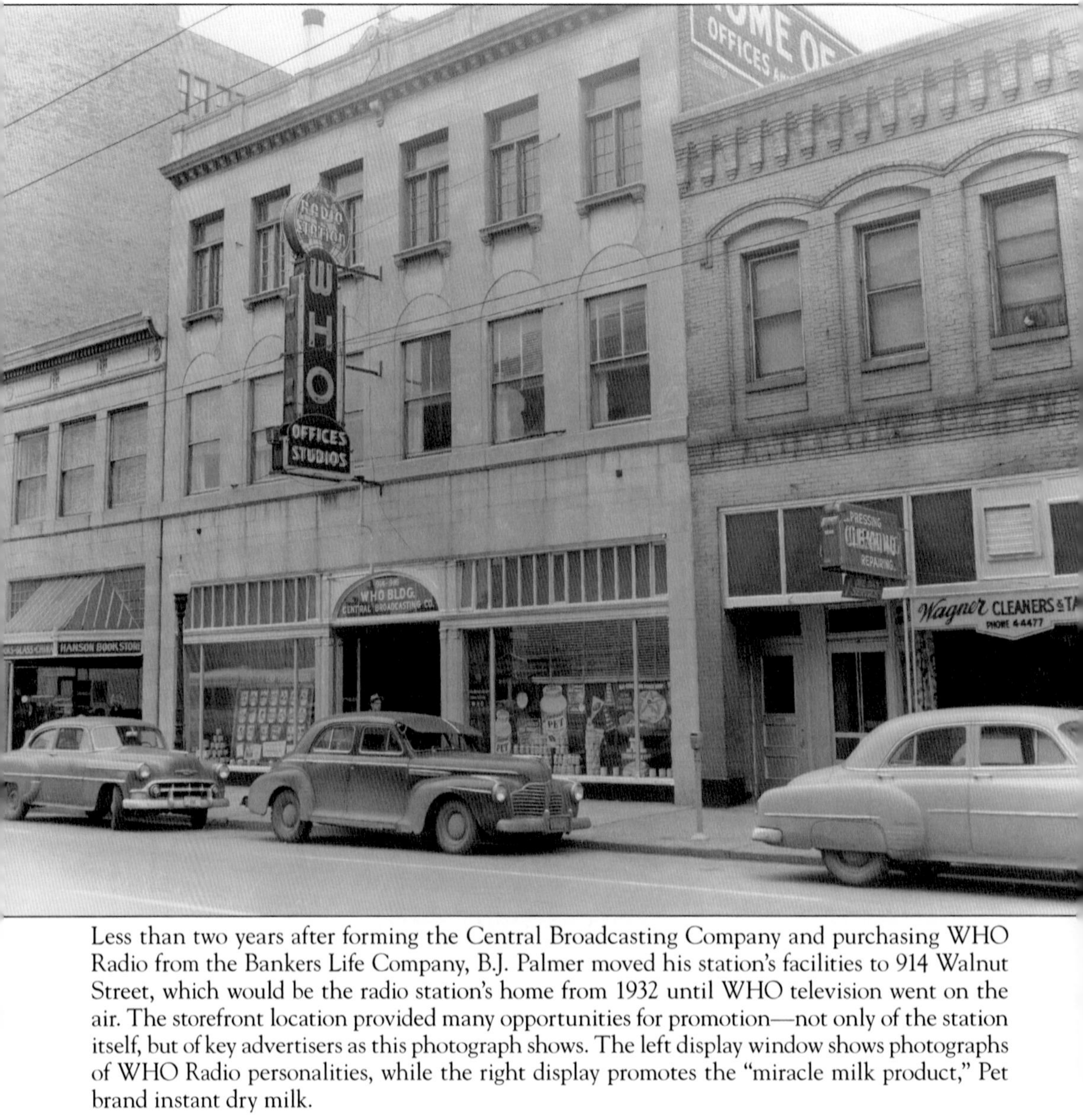

Less than two years after forming the Central Broadcasting Company and purchasing WHO Radio from the Bankers Life Company, B.J. Palmer moved his station's facilities to 914 Walnut Street, which would be the radio station's home from 1932 until WHO television went on the air. The storefront location provided many opportunities for promotion—not only of the station itself, but of key advertisers as this photograph shows. The left display window shows photographs of WHO Radio personalities, while the right display promotes the "miracle milk product," Pet brand instant dry milk.

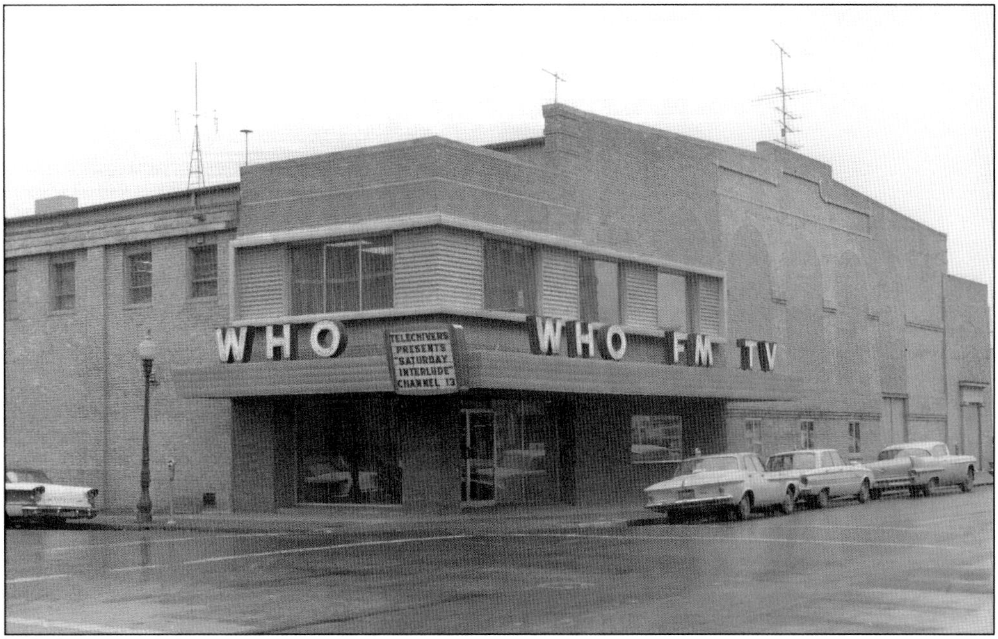

With the advent of television, the WHO Broadcasting Company moved two blocks away to 1100 Walnut Street, a building that formerly housed the Midtown Roller Rink. The former roller rink was ideal for television studios, which required a large, open space with high ceilings and a smooth floor. Radio studios and offices were incorporated into a second level of the building. The photograph above shows the building as it looked when the stations moved there in 1954. In 1976, the building underwent extensive renovation, as seen in the photograph below. This site was home to the WHO stations until they moved to new facilities, located at 1801 Grand Avenue, in 1981.

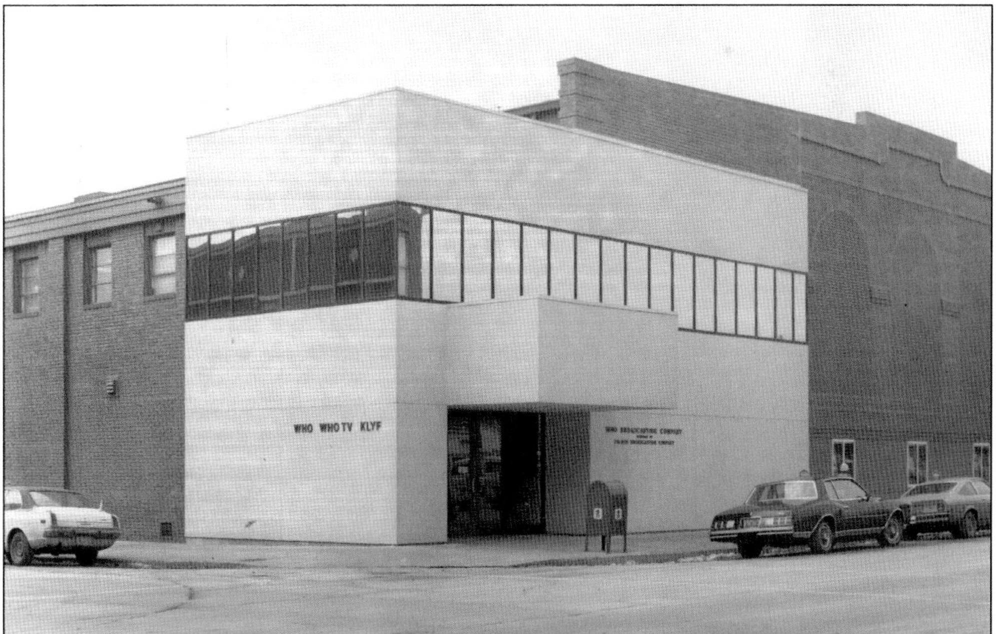

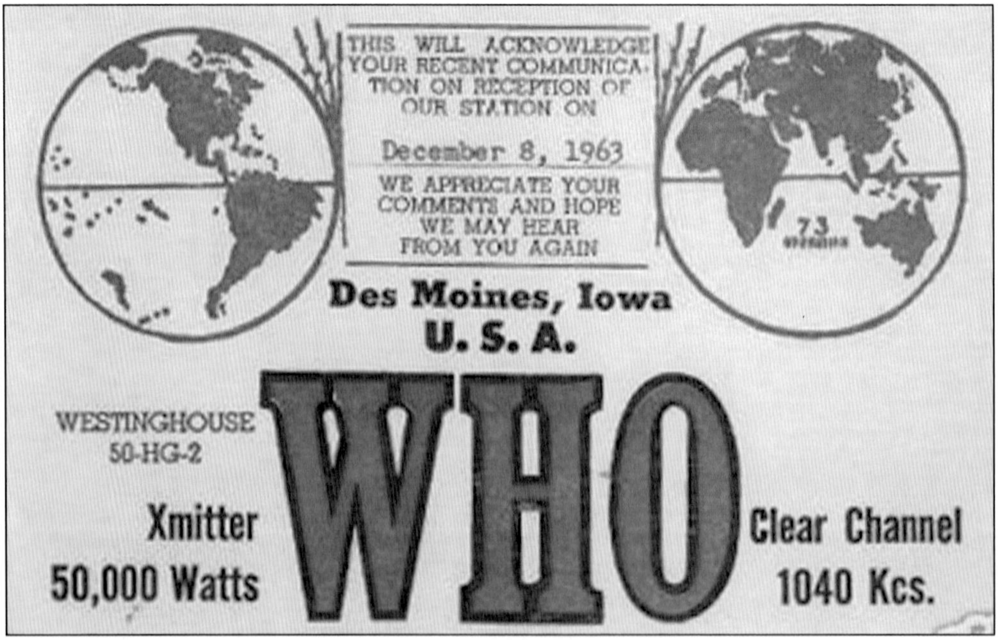

In a popular activity of the time, hobbyists known as DXers competed to see if their radio set could receive distant stations. The listener would send a letter to the station, giving the day, date, and time they heard the station and describing what was being broadcast. If the station confirmed the accuracy of the transmission, the listener would receive a postcard from the station. The photograph above shows one of those postcards from 1963, while the photograph below demonstrates that the practice was still in vogue a dozen years later. The advent of digital technology today renders the ability to draw in a remote station by fine-tuning the dial impossible.

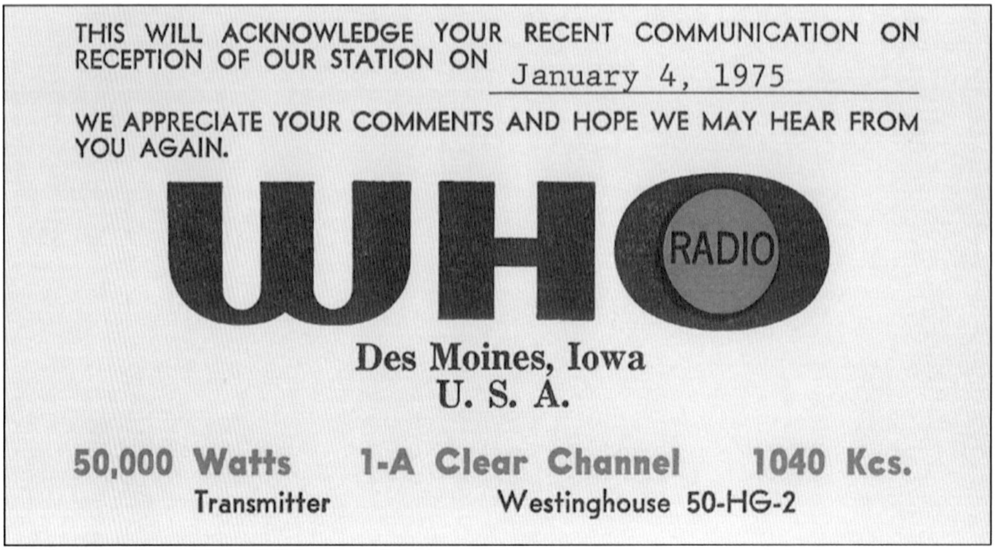

Many a child spent part of their youth collecting US postage stamps. The popularity of stamp collecting extended to tracking reception of radio stations, a trend capitalized on by both the EKKO and Bryant companies. The radio verification stamp served the same purpose as confirmation postcards. Stamps came in a variety of colors, and listeners collected the stamps in albums, just as with the stamps found on letters. EKKO stamps were initially given out by stations as confirmation of a listener hearing the station. Bryant stamps, which first appeared in 1925 after the EKKO stamps were well established, came as a complete set with an album, and collectors were told to paste the stamps into the album when they heard a station. Bryant stamps were only available until 1927, while EKKO stamps were available in one form or another into the 1950s.

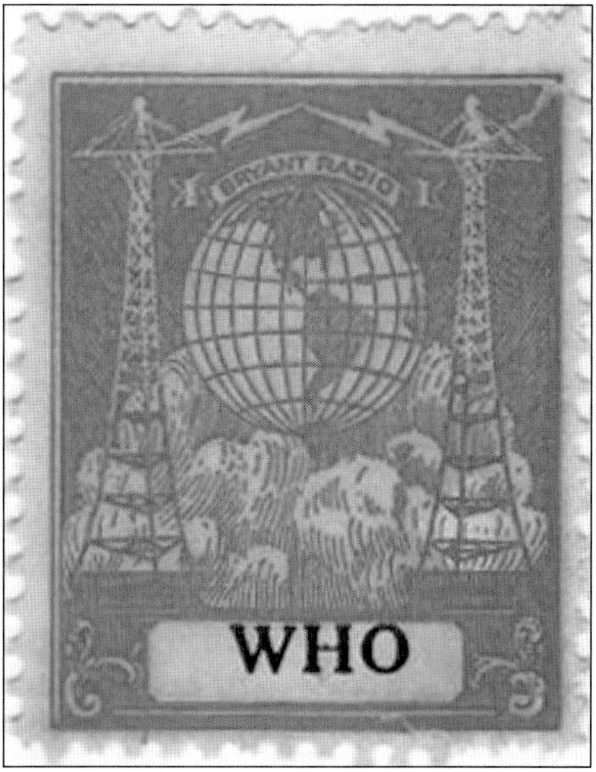

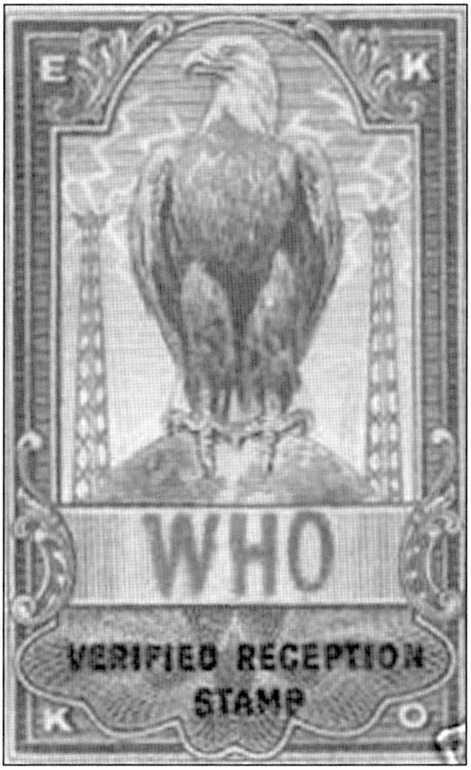

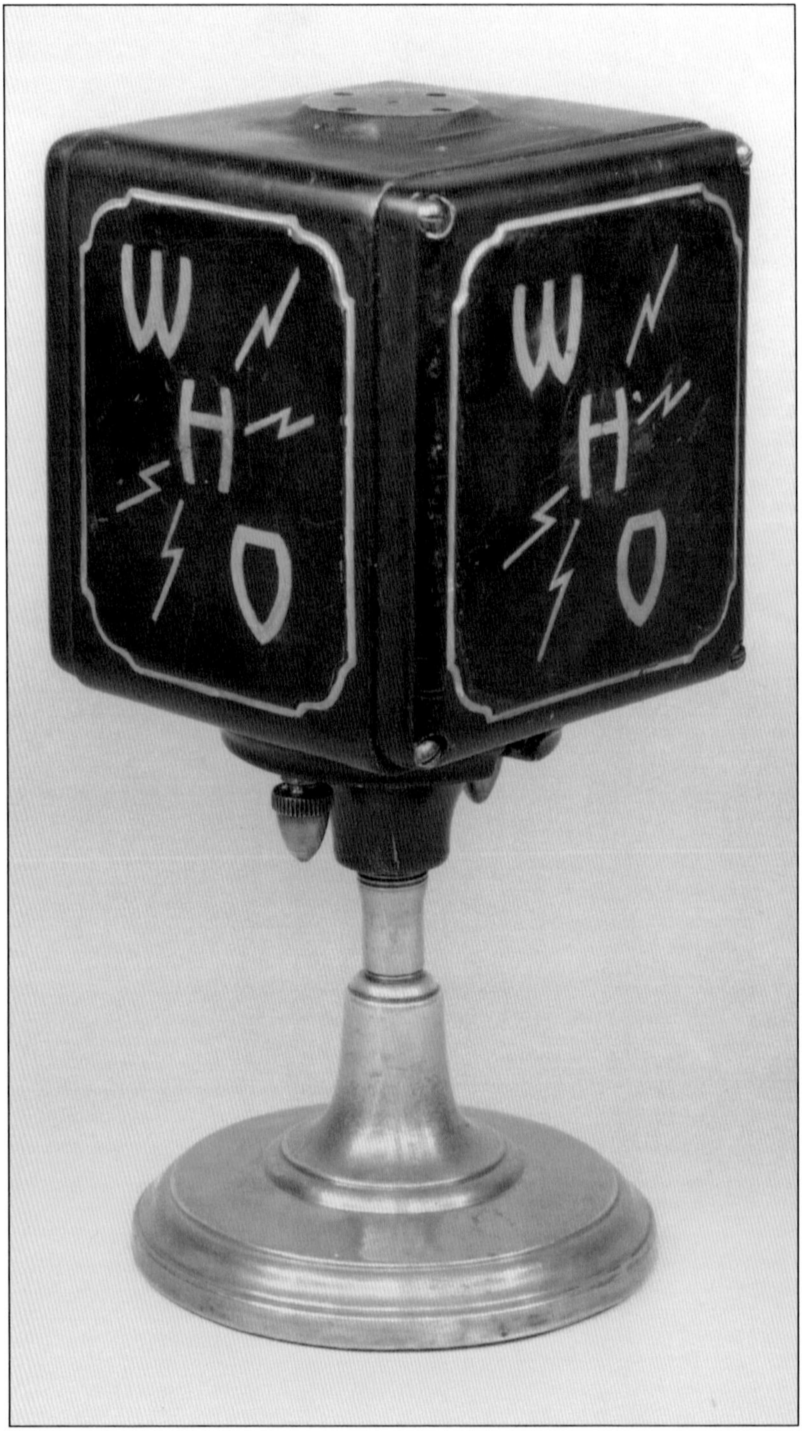

Tabletop microphones like this one were commonly used at WHO Radio in the 1930s. This particular microphone was restored and presented by station personnel to Pres. Ronald Reagan in the White House during a 1981 ceremony inducting Reagan into the national Broadcast Pioneers organization.

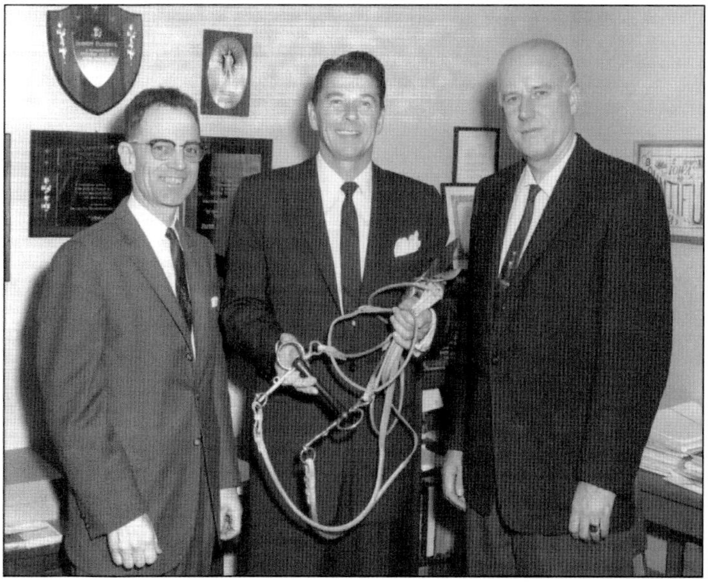

This reunion photograph of three coworkers from WHO Radio in the 1930s was taken when Ronald Reagan visited the station during a 1961 trip to Des Moines. Herb Plambeck (left) became farm director in 1936, while Jack Shelley (right) joined the news department in 1935. Reagan predated both of them, coming to WHO as sports director in early 1933.

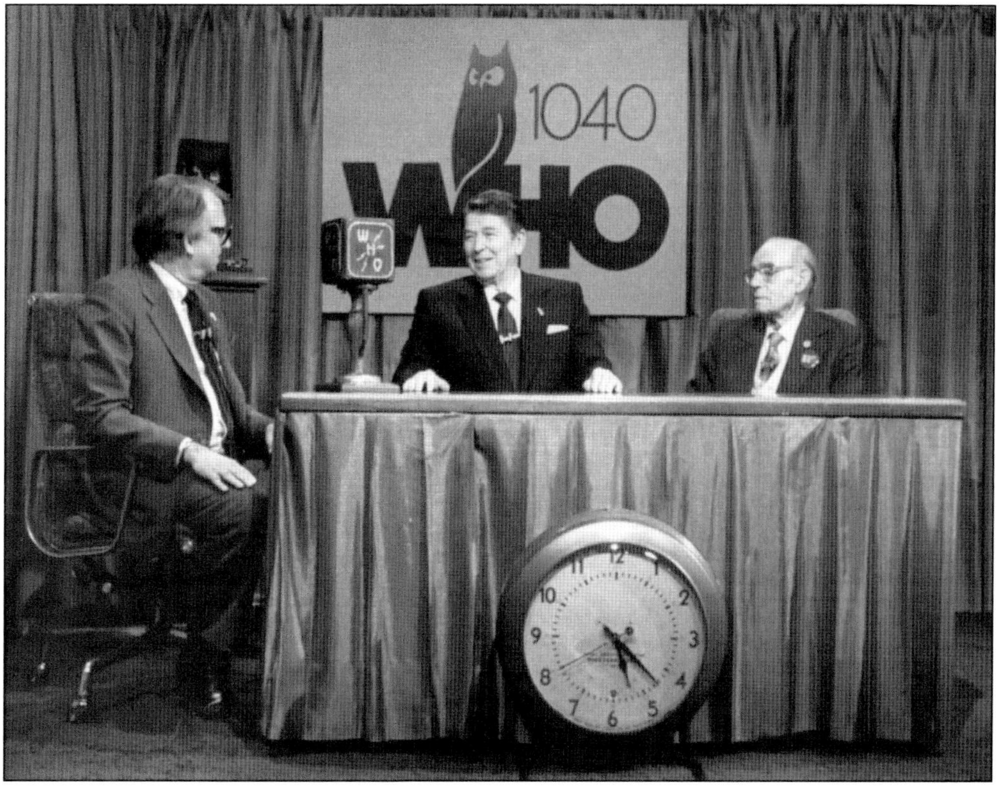

Another reunion occurred in February 1984, when Ronald Reagan, then president, visited Des Moines for the Iowa Caucuses. During his trip, he stopped for an interview at the WHO studios at 1801 Grand Avenue before speaking to supporters at Veterans Memorial Auditorium. Conducting the interview was Reagan's successor as WHO sports director, Jim Zabel (left). Also joining the conversation was 85-year-old H.R. "Charlie" Gross, who as WHO's news director worked with Reagan at the station from 1935 to 1937.

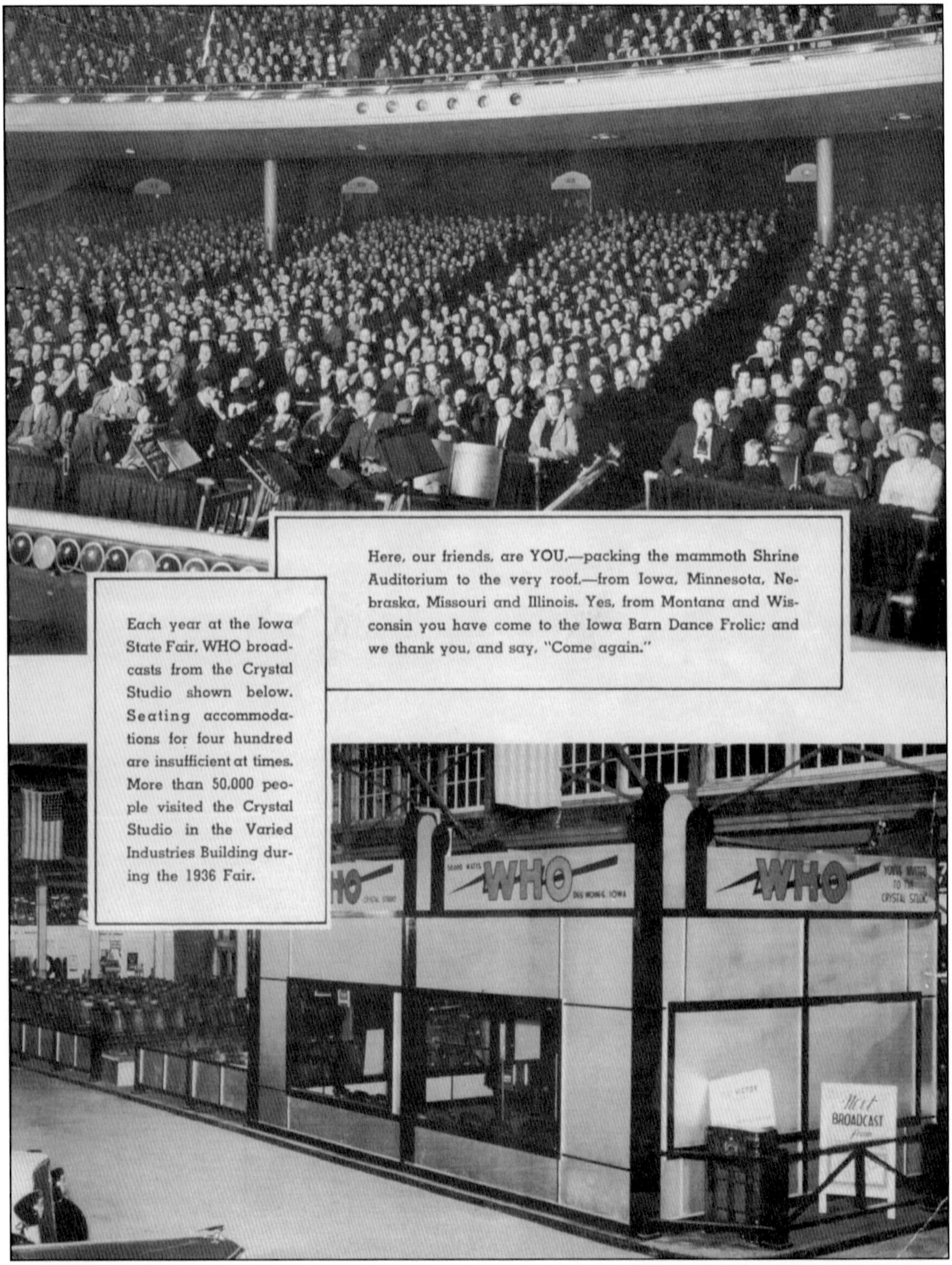

These photographs from a 1937 *Iowa Barn Dance Frolic* souvenir guide serve as a visual portrayal of the audience's commitment to the young radio station. The photograph above is from the Shrine Auditorium, which each week was filled to its 4,500-seat capacity for the Saturday *Barn Dance* broadcasts. The image below shows the original Iowa State Fair Crystal Studio in the Varied Industries Building, which counted 50,000 visitors during the 1936 fair alone.

Two

AN INFORMATION SOURCE

As radio evolved from merely a hobby for a few enthusiasts to an integral part of the home, the monopoly newspapers held on providing information to the public also changed.

By the time readers received their newspapers, the information was already a number of hours old. The immediacy of radio, therefore, presented a serious challenge to traditional print media sources.

To supplement the local coverage reporters provided, newspapers received much of their information from various wire services, such as the Associated Press (AP), United Press (UP), and International News Service (INS).

Radio stations, which have consistently been licensed by the federal government to serve the "public interest, convenience, and necessity," started delivering news on the air and sought to become clients of the wire services as well. The wire services were eager to generate more revenue and began to supply radio stations with material in direct competition with their newspaper clients in the same city.

The newspapers, which were the prime revenue source for the wires, objected strenuously, engaging in what historians have called a decade-long press-radio war. Newspapers threatened to drop one wire service or another if that service sold material to radio stations.

One noteworthy example concerned WHO Radio. In the late 1930s, the station's news director, H.R. Gross, was negotiating with UP, which saw the value of radio for promoting its products and was more willing to work with stations than the AP. The Des Moines Register & Tribune Company (R&T), which published morning and afternoon newspapers, objected and threatened to cancel its membership if UP sold material to Gross and WHO.

The wire service did not blink, and WHO Radio became a UP client. The R&T immediately dropped UP and never again utilized the service despite the end of the war between print and broadcast media. Ironically, the attempts by newspapers to stifle broadcast journalism, in the end, may have strengthened radio. In the absence of wire copy, stations had to work harder and hire more staff, which helped to establish broadcast journalism as an important source for information—and the WHO Radio staff went on to become one of the nation's strongest local news departments in America.

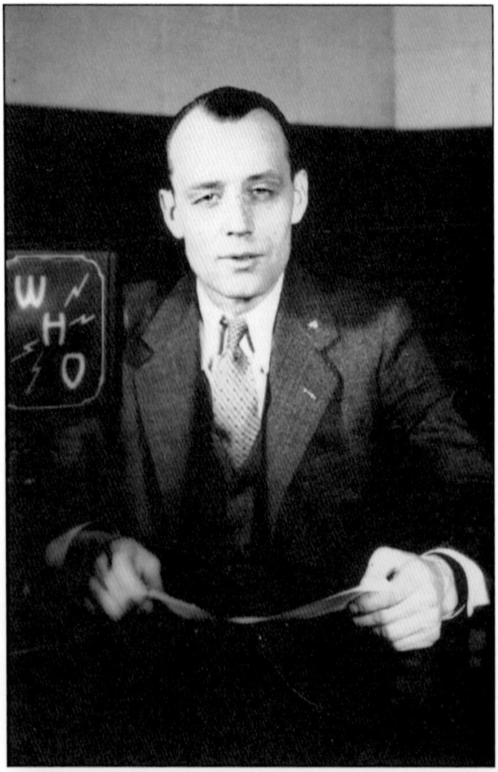

The founding member of the WHO Radio news department was H.R. Gross, whose late-evening newscast *Tomorrow's News Tonight* was listened to throughout the country thanks to WHO's strong nighttime signal. Gross joined WHO in 1935 and soon was responsible for hiring other legendary broadcasters such as Jack Shelley and Herb Plambeck. Always interested in politics, Gross left WHO in April 1940 to run for governor of Iowa; barely campaigning, he lost a close battle in the Republican primary to incumbent George A. Wilson. Voting records show that Gross won in those counties where WHO's signal was strong, giving early indication of the ability of radio to help propel candidates to office. From there, Gross reported news on another station with a powerhouse signal, WLW in Cincinnati, before returning to Iowa and 50,000-watt Waterloo station KXEL. After building a reputation there, Gross again tried his hand at politics and was elected to Congress from Iowa's Northeastern District in 1948. He served 13 terms, retiring in 1974 with a reputation as a fiscal watchdog.

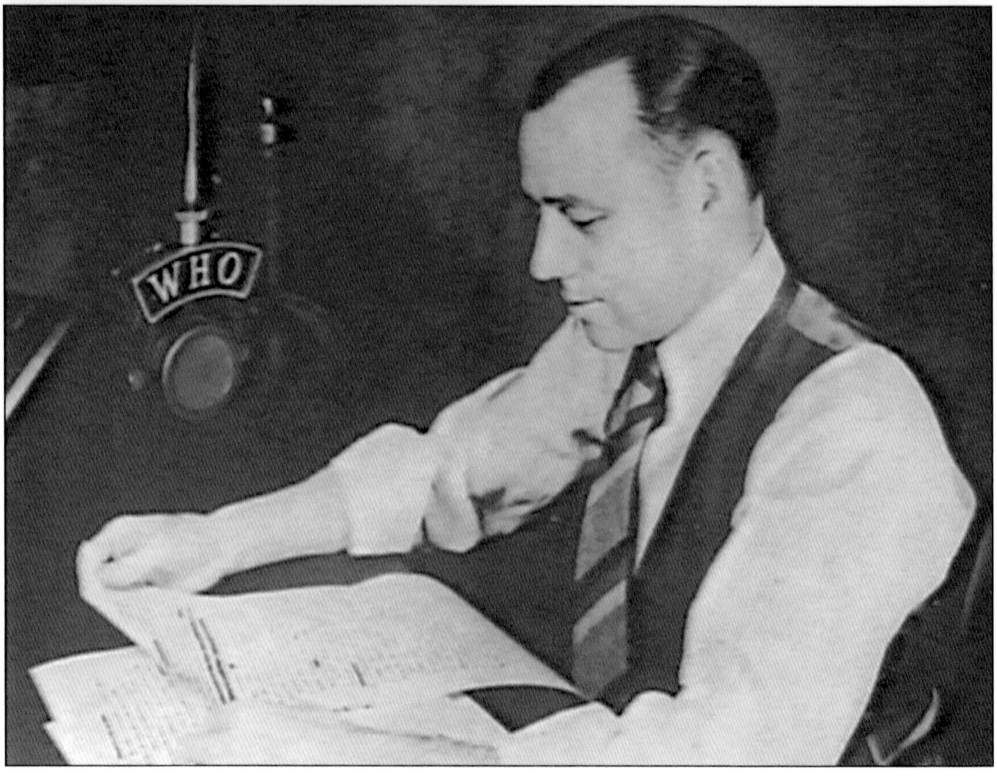

One of the most influential broadcast journalists in American history was Jack Shelley, who joined the WHO Radio staff in 1935 after completing study at the University of Missouri and working in newspapers for a year. A native of Boone, Shelley would go on to cover some of the most historic events in history, including the Battle of the Bulge, the Japanese surrender on the battleship USS *Missouri*, atomic bomb tests at Yucca Flat, Nevada, the visit of Soviet premier Nikita Khruschev to Iowa, and more during his 30 years at the station. His recorded interviews with the crew of the *Enola Gay* were the first to be transmitted back to America following the dropping of the atomic bombs on Japan. "You have to remember that in those days, in the 1930s, the vast majority of our audience found radio news something brand new and very exciting," Shelley once recalled. "All these people who lived in small towns and on the farms in Iowa had never had anything that brought news to them so quickly."

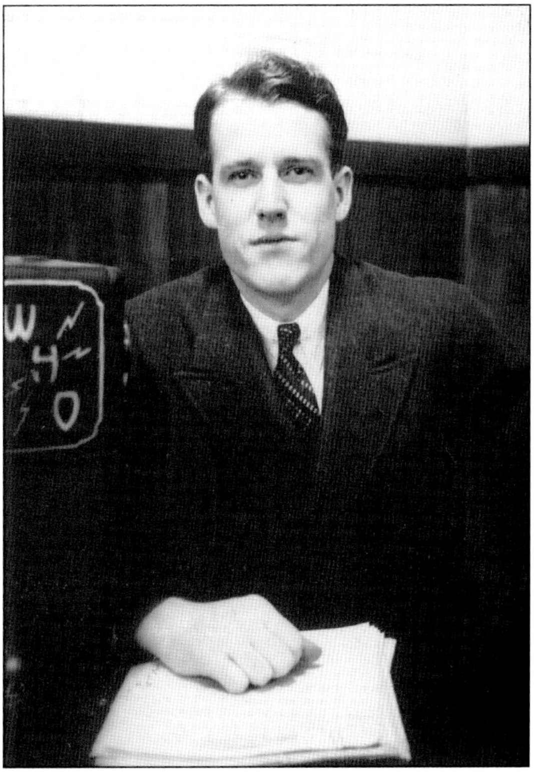

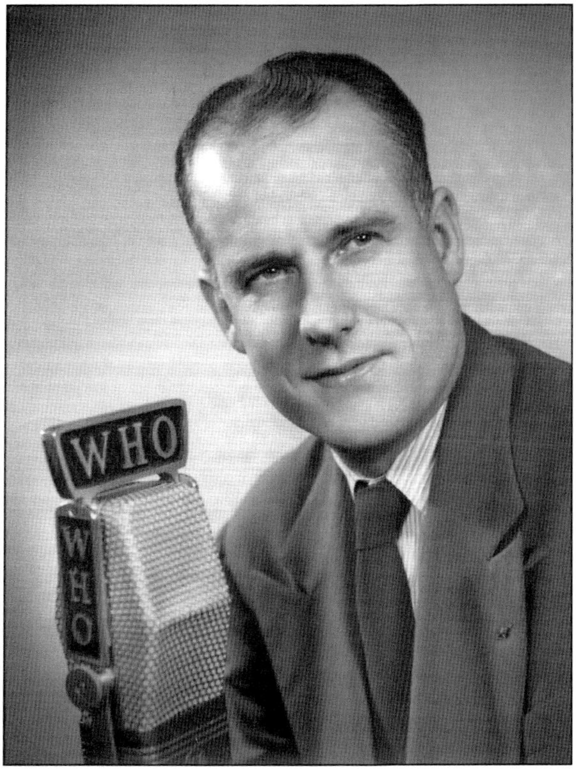

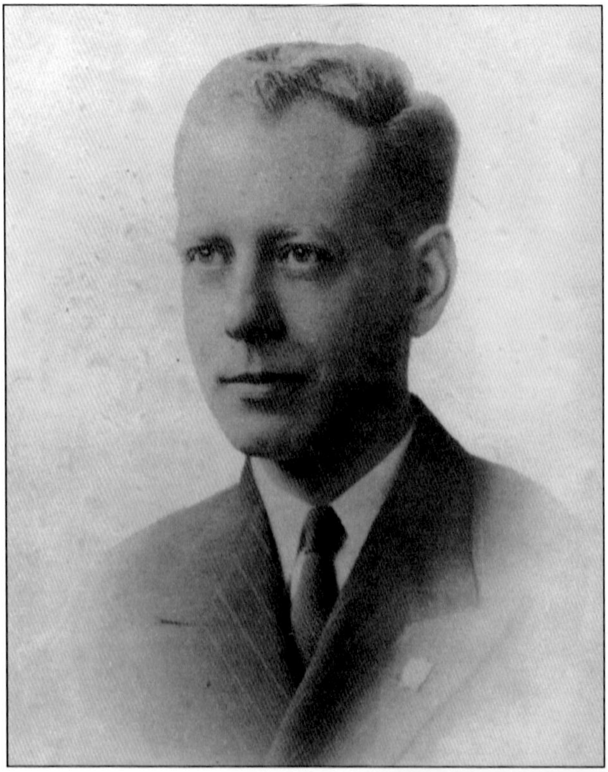

Bob Burlingame (left) was a well-known figure in Des Moines for decades and was the host of the nightly 10:30 *Bob Burlingame Reports* program during the early 1940s. M.L. Nelsen (below) was a key figure in the news department during the 1940s and 1950s, becoming Jack Shelley's top assistant. The news programming became a foundation of the WHO program schedule, and listeners often commented on the news and entertainment programming they heard on the air. More than 700,000 letters were received at WHO during 1936—enough that a stack of them would reach more than 400 feet in the air. In Dr. Whan's 1947 Iowa Radio Audience Survey, WHO was named as the station "listened to most," with 47.7 percent of Iowans tuning in for daytime programming and up to 56.9 percent at nighttime.

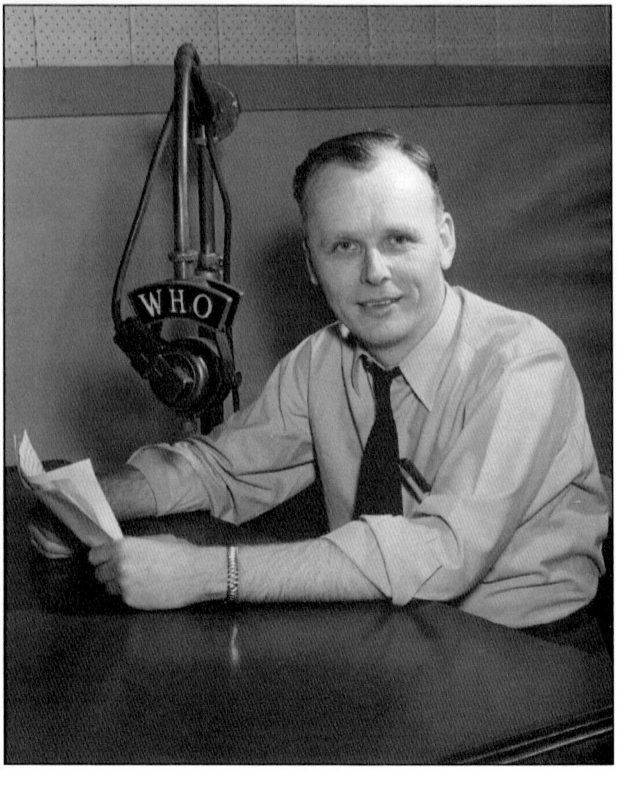

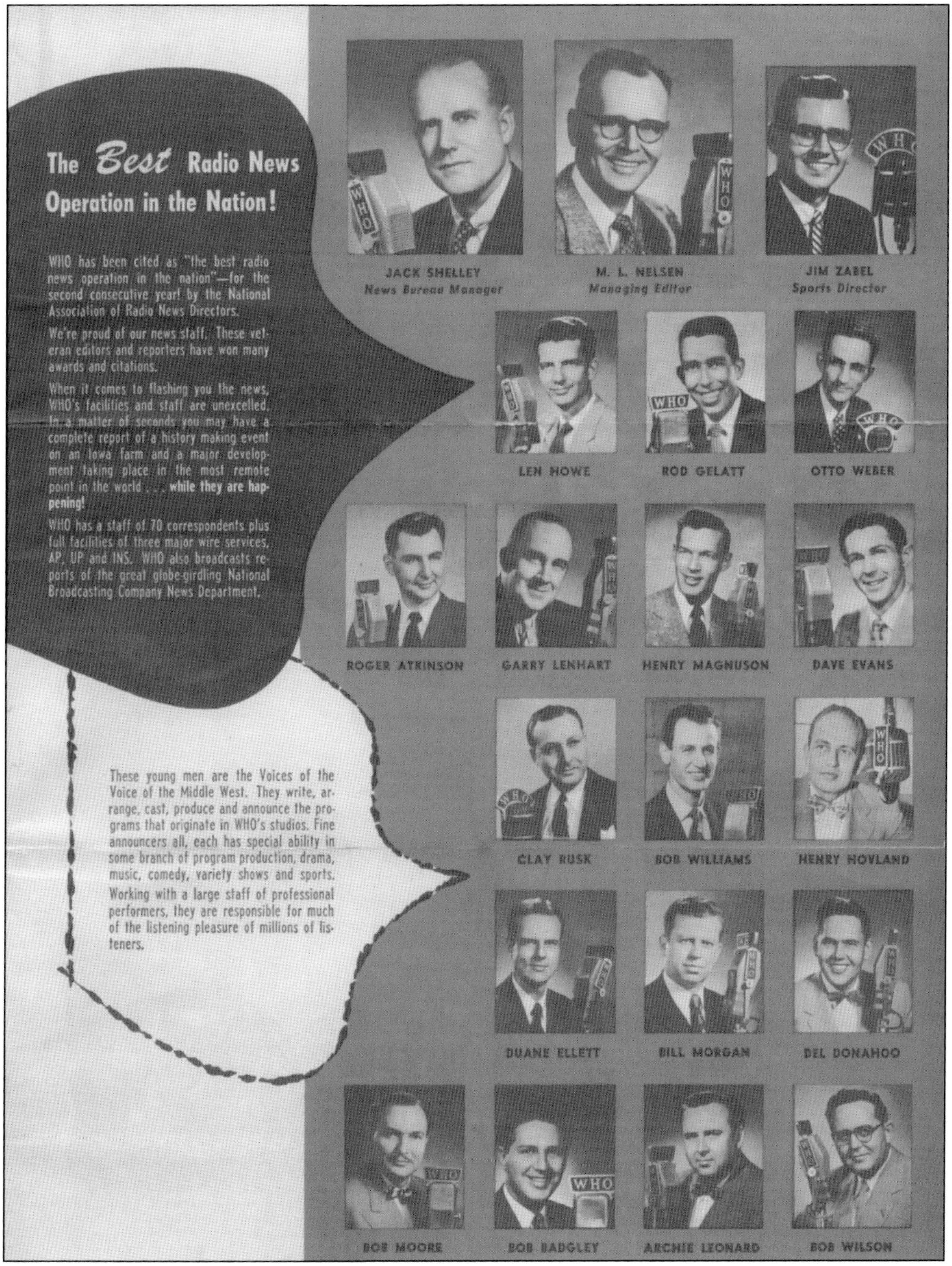

"The best radio news operation in the nation," boasts this station promotional piece from about 1950. The flyer identifies a number of announcers and newscasters, including Rod Gelatt, Otto Weber, Henry Magnuson, and Dave Evans. The Best Radio News Operation award was presented to the station by the Association of Radio News Directors, a group cofounded by Jack Shelley, who also served as its third president. The international organization is now known as the Radio Television Digital News Association (RTDNA).

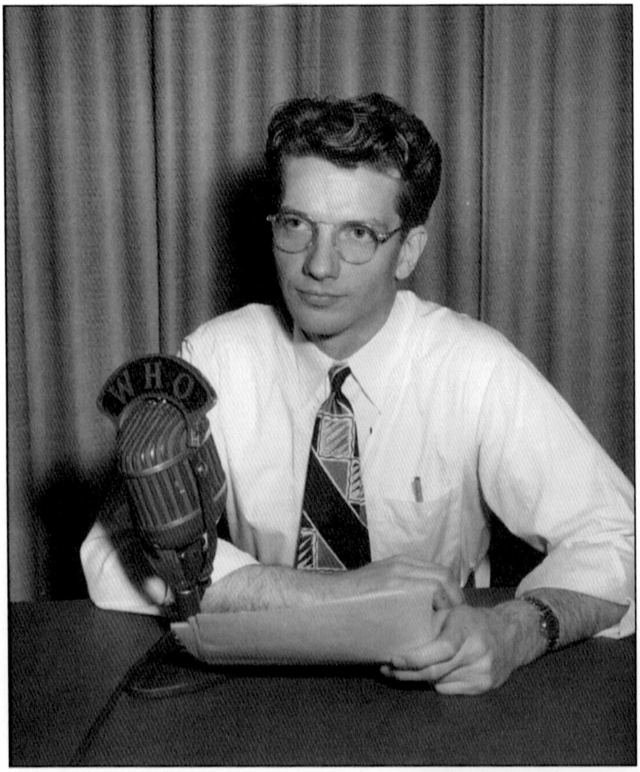

Leonard "Len" Howe joined the WHO Radio staff in 1938. After serving in World War II, Howe returned to the station and served seven years as editor of the popular *Morning News Roundup* program. Later, as managing editor of the department, he anchored the early-evening newscast on WHO Radio. A station biography calls Howe the "Chet Huntley of the Middle West" thanks to a "striking" resemblance to the NBC anchor in both appearance and delivery.

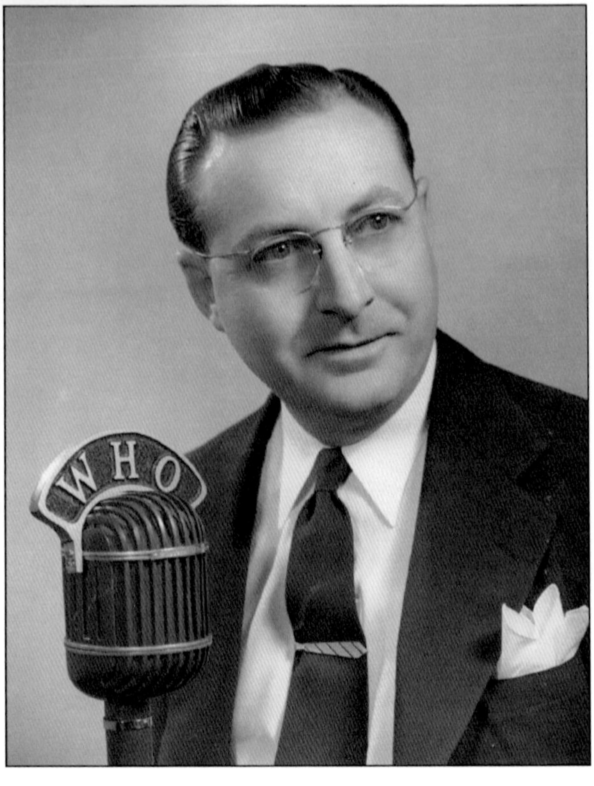

Clay Rusk got his first job in radio in 1937 when he won an announcer contest at Marshalltown radio station KFJB. Rusk came to WHO in 1942 and served in the radio news department, and as host of the popular *Town and Country Quiz* program, before moving to television as a news and weather presenter when WHO-TV signed on in 1954.

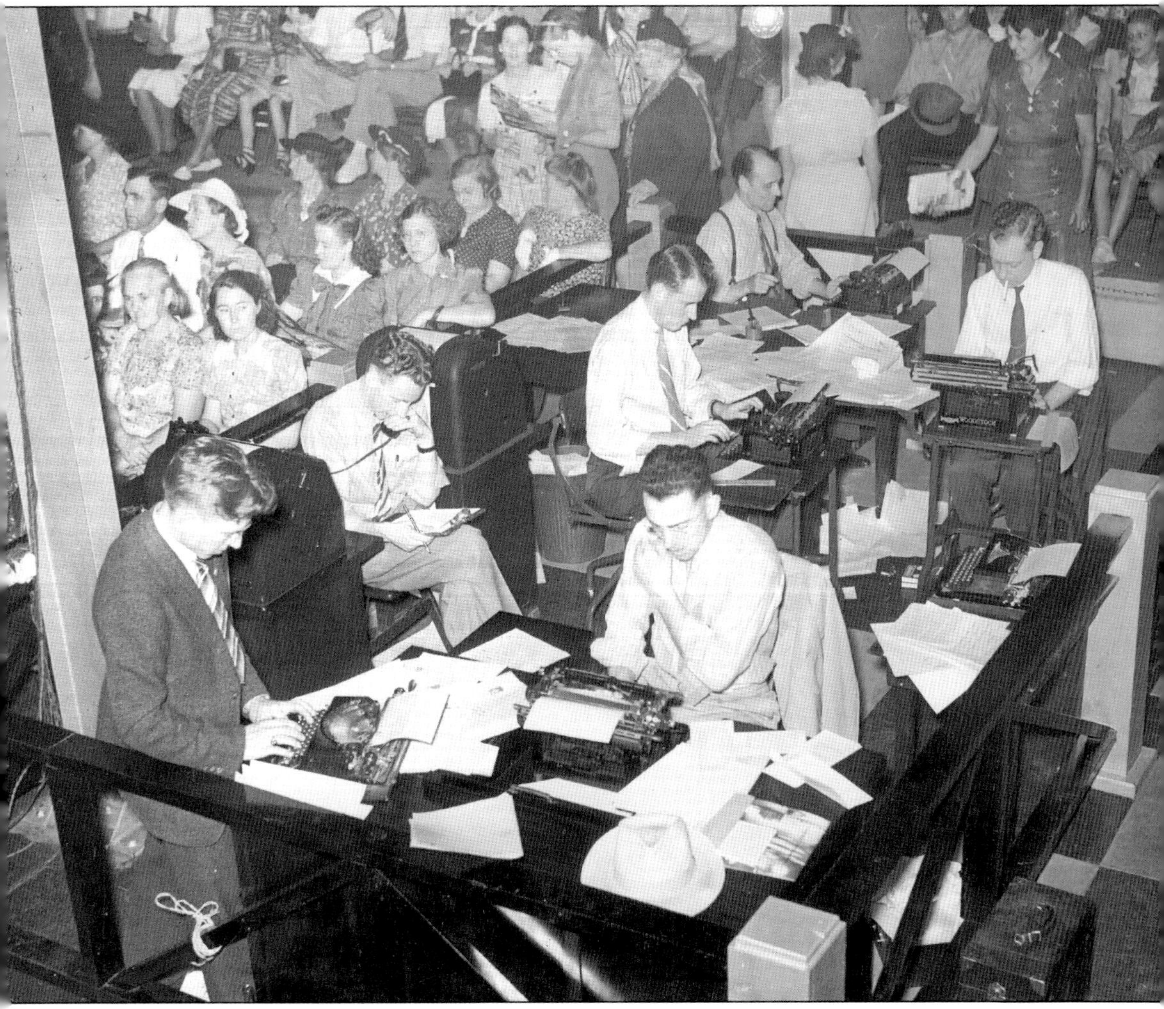

During the Iowa State Fair in the 1930s, the entire WHO news department moved to the station's original Crystal Studio at the fairgrounds. Seen in this 1937 photograph in rather cramped quarters are farm director Herb Plambeck (front right, in the striped shirt), news editor Jack Shelley (at the typewriter directly behind Plambeck), and news director H.R. Gross (in suspenders, directly behind Shelley).

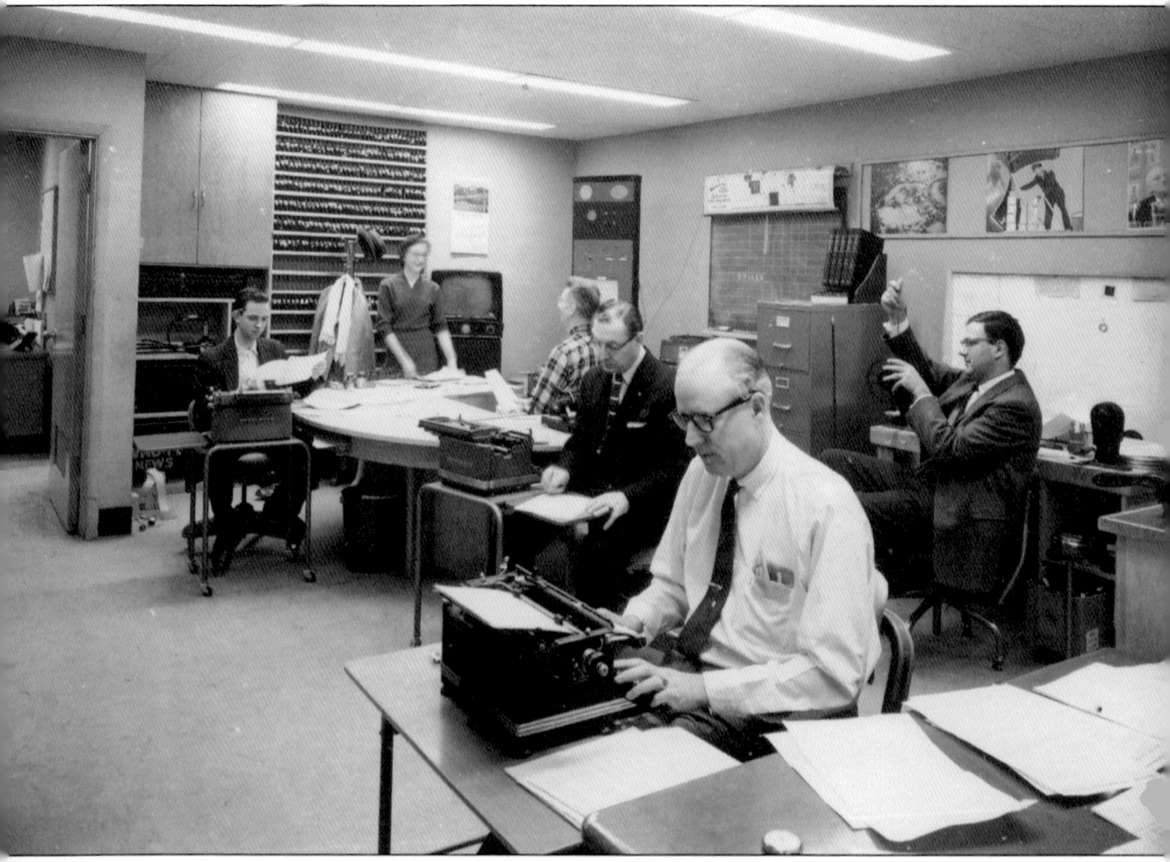

The combined WHO radio and television newsroom at 1100 Walnut Street is seen in this photograph from January 1958. Vern Bodelund is at the far left, while Jay Hytone is at far right; in the center are, from background to foreground, Len Howe, Clay Rusk, and Jack Shelley.

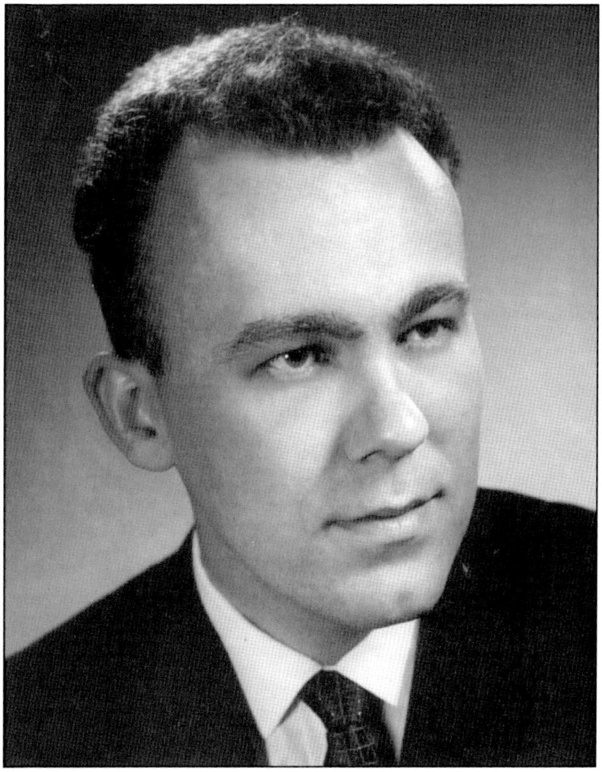

Everett "Ev" Hickman joined the WHO stations in 1955. A graduate of Drake University, Hickman spent his entire career at WHO, including a stint hosting a record show as one of the WHO Music Men and later as the editorialist for WHO-TV. He concluded his career anchoring the evening news at WHO Radio. Hickman won the Jack Shelley Award for lifetime achievement from the Iowa Broadcast News Association in 1992.

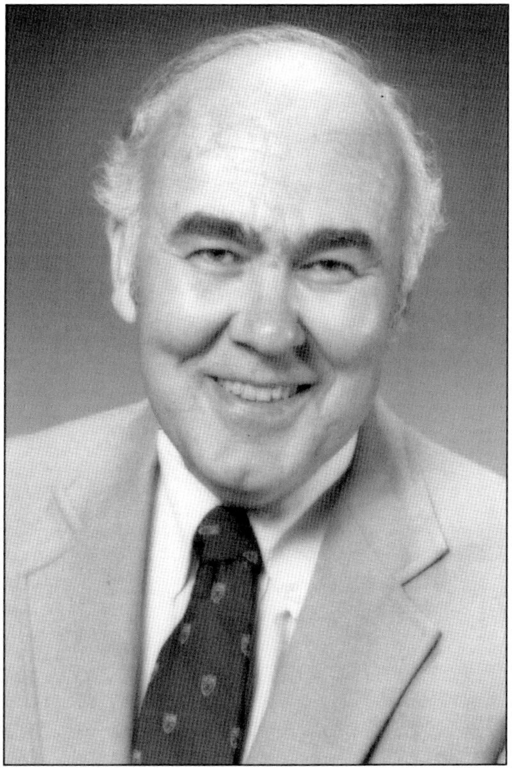

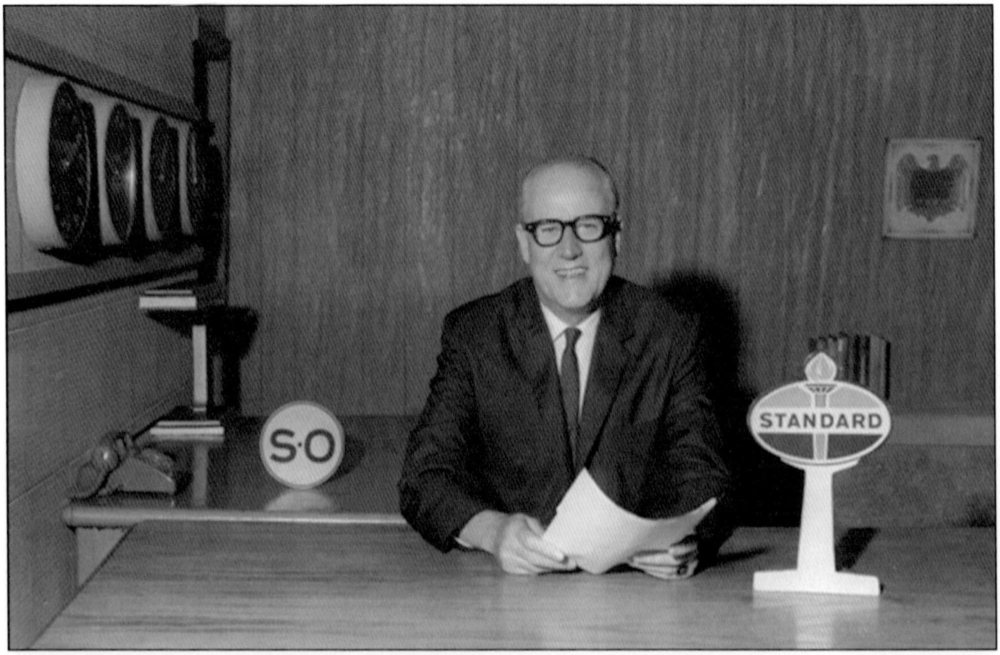

As manager of the entire WHO news operation and anchor of the signature 12:30 p.m. radio newscast, Jack Shelley long resisted the pressure to move to television as a news anchor. Ultimately, he became the station's 10:00 p.m. news anchor while continuing the midday radio newscast with which he had become so identified. These photographs show Shelley at work in the television studios at 1100 Walnut Street. The photograph above shows a 1960s news set with signage for Standard Oil, the newscast sponsor, and the photograph below depicts Shelley behind a slightly earlier television anchor desk.

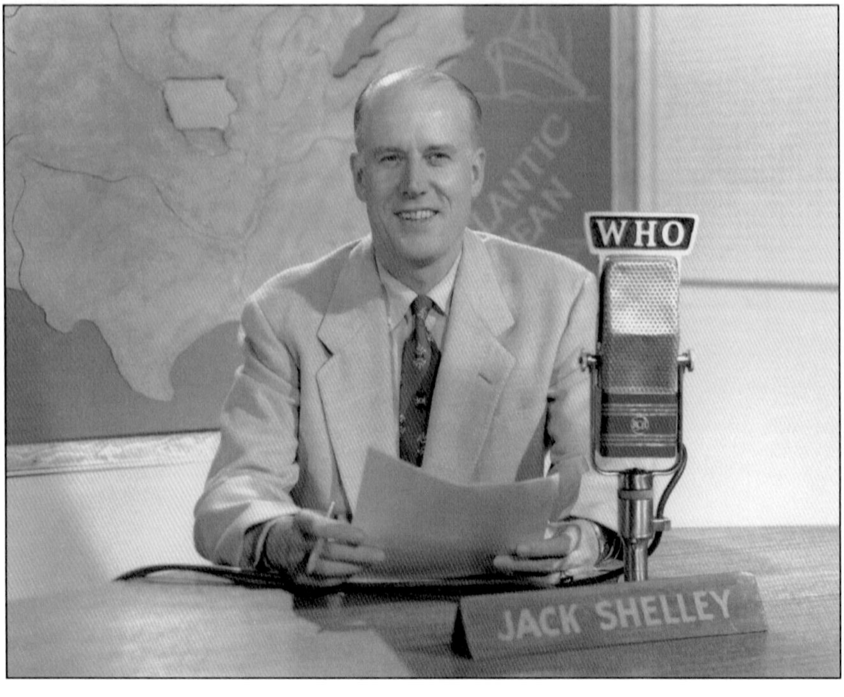

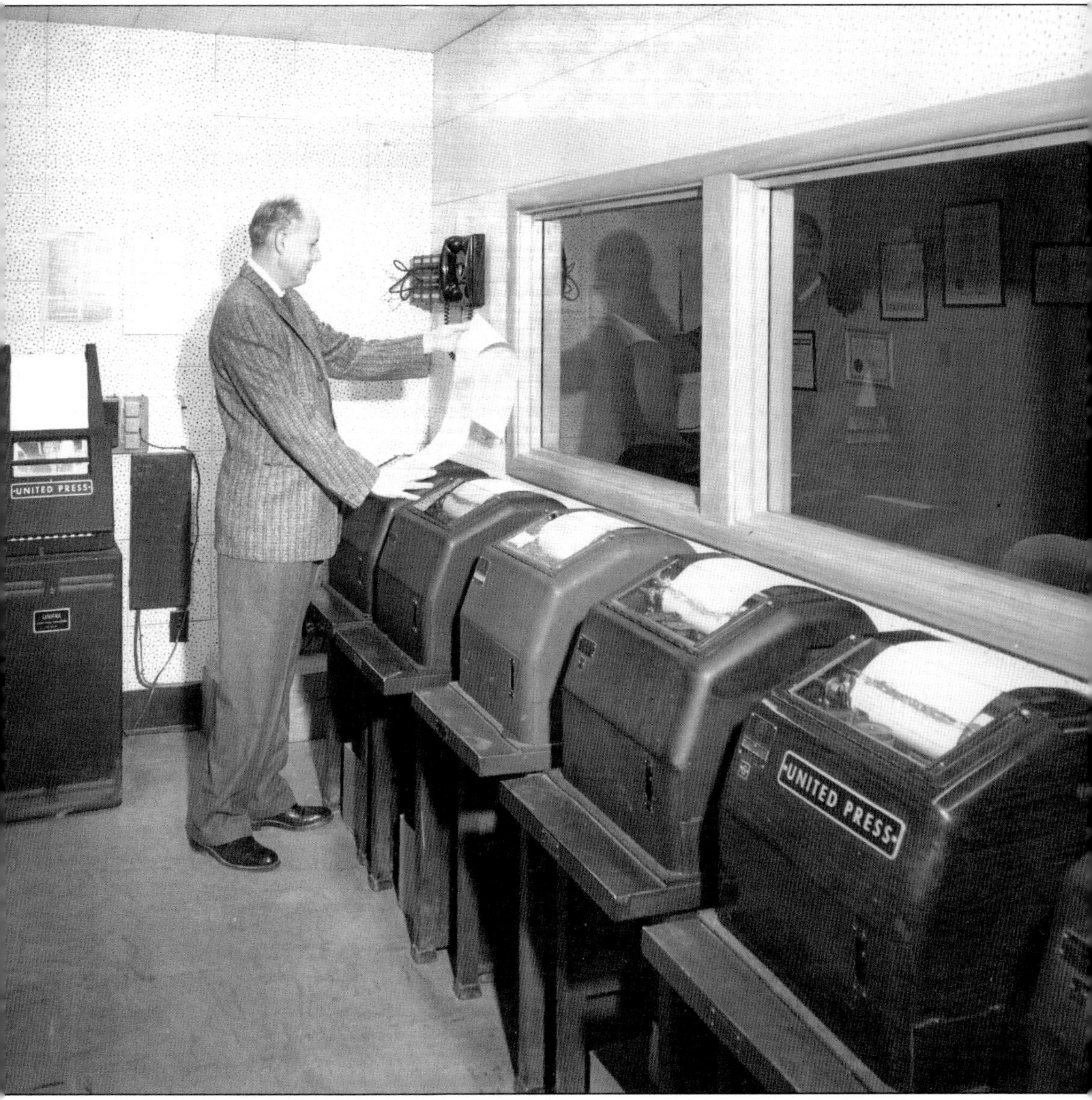

WHO news director Jack Shelley is checking one of the various Teletype wires that brought national and international news to the station. After 30 years in the WHO news department, at age 53 Jack Shelley left daily broadcasting for a new career as a professor, teaching broadcast journalism at Iowa State University (ISU) in Ames. A faculty member at ISU from 1965 until reaching the then-mandatory retirement age of 70 in 1982, Shelley was responsible for teaching the craft to hundreds of today's practicing journalists. In retirement, he was still active in the broadcasting community, appearing regularly at conferences until shortly before his death in September 2010 at age 98. The top award in Iowa broadcast journalism—the Iowa Broadcast News Association's Jack Shelley Award—has been presented annually in his honor since 1972.

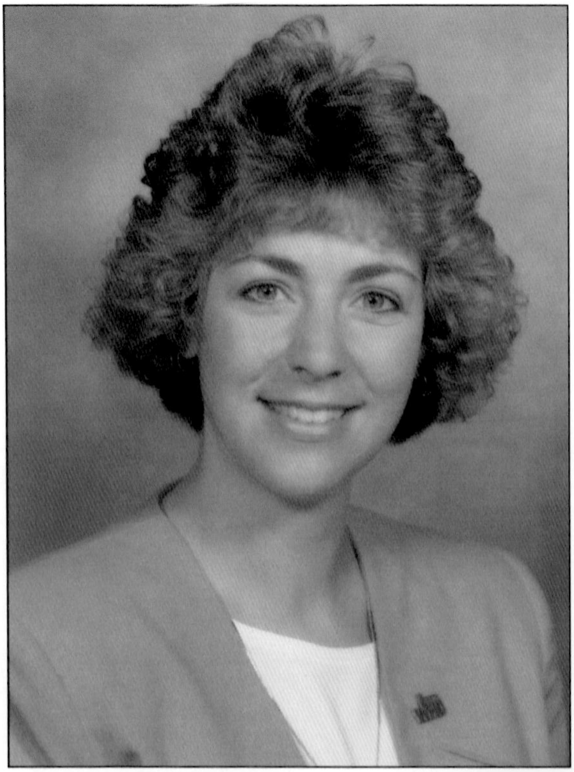

Jodi Chapman (left) was heard regularly anchoring and reporting for WHO Radio newscasts for more than a decade starting in the 1990s. Kevin Teale (below) was political reporter and anchor at WHO Radio from 1984 to 1991 as part of a 12-year broadcasting career before moving into public-sector communications, including a 14-year stint as communications director for the Iowa Department of Public Health.

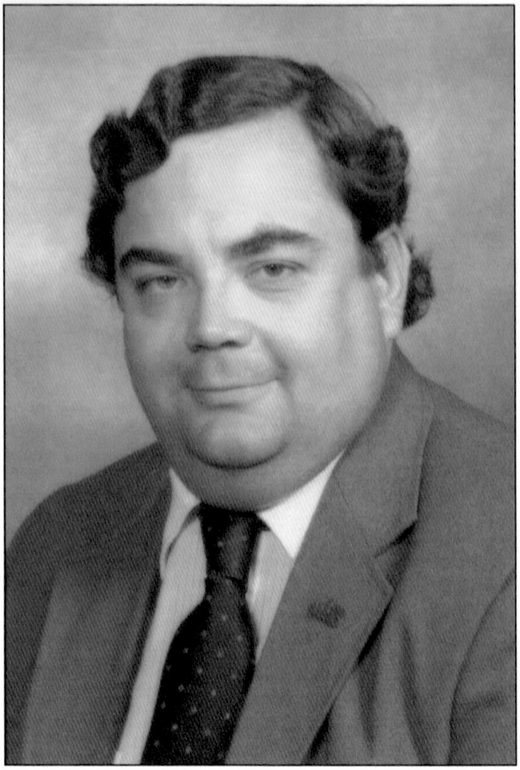

Bob Wilbanks came to WHO Radio in 1960 and succeeded Jack Shelley as news director for radio and television in 1965. Wilbanks anchored the 6:00 p.m. television newscast for several years. He won the Jack Shelley Award for lifetime achievement from the Iowa Broadcast News Association in 1979.

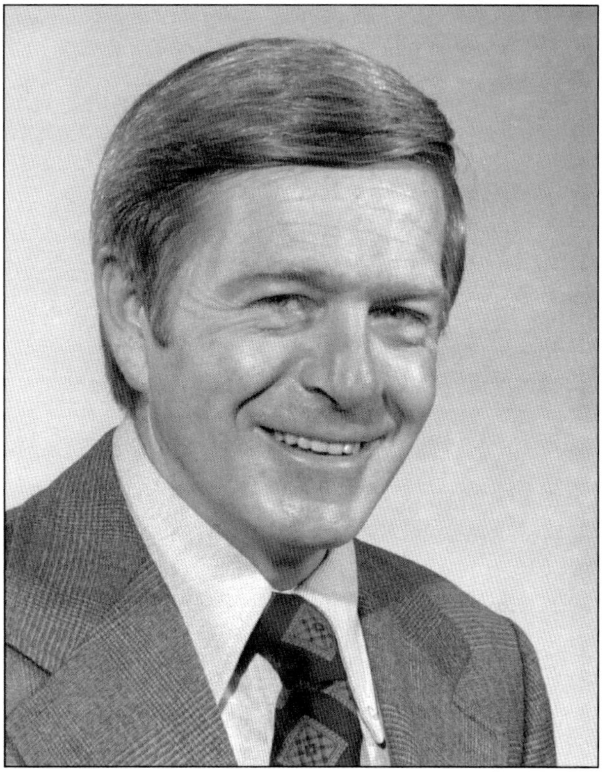

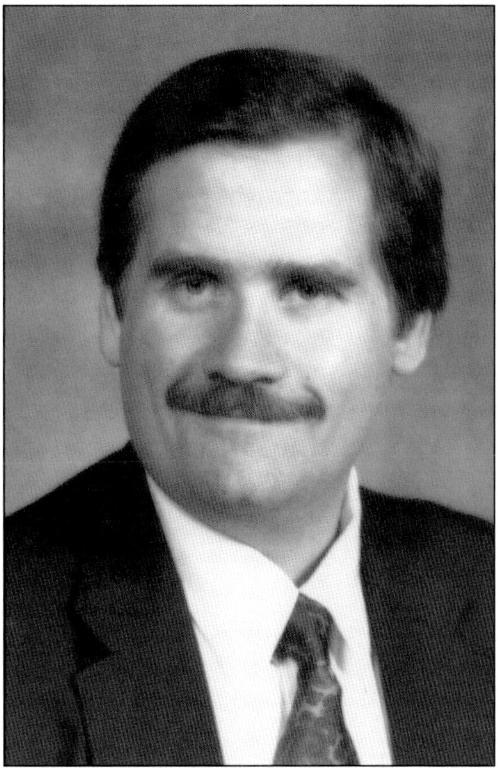

Gary Barrett anchored news and interview programs on WHO Radio in the 1980s and 1990s, including statehouse reporting. He currently anchors newscasts on the station and served as organizer and moderator of a US Senate candidate debate in 2010.

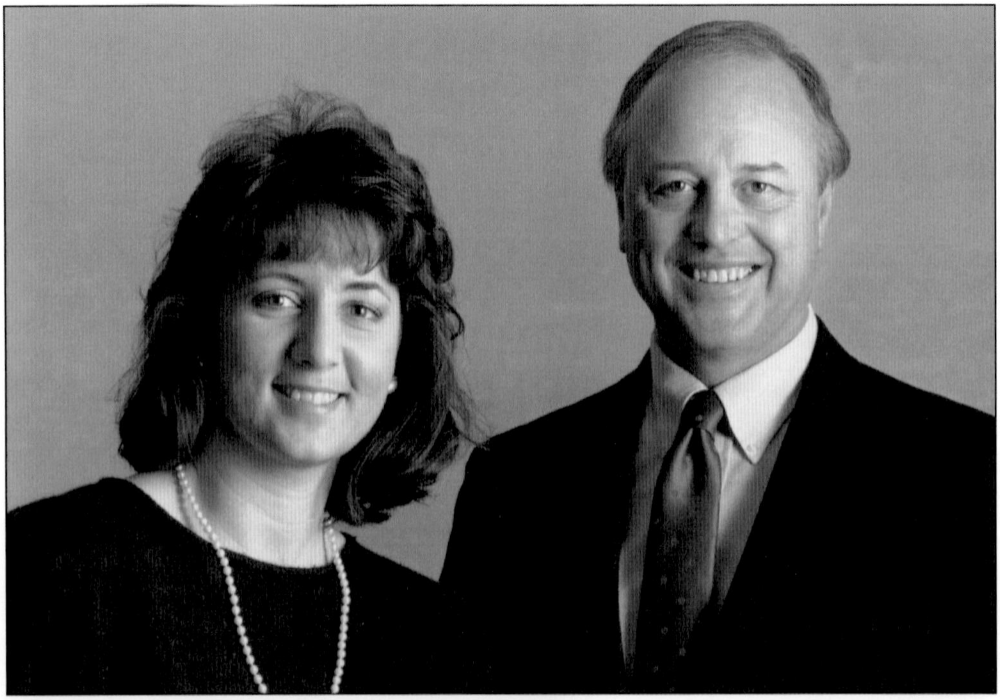

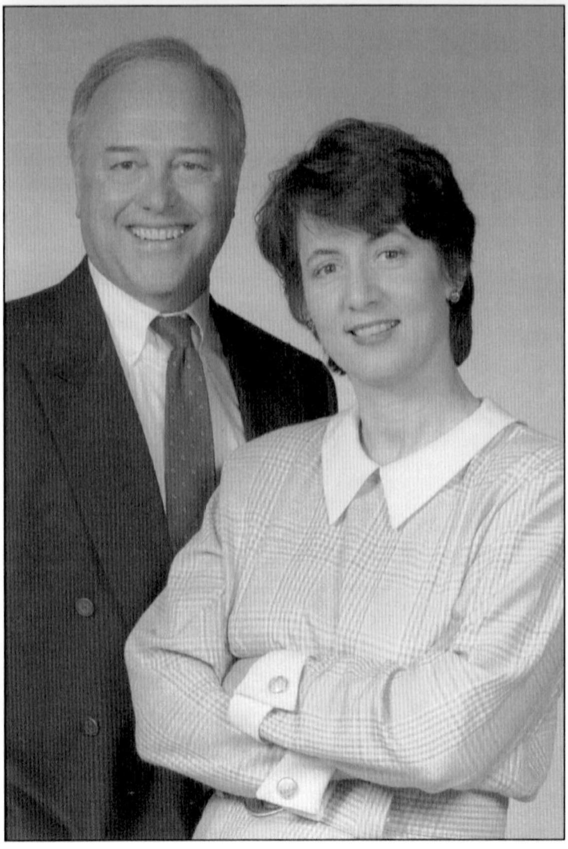

For nearly 20 years, listeners heard a mix of news, information, and interviews from 4:00 p.m. to 6:00 p.m. weekdays on *Drive Time Des Moines*, hosted for its entire run by Sue Pritchard Danielson and Jerry Reno. The image above was taken in 1991, while the photograph at left shows the duo in 1996. The program ended in 2006. Danielson continues to report and anchor news for WHO Radio.

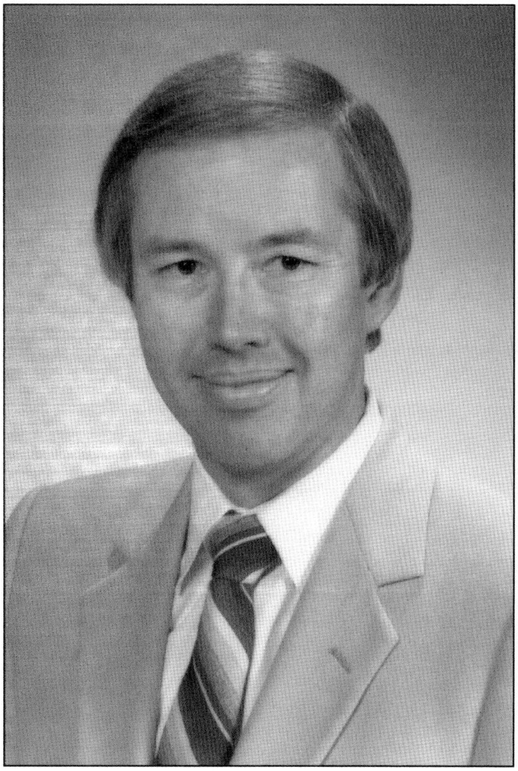

Starting in the mid-1980s, Jess Peterson anchored daily morning newscasts on WHO Radio for nearly two decades, including for many years on the morning show cohosted by Van Harden.

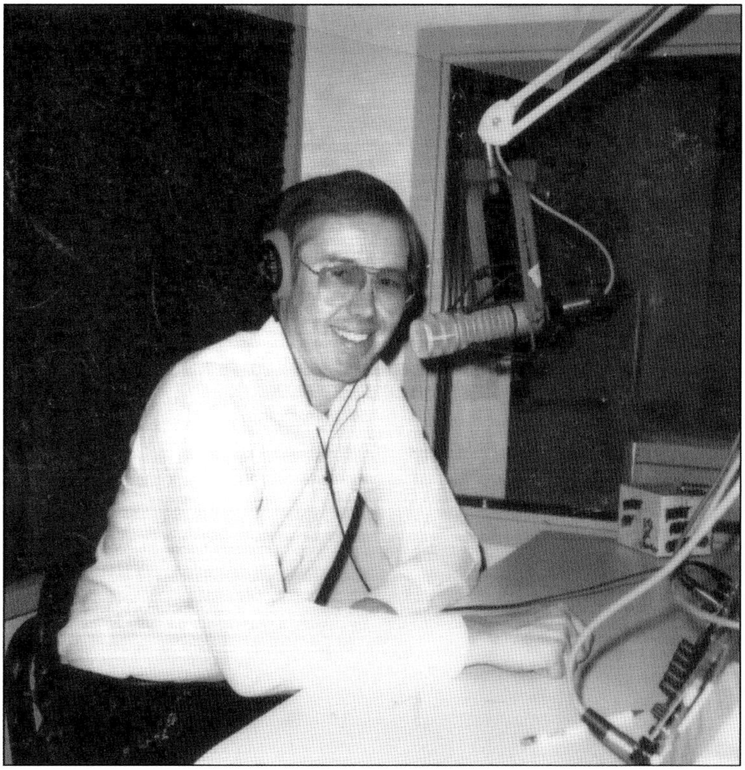

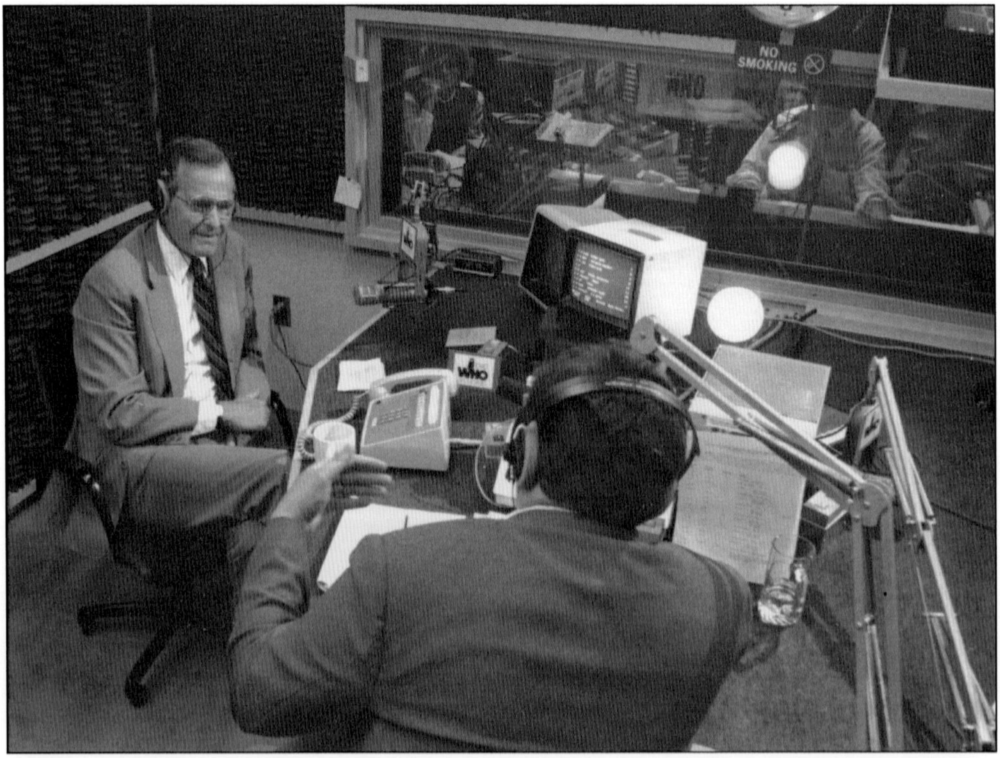

US presidents have found the WHO Radio microphones to be important stops as they sought to get their messages to the public. In the above September 1987 photograph, then-Vice President George H.W. Bush is in the studio during his campaign for the 1988 presidential nomination; the photograph below shows WHO's Bob Quinn interviewing Pres. Bill Clinton in May 1993. Clinton would visit the WHO studios later that summer during a visit to Des Moines to view in person the record flooding in Iowa's capital city.

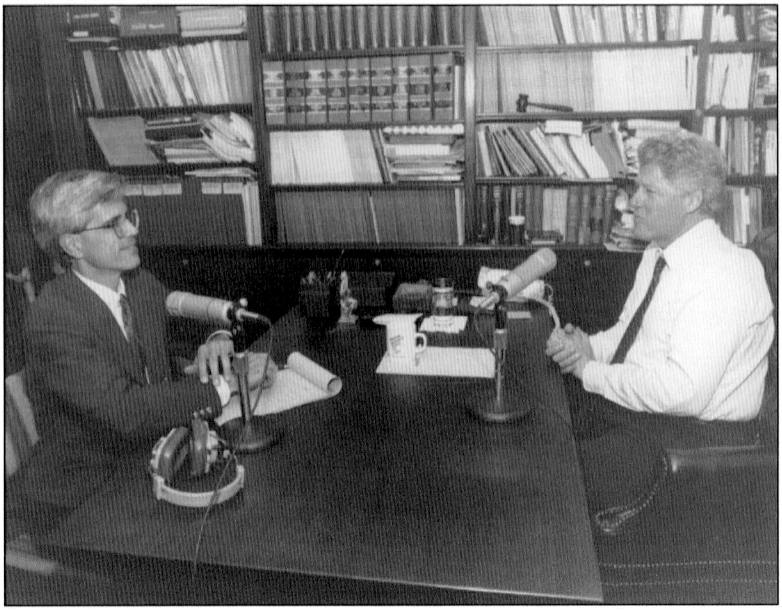

Three

The View from the Press Box

In the early days of radio, stations did not have the luxury of audiotape or computers, so all programming was live in one form or another. This meant a station needed to fill many hours of airtime each day.

One way early broadcasters quickly learned to fill time was through broadcasting sporting events. Not only did it fill a gap in a station's broadcast schedule, but it also was popular with audiences.

Games were typically broadcast on a single station; at the time, there was no way to easily connect a number of stations in what today is called a network. That led to re-creation of game events, and among the most famous were the ones done at WHO Radio by a future president of the United States.

The station would receive the pitch-by-pitch account of the game via telegraph. A telegraph operator at the station would write down the information received by Morse code and pass it to the announcer, who would act as if he were at the ballpark and describe the action based solely on the telegraph transmission. Primitive sound effects were employed, like a stick striking a block of wood to simulate a hit.

The challenge was for the announcer to provide enough description and commentary to lead a listening audience to feel like they were really at the game. The announcer never actually claimed he was at the ballpark, and the station was careful to promote these broadcasts as re-creations of the game, but given that radio was then known as the theater of the mind, the re-creation had to be as real as possible.

One of the other challenges was to respond to technical issues—like the telegraph going dead. Ronald Reagan often told a story of re-creating a Cubs-Cardinals game in the bottom of the ninth inning when all of a sudden the game feed stopped coming down the wire. Reagan filled the time by pretending the batter was simply fouling off pitches until the signal was restored.

Game re-creations were common, even into the 1960s and particularly on stations that covered minor-league baseball teams. The announcer was in the local stadium for home games but re-created road games as a cost-saving measure.

Reagan also broadcast from stadiums, including University of Iowa football games. One boy who listened to those broadcasts at his home in Davenport would grow up to take Reagan's place—and for many Iowans, his was the "Voice of the Hawkeyes" for more than 50 years.

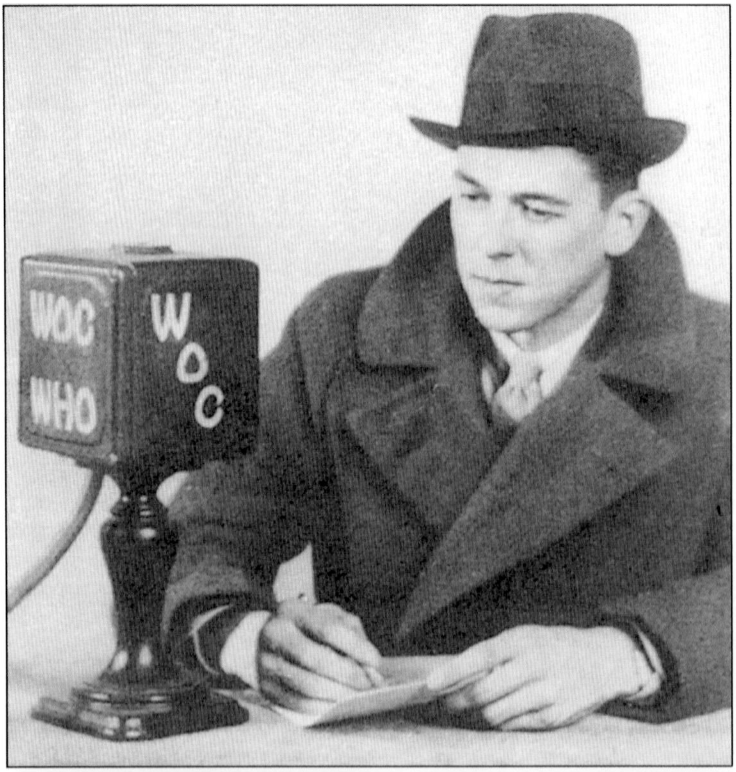

The first sports director at WHO Radio, Ronald Reagan, gained a large following during his four years at the Des Moines station. Reagan was hired by WOC Radio in Davenport in 1932; at age 21, he was hired to broadcast University of Iowa football games at a rate of $5 per game. He soon was promoted to a full-time announcer's job and paid $100 per month. Reagan moved from Davenport with the rest of the WOC staff when the operations were combined in Des Moines in early 1933.

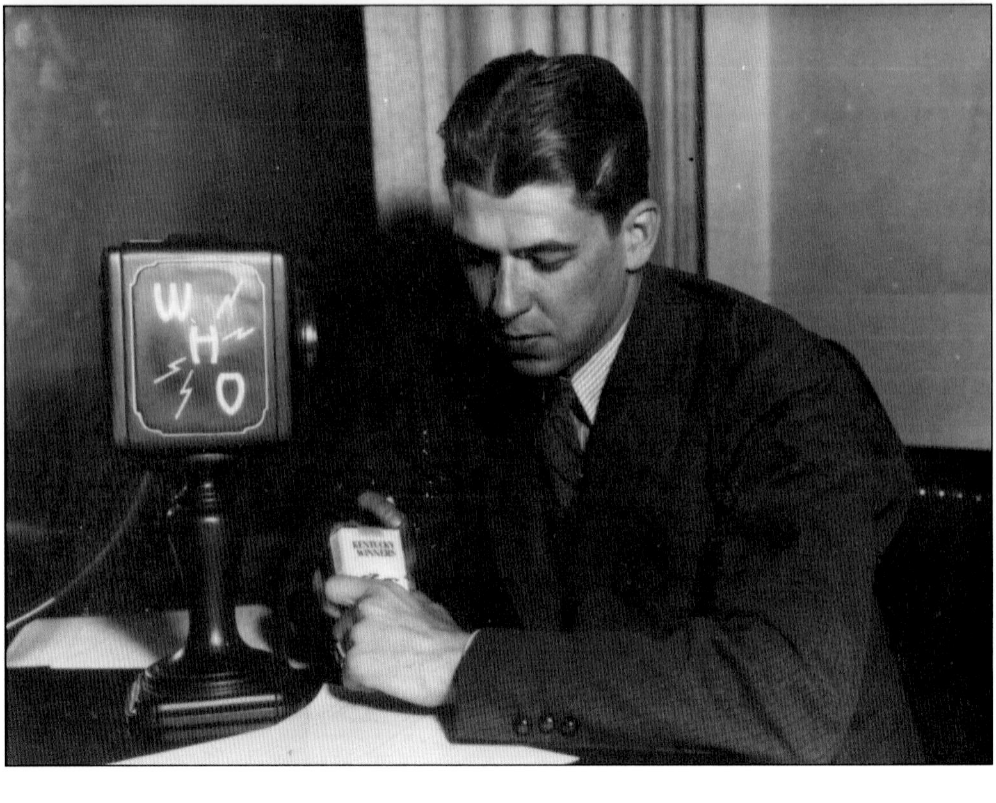

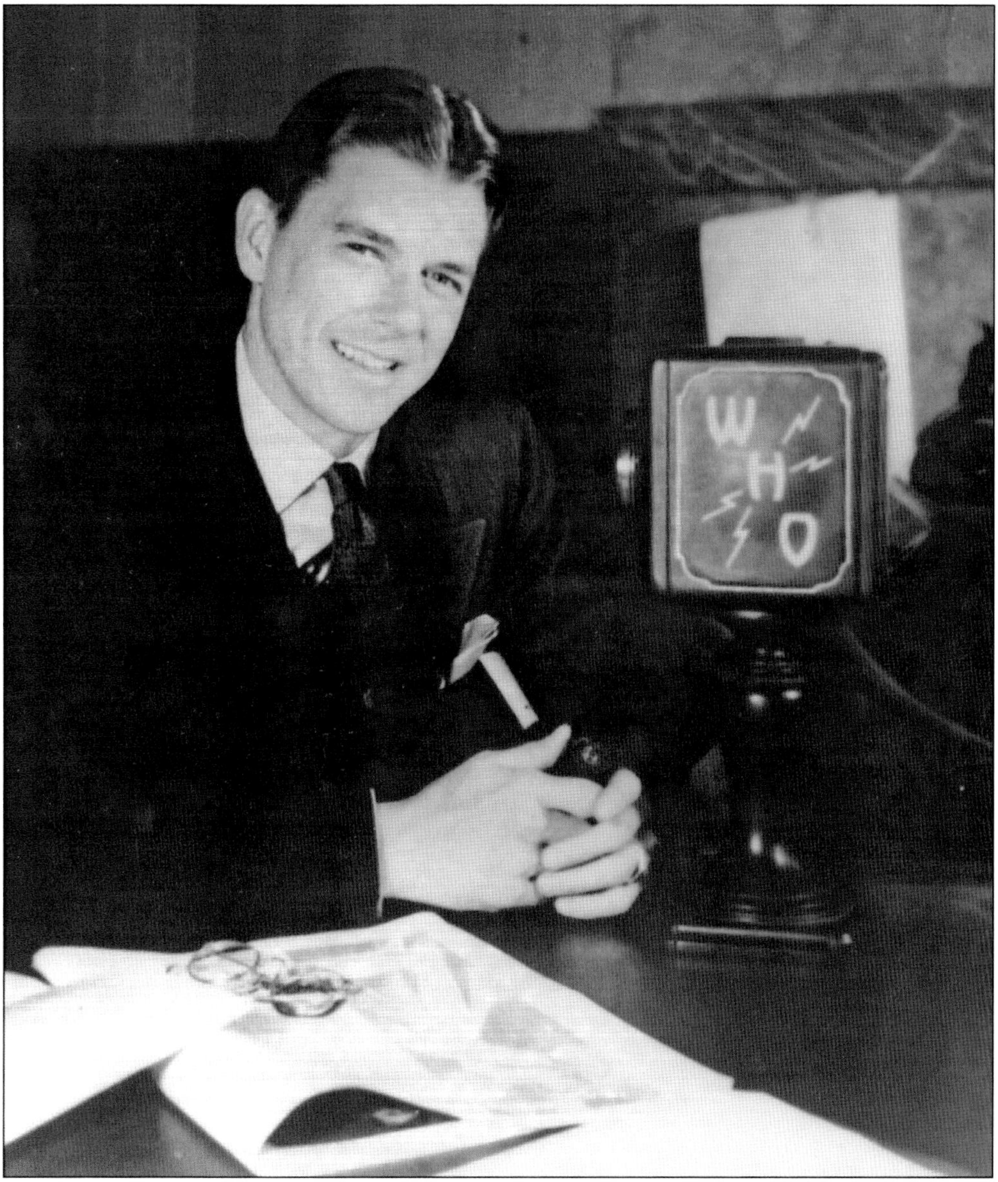

"Dutch Reagan, himself a varsity man, has a comprehensive knowledge of sports in general, and ability to put into swift running words the rapidly moving activities of sports events from an unbiased observer's viewpoint," according to WHO station promotional materials of the era. Reagan was the voice of Hawkeye football from 1932 to 1937 and broadcast live events, such as the Drake Relays, in addition to his famous baseball game re-creations (some of which were done in front of a live audience at the Iowa State Fair). Reagan reportedly closed his late-night broadcasts on WHO with a coded message that told friends whether he would show up at his favorite hangout, the Moonlight Inn at Seventy-third Street and University Avenue, that night.

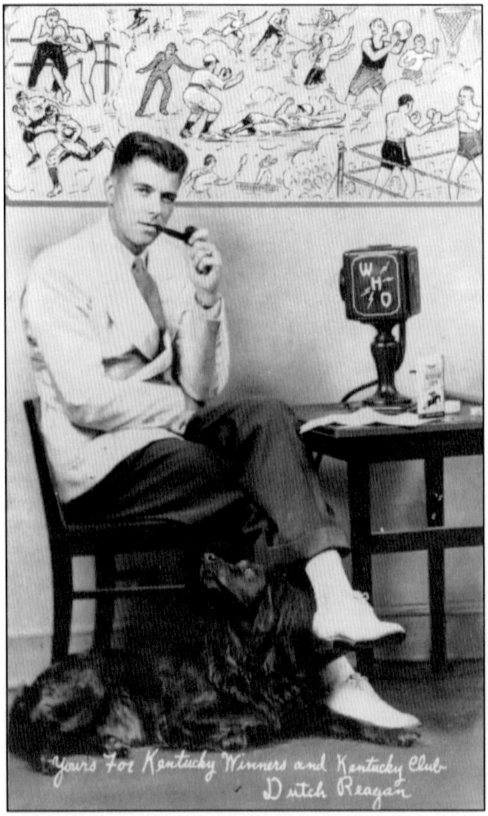

This postcard was printed by the station to be sent in response to listeners' letters. Reading, "Yours for Kentucky Winners and Kentucky Club—Dutch Reagan," the postcard also served as a promotion for the tobacco company, no doubt why Reagan was prominently posed with a pipe. Kentucky Club was one of the sponsors of Reagan's broadcasts.

In this rare photograph from the 1934 Drake Relays, Reagan is seen in the center, with trademark hat, calling the action live from the Drake Stadium field. At left is Reed Snyder, WHO's chief engineer, and at right is Harold Fair, the station's program manager. The use of the WOC/WHO microphone depicts the dual call letters still in effect for the stations at that time.

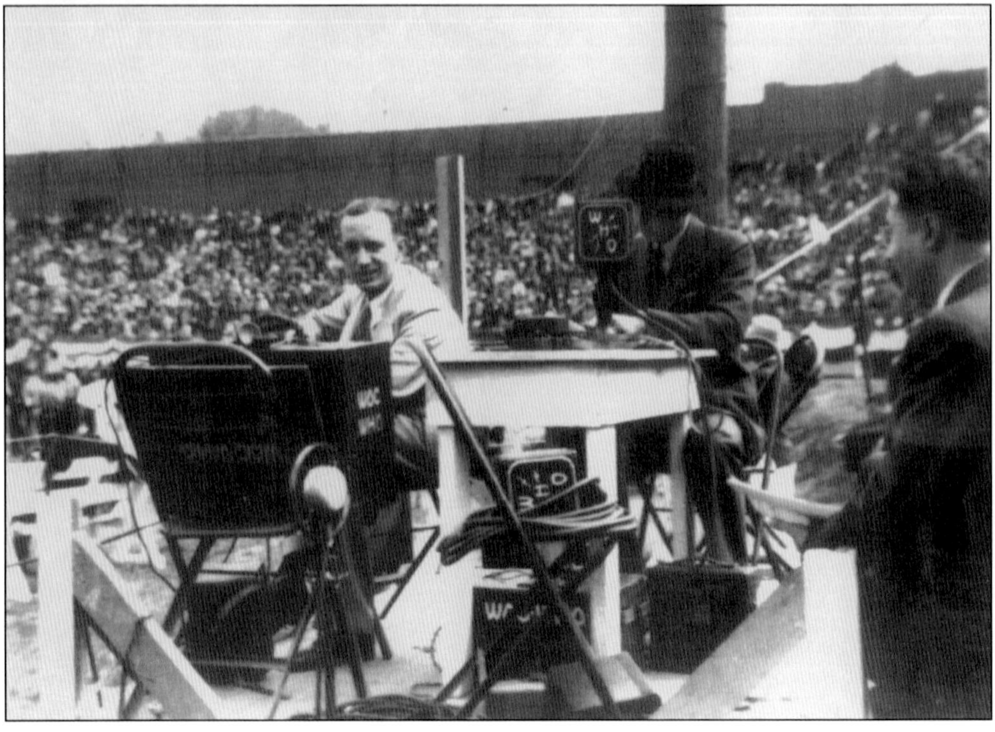

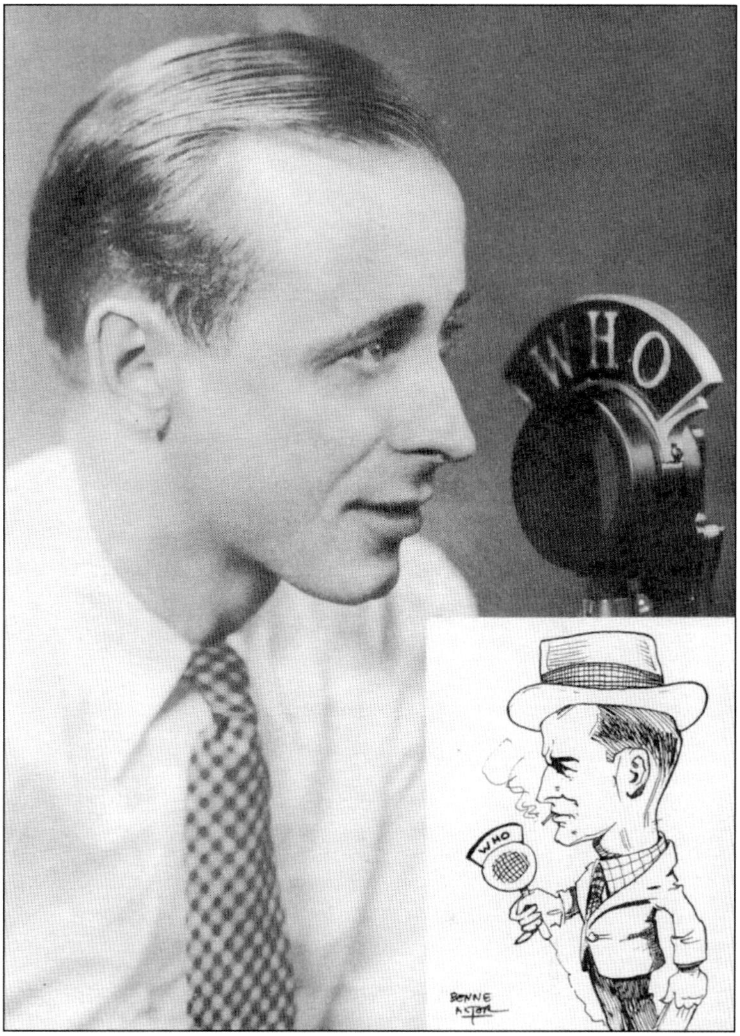

Bill Brown succeeded Ronald Reagan as WHO Radio sports director. At right, from a 1939 promotional brochure, Brown is seen at the microphone with an inset caricature drawn by Benne Alter, who would become a well-known personality in his own right at WMT Radio in Cedar Rapids. Below, Brown is seated by a pile of Wheaties cereal box tops submitted as entries in a contest conducted in connection with Wheaties' sponsorship of the baseball games Brown re-created on air.

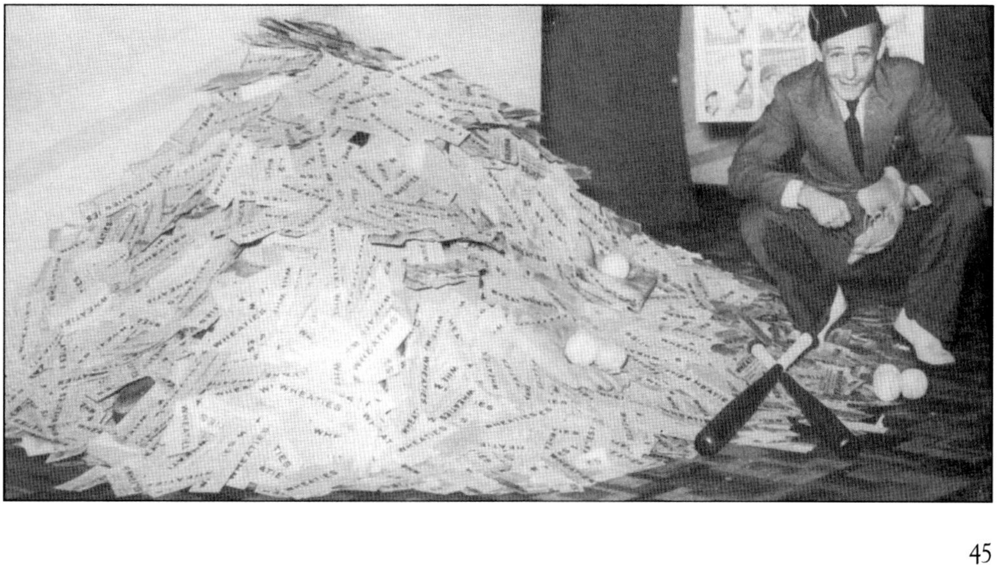

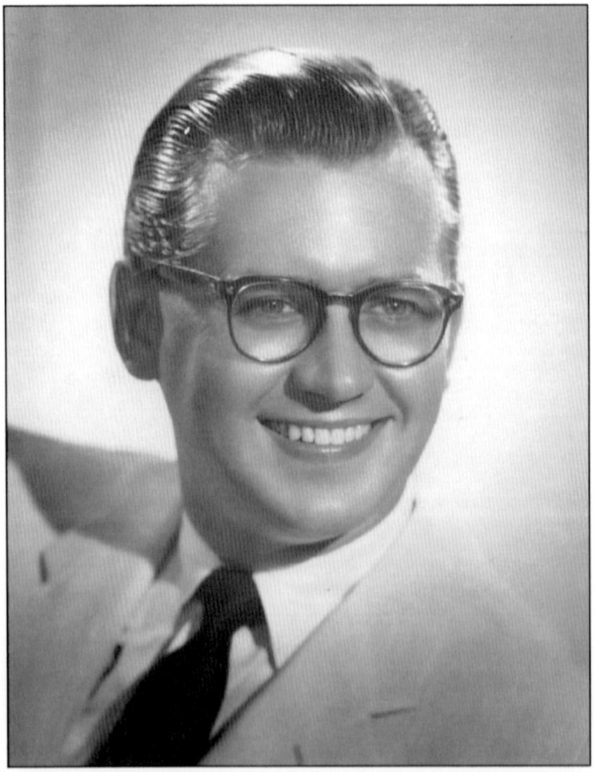

Fresh from the University of Iowa, James F. "Jim" Zabel began work for WHO Radio on May 18, 1944—and has been a fixture on the station ever since. As the station's sports director, Zabel personally called some 6,000 play-by-play events, including every Iowa football and basketball game for a half century. In the 1960s and 1970s, the versatile talent also hosted a daily radio talk show focusing on general contemporary topics. While many remember Zabel as anchoring sportscasts on WHO-TV, fewer recall that he served a stint in the 1950s as the television late-news anchor while also serving as radio sports director.

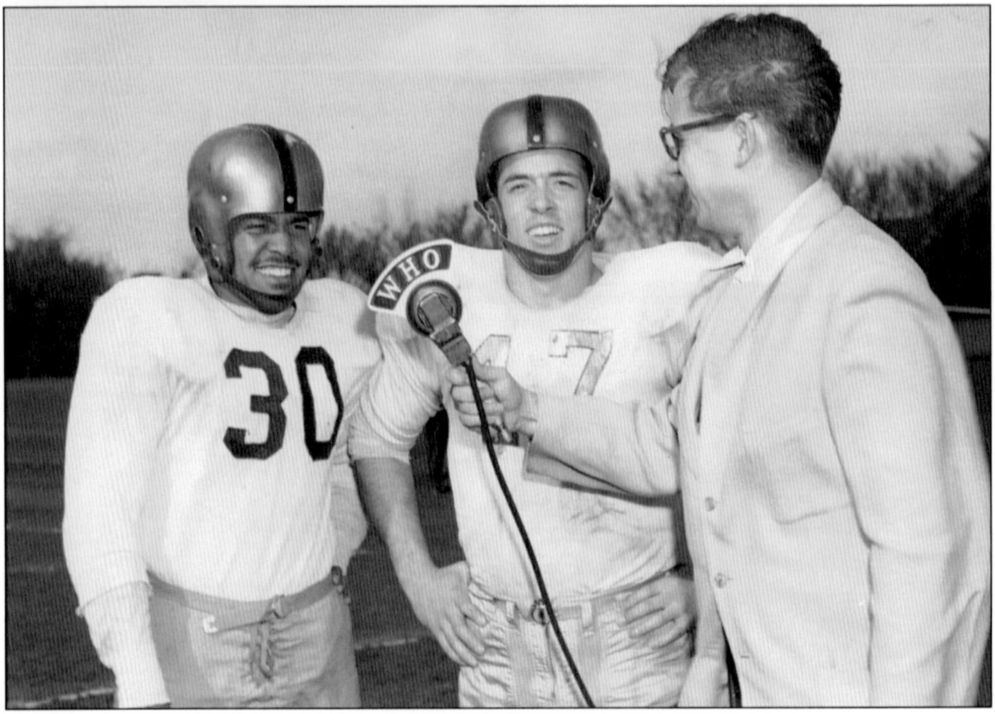

Not that long out of college himself, a 29-year-old Jim Zabel is seen interviewing 1950 University of Iowa football left halfback Don Commack (left) and center John Towner.

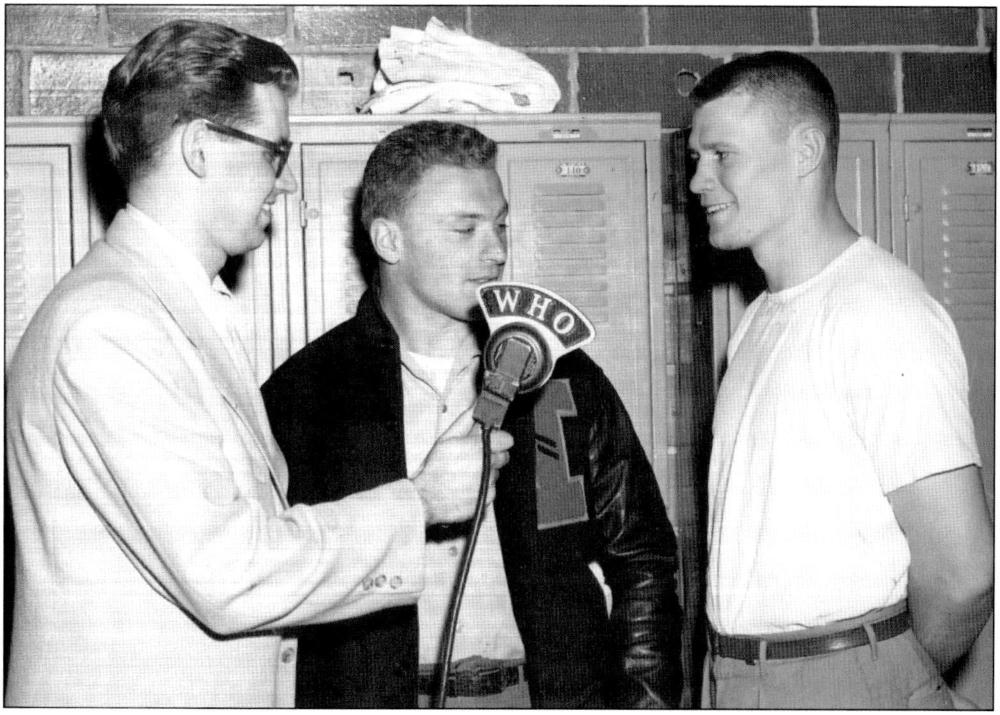

Sports director Jim Zabel conducts a locker room interview with Hawkeye right halfback Jerry Faske (center) and fullback Gerald Nordman in this 1950 photograph.

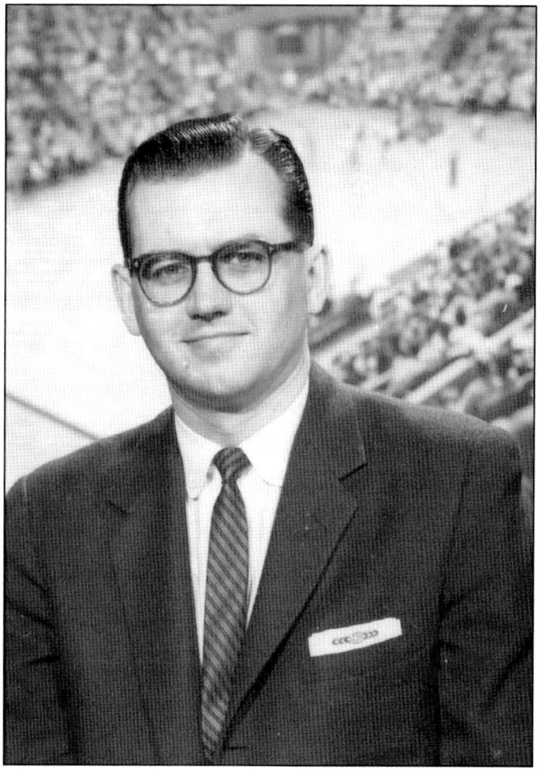

Jim Zabel was at home courtside at Veterans Memorial Auditorium as the radio and television voice of the state high school boys' and girls' basketball tournaments for 52 years. Winner of the National Association of Broadcasters Marconi Award as Personality of the Year in 1993, Zabel is also a member of the Iowa Broadcasters Association Hall of Fame. Included in a select group for the *Golden Voices of Football* book project were two of Zabel's legendary game calls: the Iowa-Notre Dame game in 1953 and the Iowa-Ohio State game in 1987. He also hosted the nation's longest-running show of its kind, *Let's Go Bowling,* on WHO-TV for 33 years. And who can forget the two incarnations of the weekly *Beat the Bear* sports prediction shows? At a time when many would have been content to relax, Zabel took on duties as the radio play-by-play voice of the original Iowa Barnstormers, calling 150 games in the 1990s, including two Arena Bowl appearances.

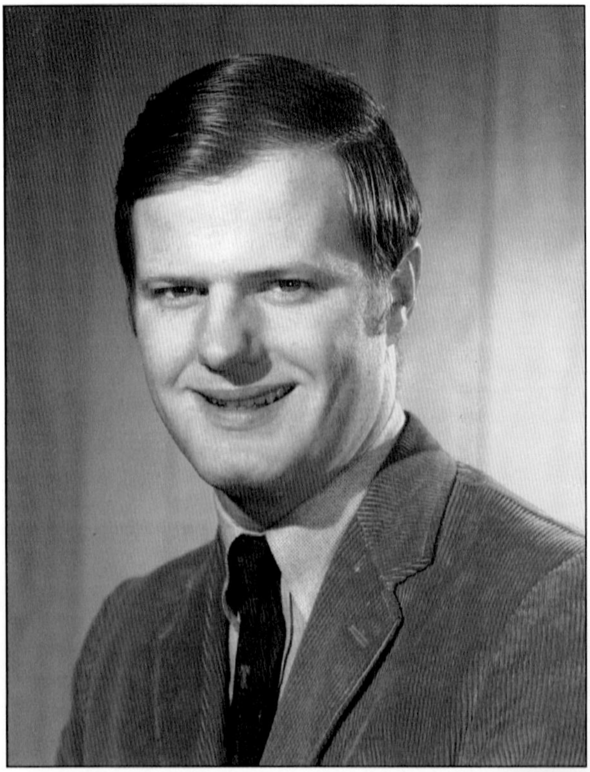

Mike Newell served as assistant sports director at WHO from 1968 to 1974, doing nightly radio sportscasts and filling in on WHO-TV as needed; he also called Iowa, Iowa State, and Drake basketball games. From 1981 to 2003, Newell was the play-by-play voice of Iowa women's basketball, morning radio sports anchor, and host of the popular *Sound-Off* call-in program, which followed Iowa football games on Saturdays.

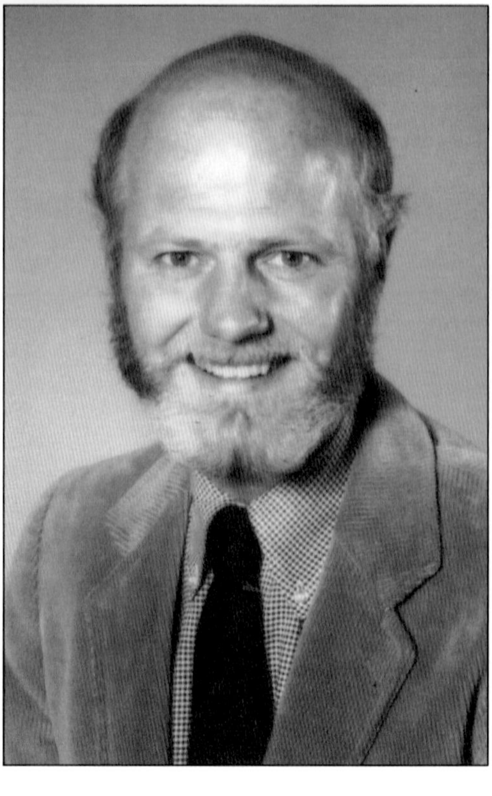

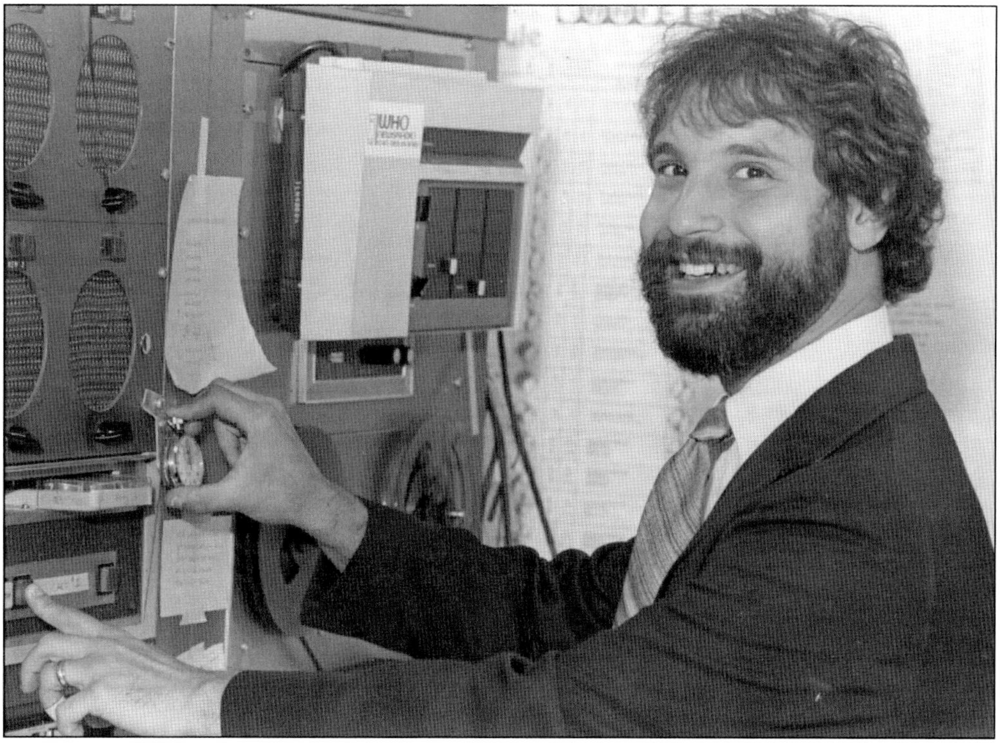

Larry Cotlar has been in sports radio since 1980, including time with WHO Radio as a sports anchor and play-by-play voice from November 1980 to December 1990. He is presently involved in a variety of Des Moines sports-media projects, including a daily radio talk program and color commentary for Iowa Barnstormers Arena Football League games.

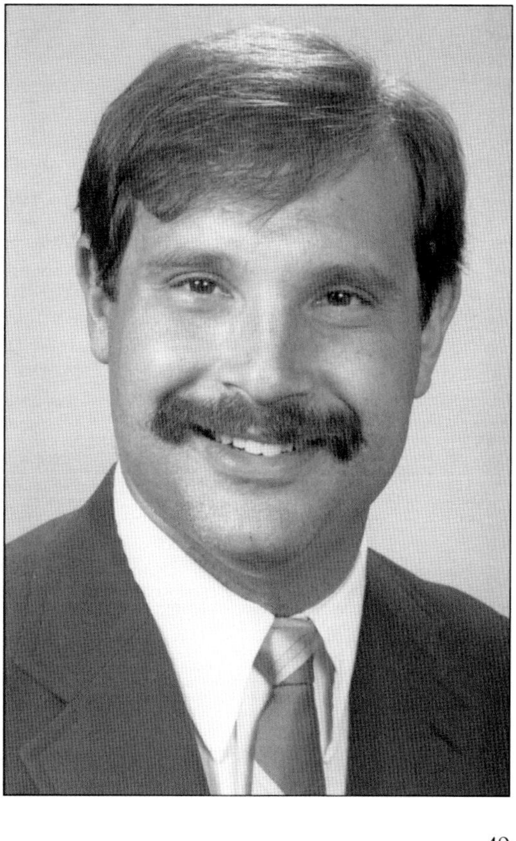

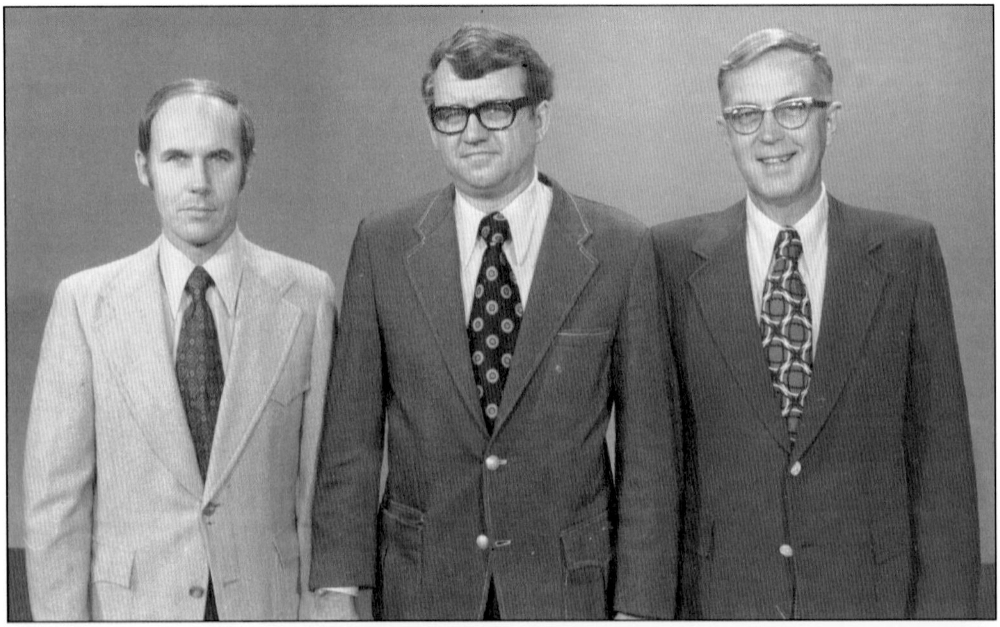

Jim Zabel (center) poses with Dick Schultz (left) and Maury John, two of the state's well-known men's basketball coaches. Schultz coached the University of Iowa team for four years, beginning in 1970, and later went on to become executive director of the NCAA. John's Drake University squad went to the 1969 Final Four, followed by two more Elite Eight finishes. He then went to coach at Iowa State, where his career was cut short by cancer in 1974.

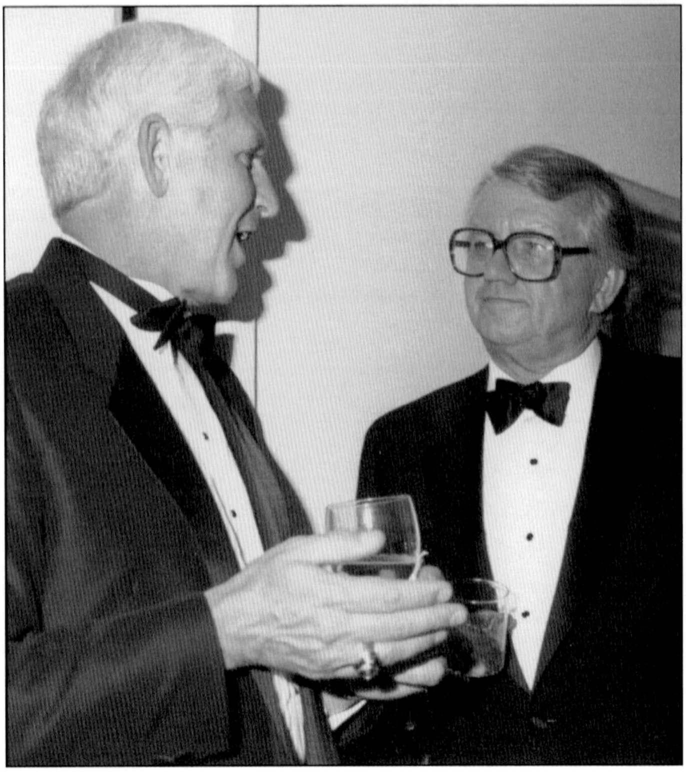

Two Hall-of-Famers meet in 1984 in this photograph. Lute Olson (left) coached men's basketball at the University of Iowa for nine seasons, taking the Hawkeyes to the NCAA tournament for the last five of those years, including an appearance in the 1980 Final Four. He coached Iowa to a 168-90 record between 1974 and 1983 and was inducted into the Naismith Memorial Basketball Hall of Fame in 2002. Jim Zabel was inducted into the Iowa Sports Hall of Fame in 2007. The occasion for the photograph was the special 40 at 1040 Roast, celebrating Zabel's 40th anniversary at WHO Radio.

Iowa football fans had suffered through 17 straight non-winning seasons by the time a Texan named Hayden Fry was hired as the school's 25th head football coach after the 1978 season. By the end of Fry's third year at the helm, the Hawkeyes had returned to Pasadena and the Rose Bowl. Fry took the Hawkeyes to 14 bowl games in his 20 years as coach, compiling a 143-89-6 record along the way. Fry (left) is pictured with Zabel at one of dozens of University of Iowa I-Club summer banquets the two attended across the state. Zabel was a frequent master of ceremonies for the events, which often featured coaches from various sports speaking about the prospects of their teams. Zabel was the play-by-play voice of Hawkeye football on WHO Radio for 49 years, ending with the 1996 season.

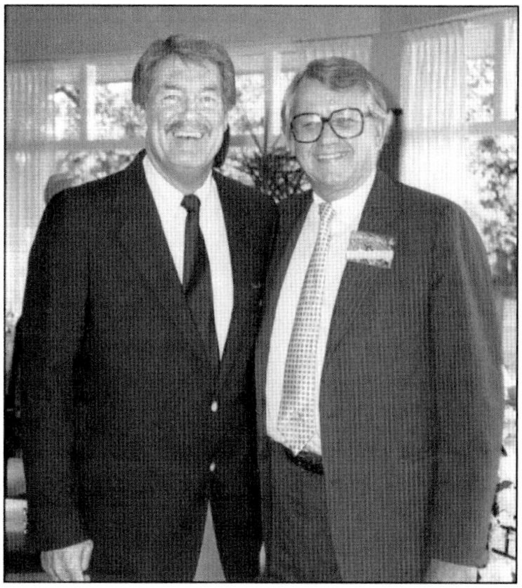

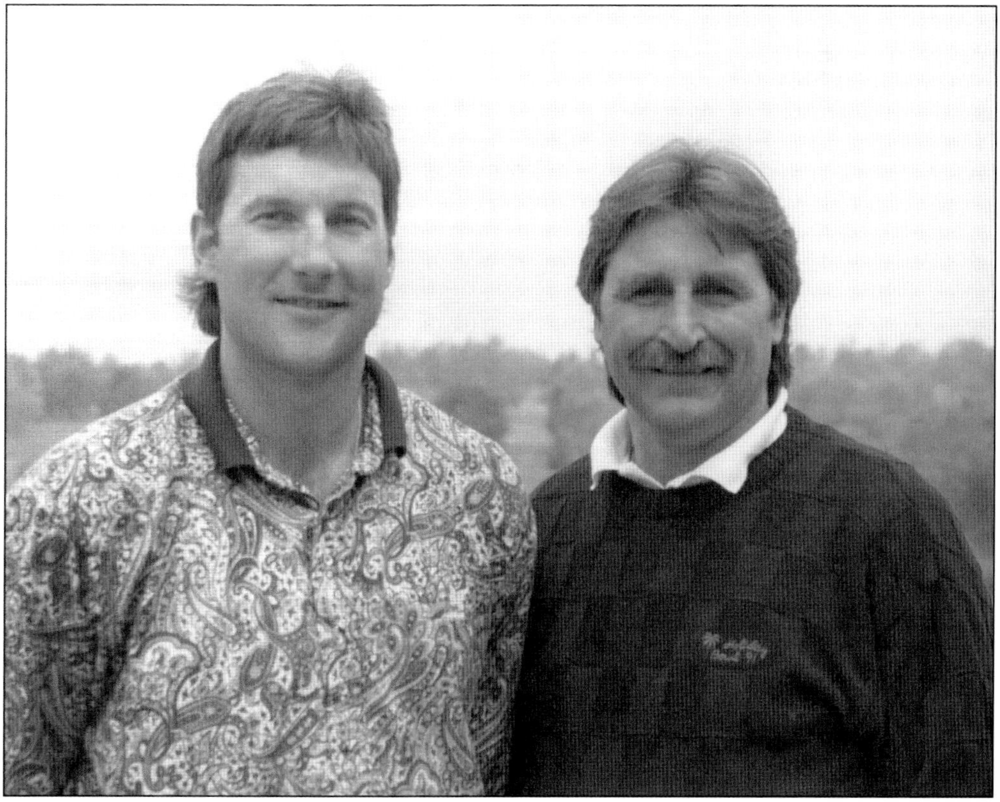

Jim Zabel's longtime broadcast partners on Hawkeye game broadcasts were athletes who went on to successful professional careers after their time wearing the black and gold uniform. Bobby Hansen (left) won a championship ring with the Chicago Bulls, while Ed Podolak (right) was on the Kansas City Chiefs team that won the 1970 Super Bowl. Podolak began as Zabel's color commentator for football in 1982; Hansen joined Zabel courtside for basketball games a decade later. Both men continue to provide commentary on Hawkeye games carried on WHO Radio, with Gary Dolphin, of Learfield Sports, providing the play-by-play call since 1996.

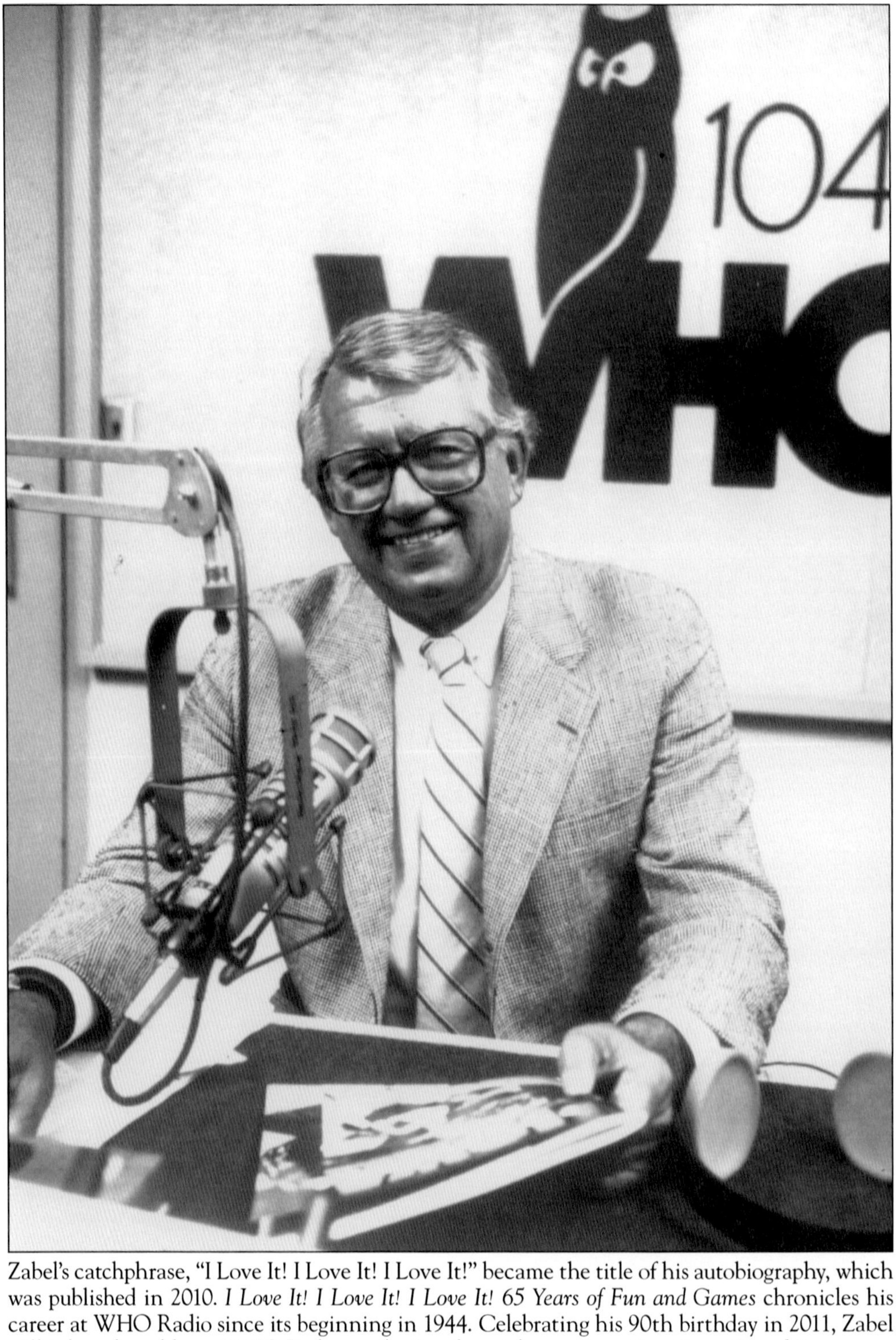

Zabel's catchphrase, "I Love It! I Love It! I Love It!" became the title of his autobiography, which was published in 2010. *I Love It! I Love It! I Love It! 65 Years of Fun and Games* chronicles his career at WHO Radio since its beginning in 1944. Celebrating his 90th birthday in 2011, Zabel still is heard weekly on WHO Radio on the Sunday night program *Two Guys Named Jim*, a two-hour show cohosted with former Iowa State University football coach Jim Walden.

Four

From the Farmstead to the Field

The first full-time radio farm department in America was established at WHO Radio in 1936. Stations had provided market information for some time before that, but given the importance of agriculture to Iowans, WHO management decided to make a stronger commitment to serving that segment of the audience.

A young newspaper reporter named Herb Plambeck was lured to the still-new medium of radio by WHO Radio news director H.R. Gross, who offered to pay Plambeck $120 a month to start—a pay cut from what he had been making. To make matters worse, Gross expected Plambeck to start the morning after his job interview.

So on August 26, 1936, Herb Plambeck delivered his first broadcast on WHO Radio, the beginning of a 34-year association with the station.

But that was just the beginning of Plambeck's eventful first day on the job. After the morning broadcast, he was assigned to do a live program at WHO's original Crystal Studio, which was a square, 10-by-10-foot, glassed-in studio in the center of the Varied Industries Building at the state fairgrounds. Before a live audience that afternoon, Plambeck organized and hosted an impromptu rooster-crowing competition.

Given that it was the middle of the afternoon, however, the roosters were in no mood to crow. It finally occurred to the rookie broadcaster that roosters mainly crow at dawn. He spied a roll of dark paper near the stage and spread it over the roosters' cage, darkening it completely. After a brief intermission, the paper was removed and the birds responded with healthy crowing, saving Plambeck from embarrassment and successfully beginning a 65-year broadcasting career that would take him around the globe and put him in the company of presidents.

A hallmark of the WHO Radio farm department has been the longevity of staff members, men who have spent their entire careers behind the WHO microphone. That has led to a level of loyalty from the audience that is unmatched in American broadcasting. And while the number of farm broadcasters has dwindled across the country (and even at WHO) as times have changed, the station's commitment to interviews, features, and market reports throughout the day, as well as a 90-minute ag-related programming block at midday, remains strong.

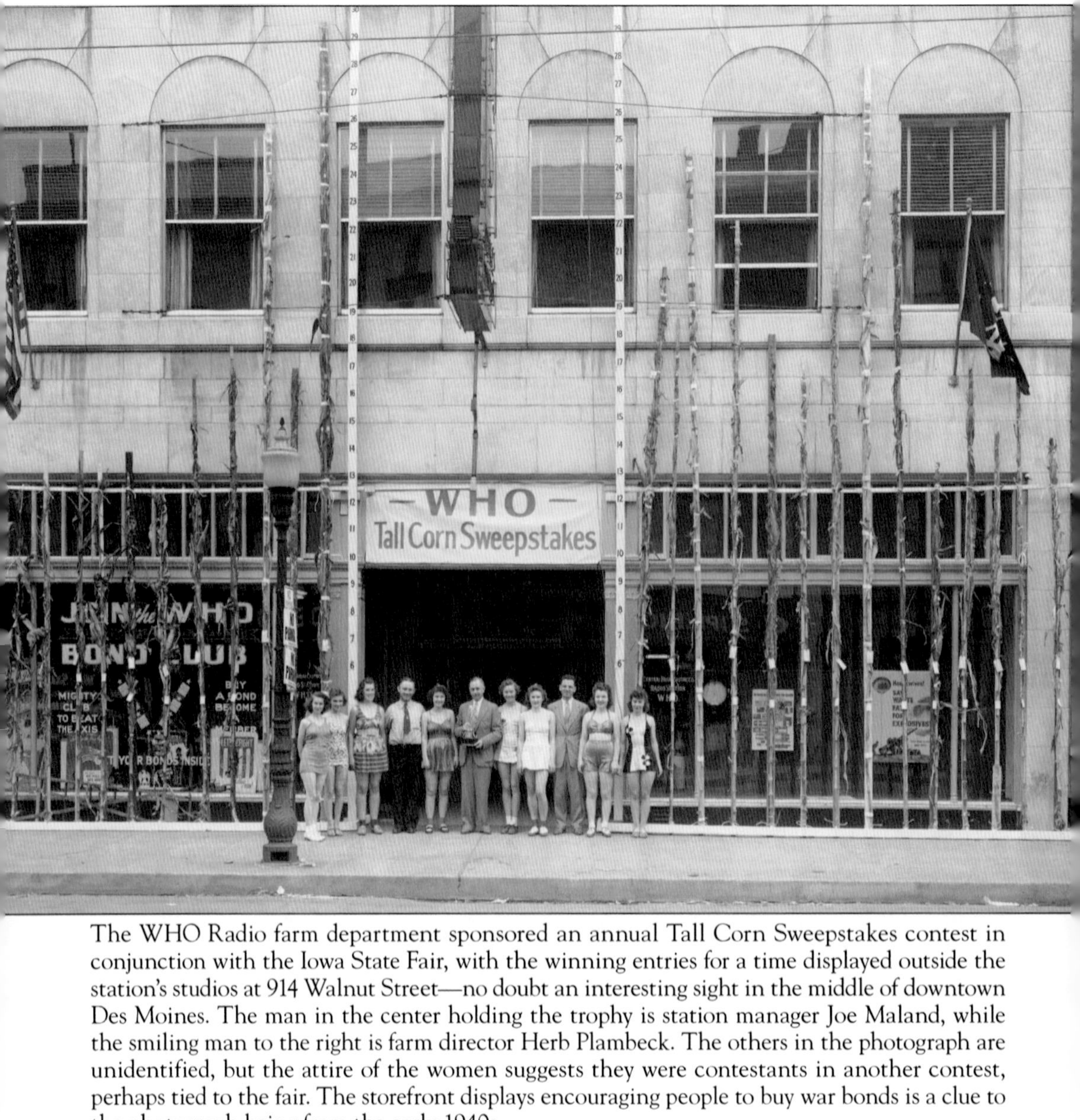

The WHO Radio farm department sponsored an annual Tall Corn Sweepstakes contest in conjunction with the Iowa State Fair, with the winning entries for a time displayed outside the station's studios at 914 Walnut Street—no doubt an interesting sight in the middle of downtown Des Moines. The man in the center holding the trophy is station manager Joe Maland, while the smiling man to the right is farm director Herb Plambeck. The others in the photograph are unidentified, but the attire of the women suggests they were contestants in another contest, perhaps tied to the fair. The storefront displays encouraging people to buy war bonds is a clue to the photograph being from the early 1940s.

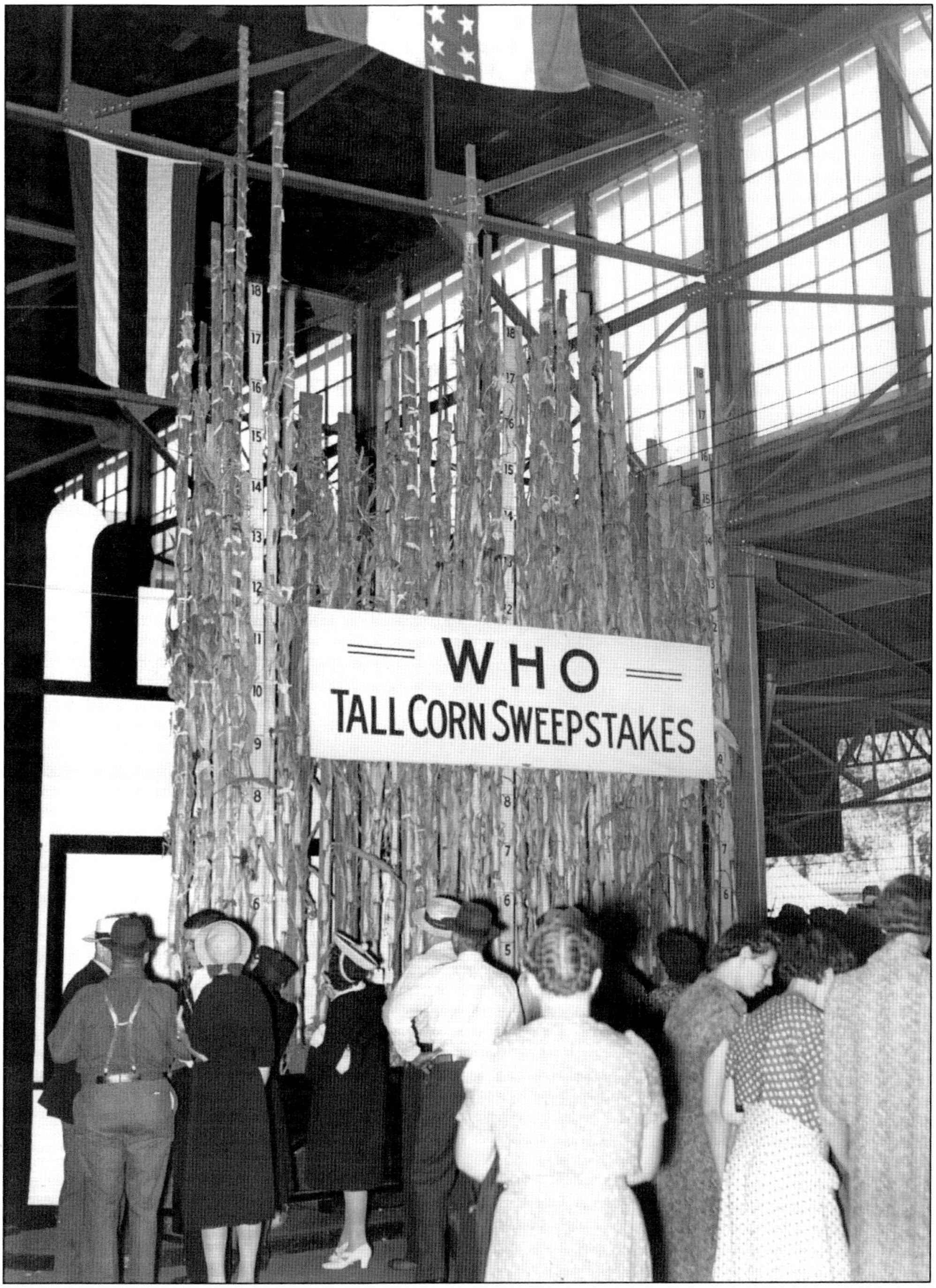

The winner of the WHO-Iowa State Fair National Tall Corn Sweepstakes would receive the Col. B.J. Palmer Trophy—naturally, it was named after the station owner. This photograph shows the 1938 contest, which was staged at the Iowa State Fairgrounds in Des Moines.

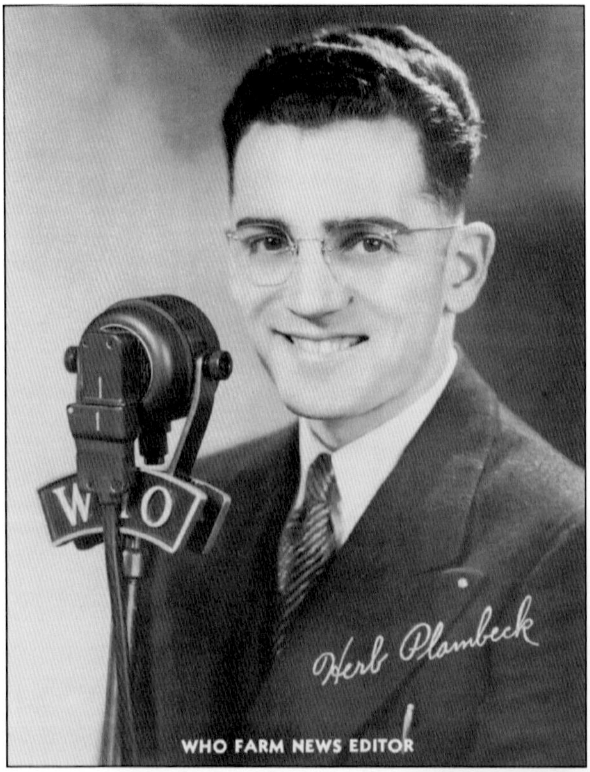

The founding director of the first radio farm news department in America was Herb Plambeck, who came to WHO in 1936 from a newspaper job in Davenport. Plambeck stayed at WHO for 34 years before leaving the station to join the staff of the US Department of Agriculture in Washington, DC. In addition to his daily work, Plambeck created the longest continuously running weekly farm program in Iowa broadcasting history, WHO's *Corn Belt Hour.* Patterned after NBC's *Farm and Home Hour,* the show aired each Saturday at noon starting in 1937. More than 12,500 guests appeared during the show's 32½-year run—a total of 1,677 shows, including when Plambeck hosted the program live from London during World War II. Plambeck also founded the annual statewide plowing matches in 1939; the first event drew 8,000 people to the match site in Mitchellville.

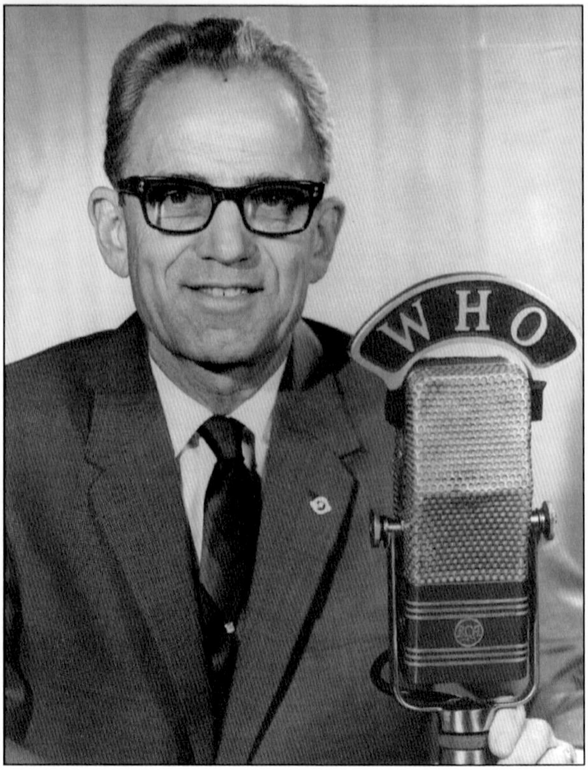

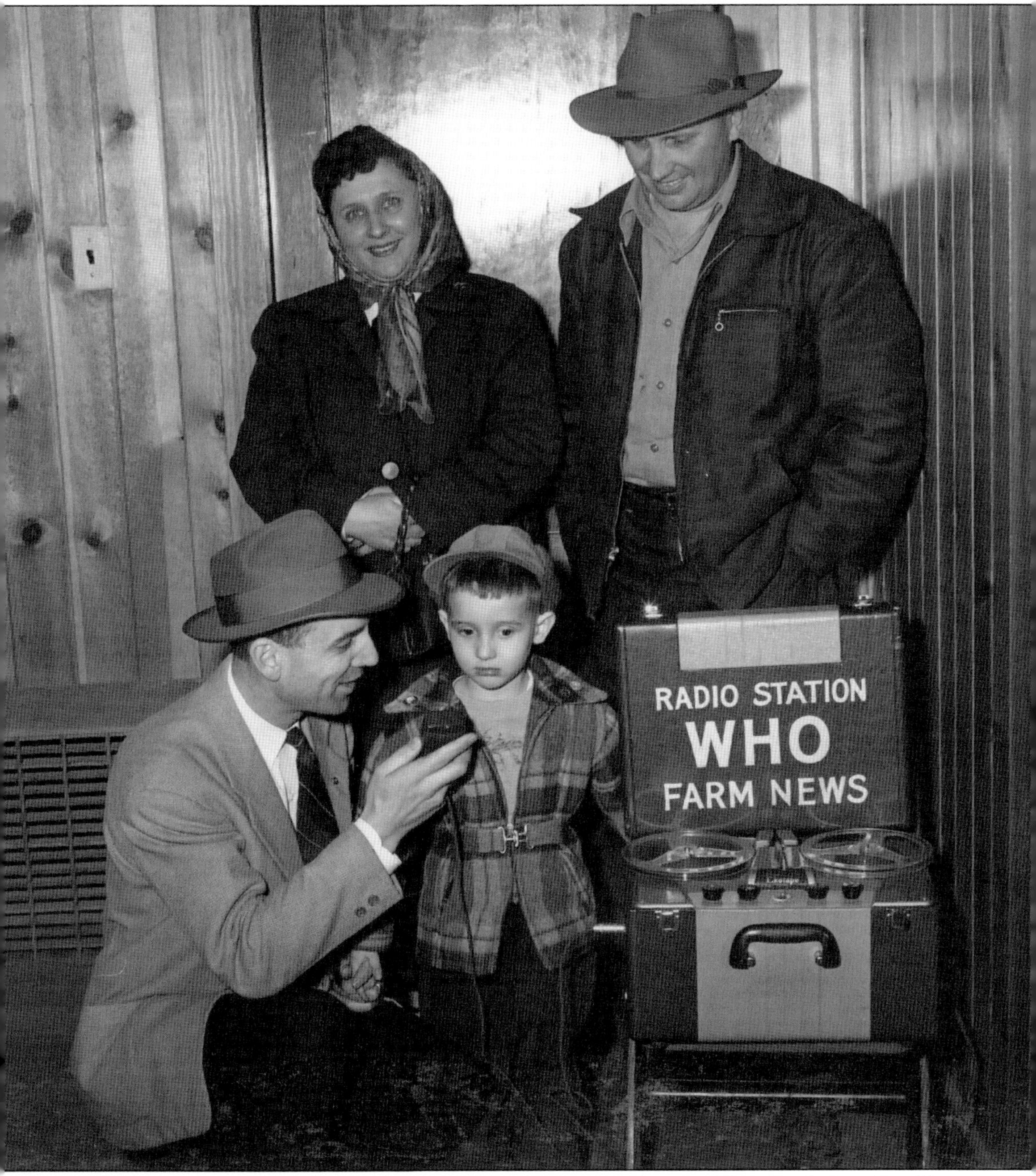

Herb Plambeck, with mobile recorder in tow, interviews an unidentified farm family from Franklin County for an Easter Sunday broadcast. In a 1979 interview, Plambeck summarized his approach to farm broadcasting: "We just felt these people out here who produce this food, the farm family, are so vital to the nation's economy, to the state's economy, to our well-being, that anything we could do to make them feel they were important was worth doing."

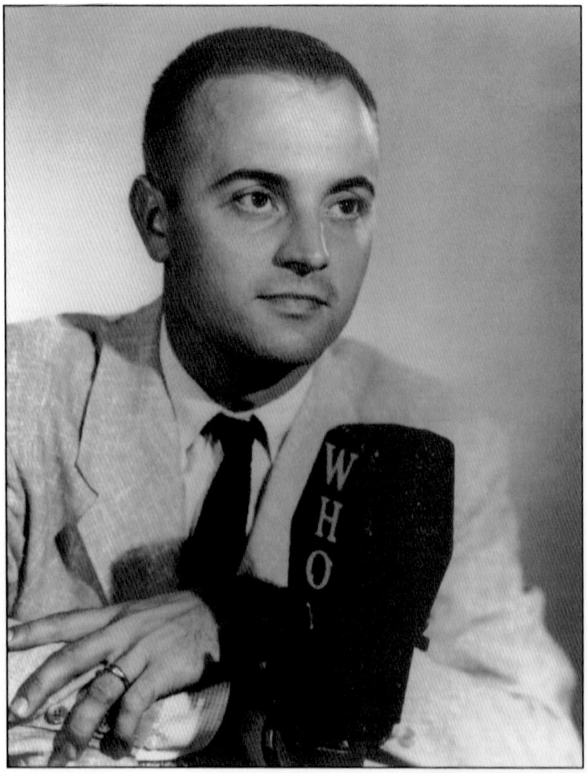

Conrad, Iowa, native Leon "Lee" Kline came to WHO's farm department in 1953. A graduate of Iowa State College with a BS degree in Agriculture Journalism, he traveled Iowa for 41 years gathering stories for his signature *Iowa Notebook* segments. Even now in retirement, Kline still contributes *Notebook* pieces regularly to WHO Radio; collections of the segments are available in a series of CDs, with proceeds benefitting Living History Farms, a working museum near Des Moines.

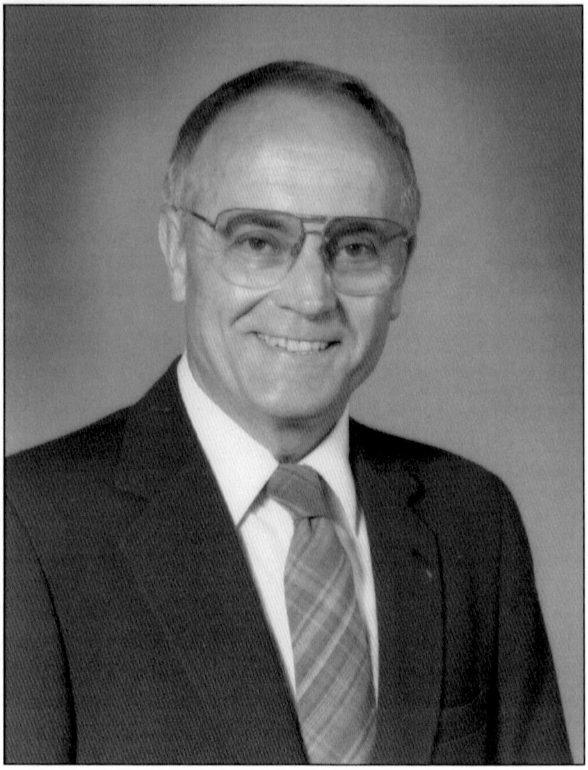

Another broadcaster who spent his professional career at WHO Radio is Keith Kirkpatrick, coming to WHO in 1951 following graduation from the State University of Iowa, where he began his broadcasting career at the university-owned radio station WSUI. Kirkpatrick became farm director in 1970 when Plambeck left to join the USDA in Washington, DC. Today, Kirkpatrick is still heard weekly on WHO Radio's Sunday morning *Sportsman's Notebook* program, which has been on the station since 1973.

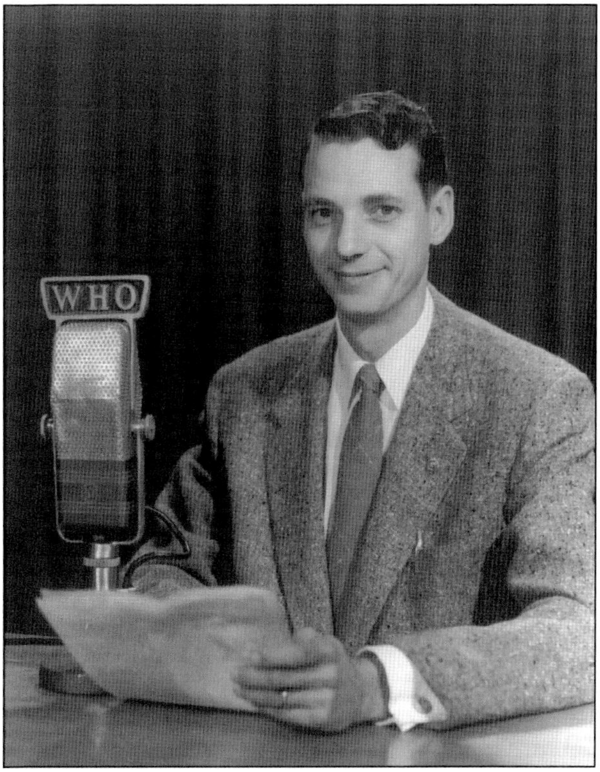

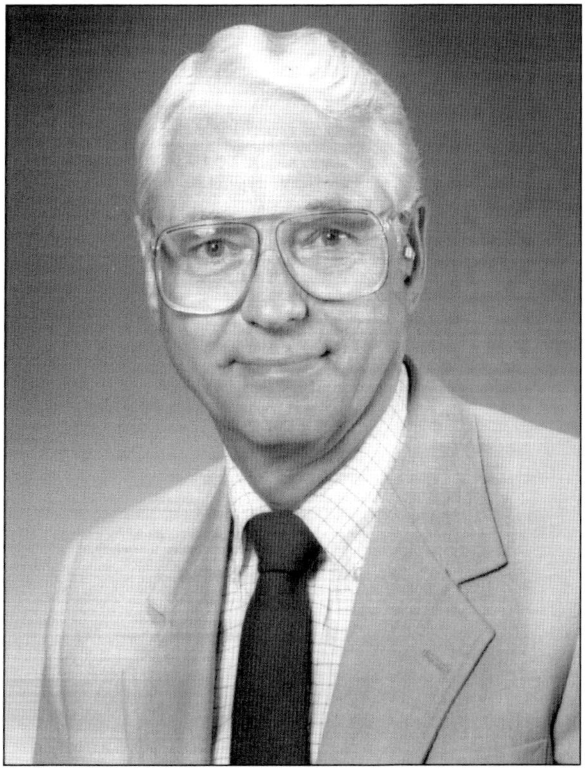

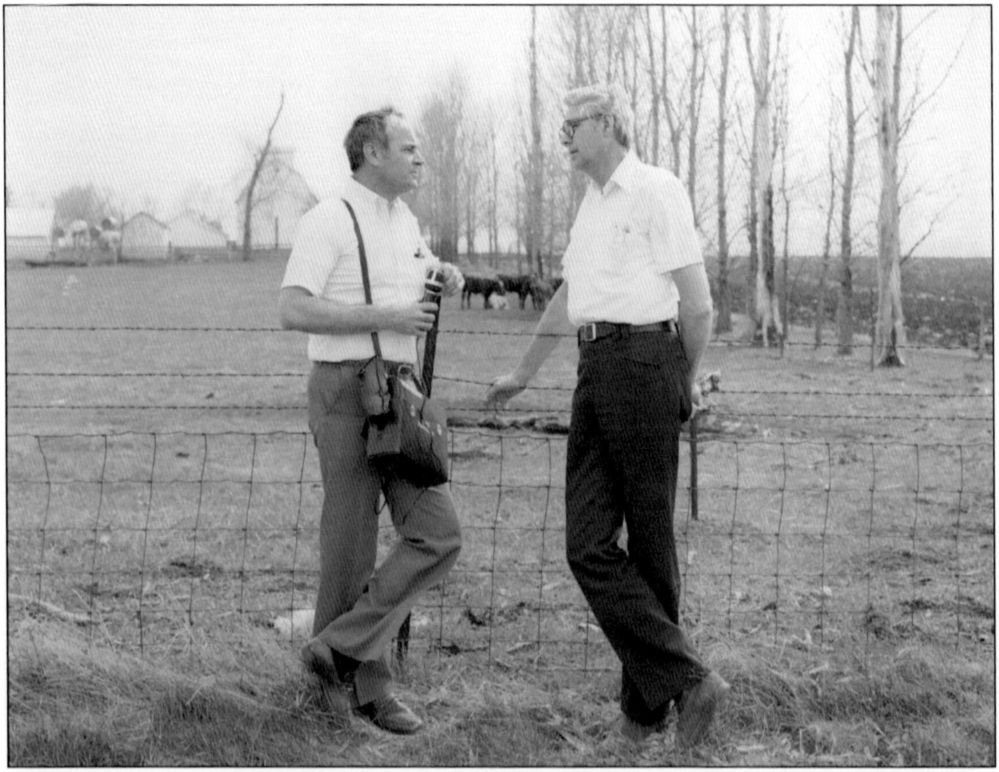

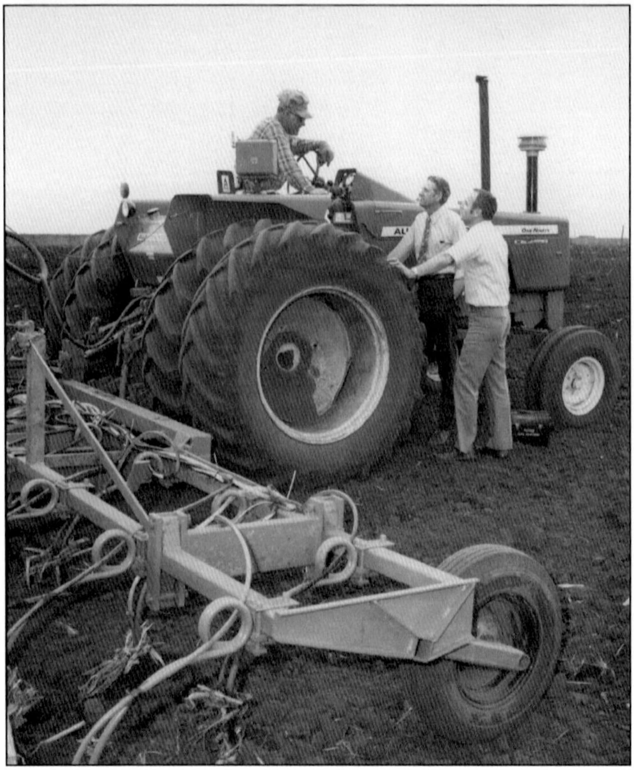

WHO Radio farm department stalwarts Lee Kline (left) and Keith Kirkpatrick appear at work in a familiar environment—the farm fields of rural Iowa. Kline retired from daily radio work in 1995 and won the Andre Award from the ISU College of Agriculture in 2005; Kirkpatrick was the station's farm director from 1970 to 1990 and was inducted into the Iowa Broadcasters Association Hall of Fame in 2002.

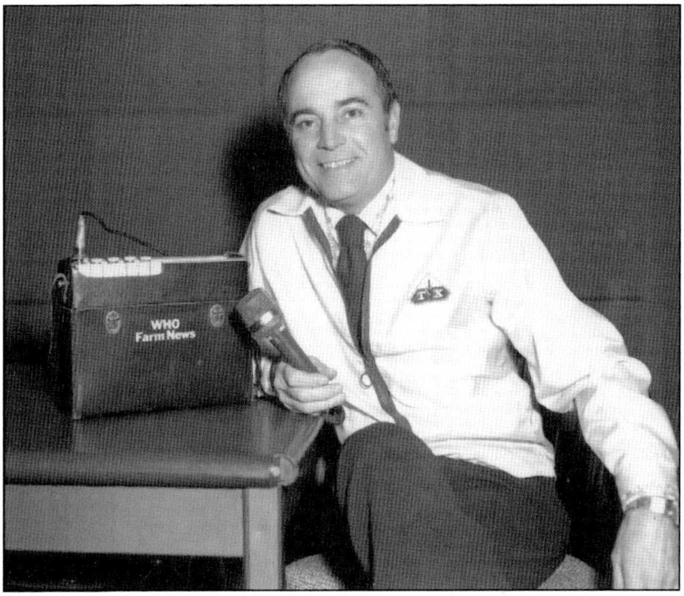

Lee Kline appears with his trusty Uher-brand reel-to-reel tape recorder that he used to record thousands of interviews with figures in Iowa agriculture. The Uher machines were the industry standard for portable recording by radio and film professionals from the 1960s to the 1980s, when audiocassette recorders became more popular.

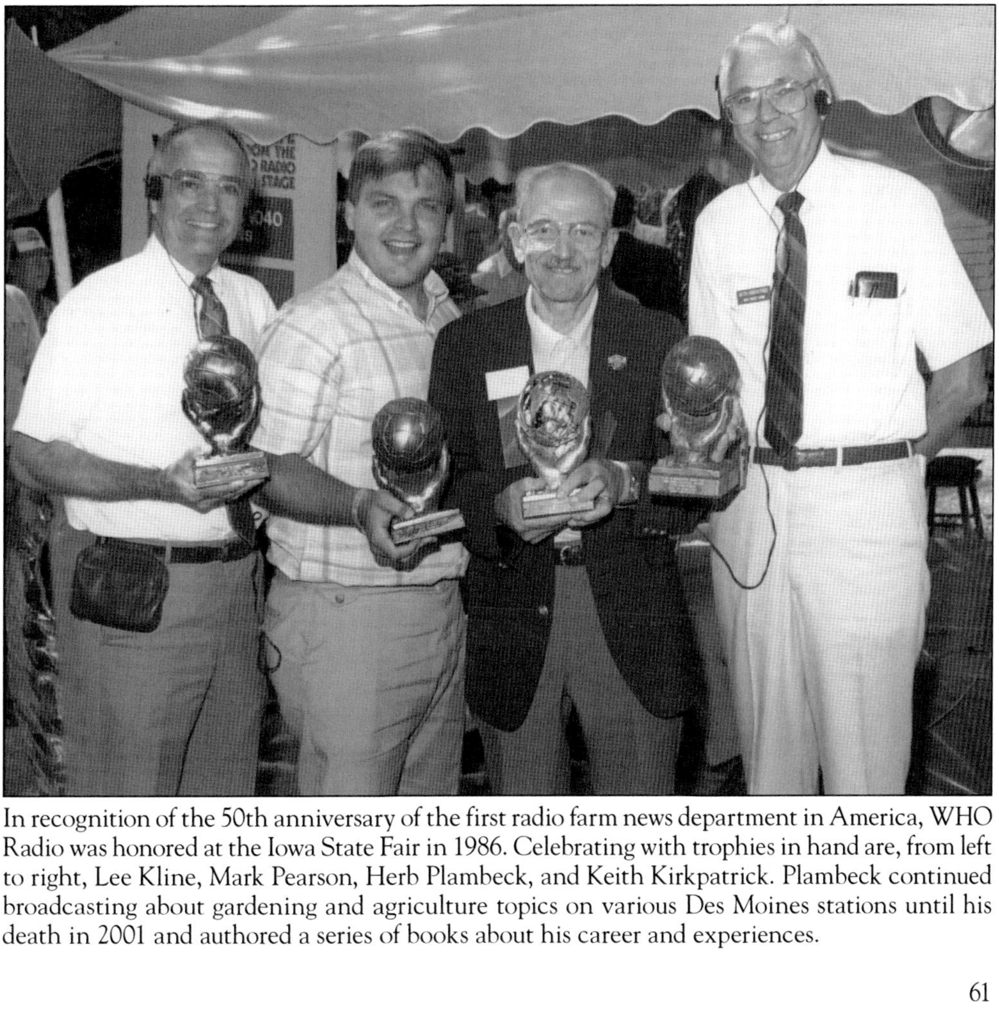

In recognition of the 50th anniversary of the first radio farm news department in America, WHO Radio was honored at the Iowa State Fair in 1986. Celebrating with trophies in hand are, from left to right, Lee Kline, Mark Pearson, Herb Plambeck, and Keith Kirkpatrick. Plambeck continued broadcasting about gardening and agriculture topics on various Des Moines stations until his death in 2001 and authored a series of books about his career and experiences.

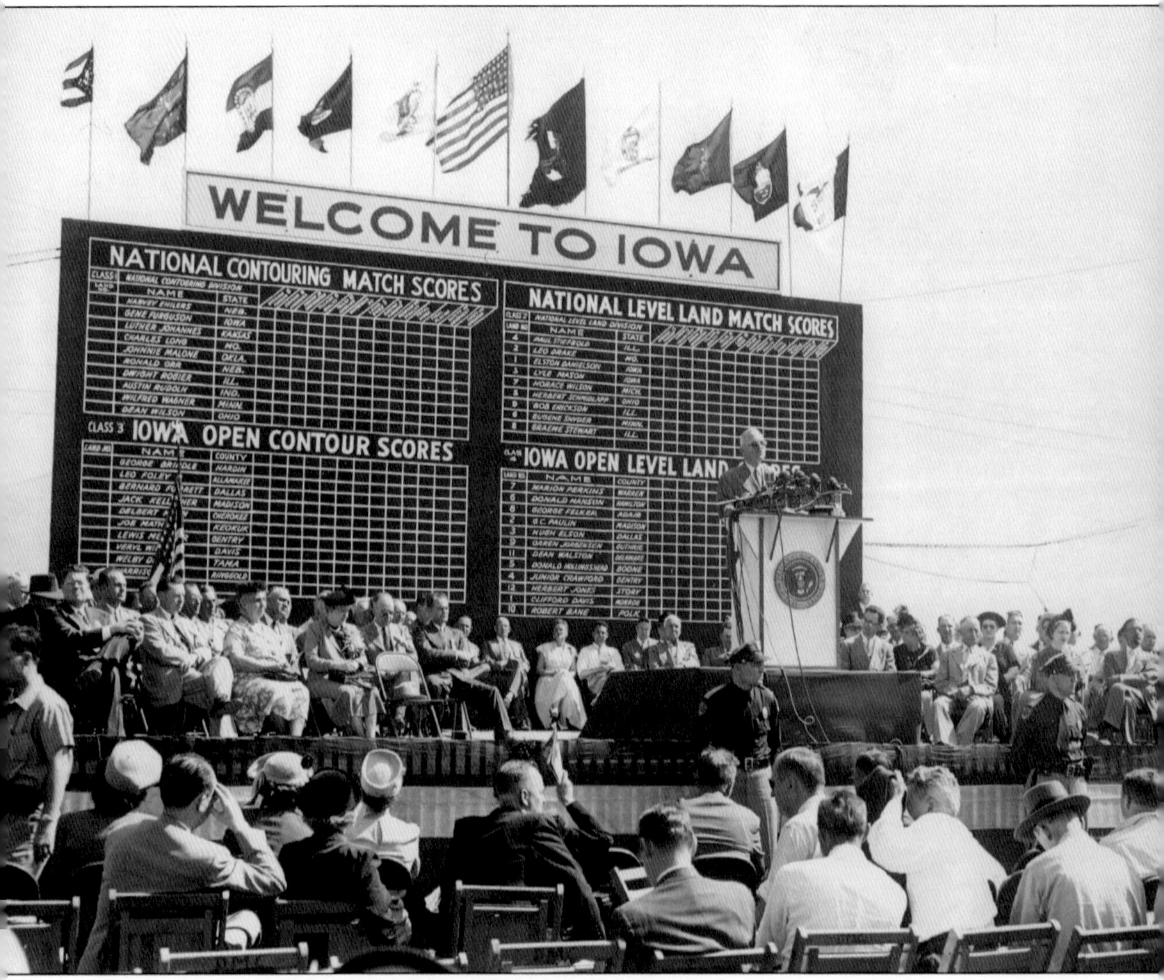

Operating under the premise that "good plowing is essential to a successful and prosperous agriculture," WHO Radio founded a series of national plowing matches in 1939. Nearly a decade later, presidential politics entered the event, as Democratic incumbent president Harry S. Truman addressed event participants.

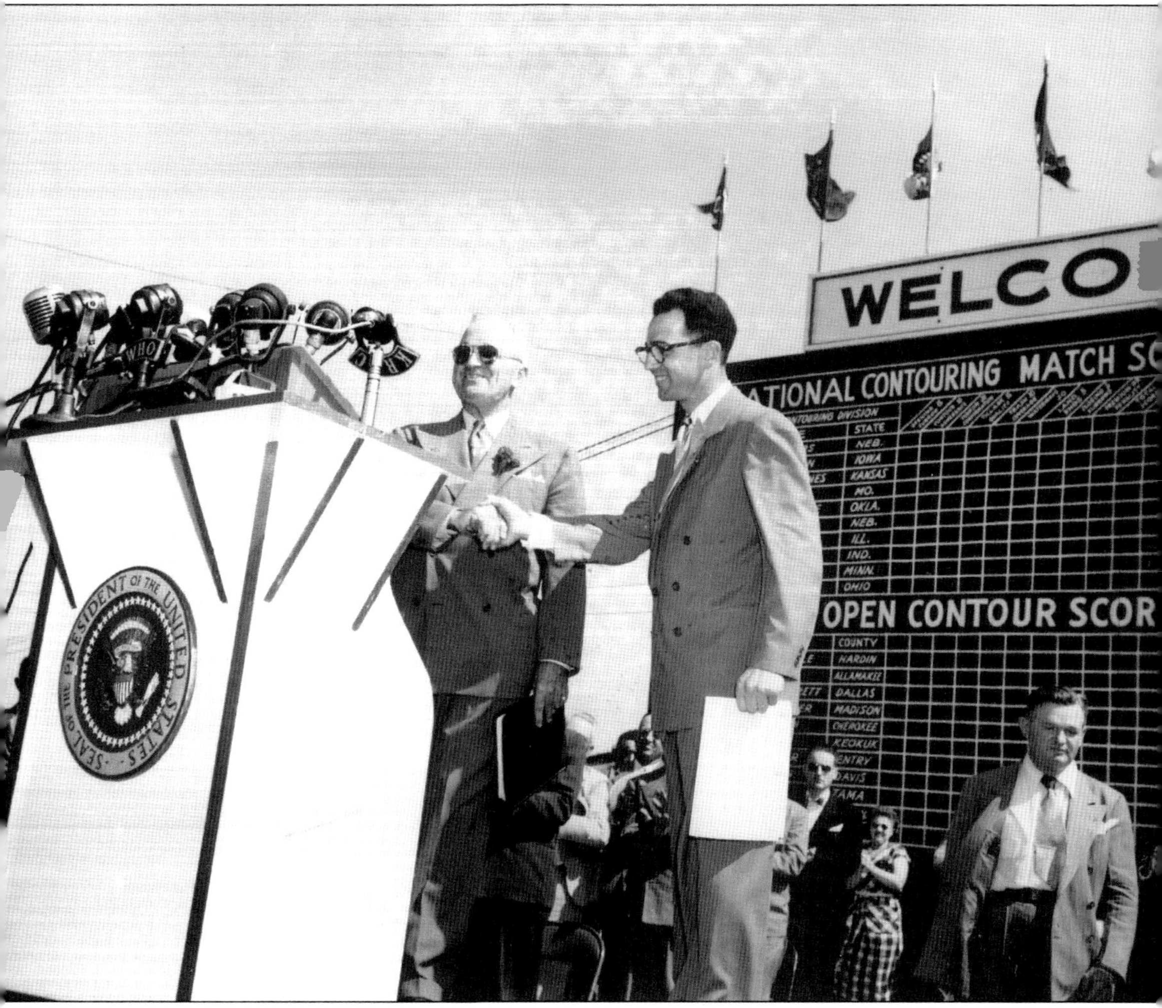

WHO Radio farm director Herb Plambeck is presenting Pres. Harry S. Truman to an estimated crowd of 75,000 at the National Soil Conservation Field Days and Plowing Matches in Dexter, Iowa, on September 18, 1948. Truman made note of his heritage from the neighboring state of Missouri and pronounced Iowa as "Ioway" during his remarks.

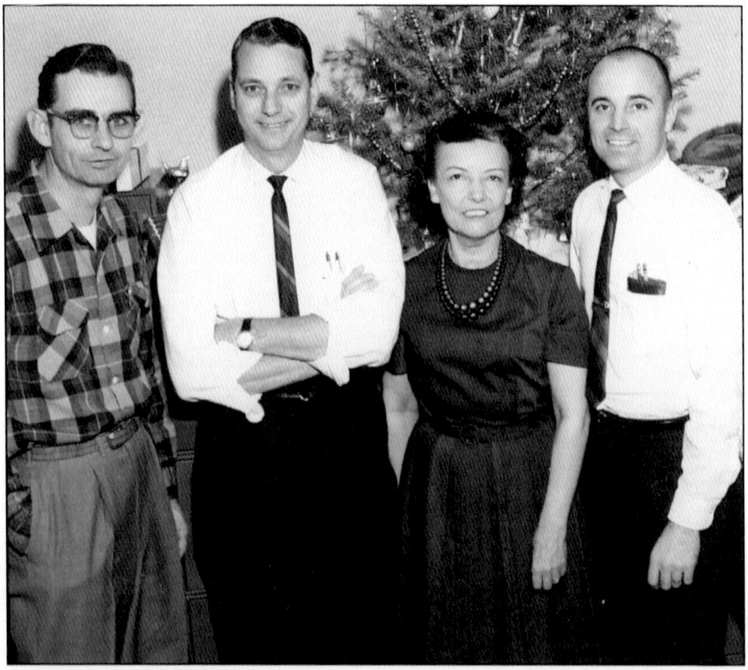

A 1950s holiday photograph of the farm staff from Herb Plambeck's extensive collection depicts, from left to right, Chet Randolph, Keith Kirkpatrick, Janet Coppock, and Lee Kline.

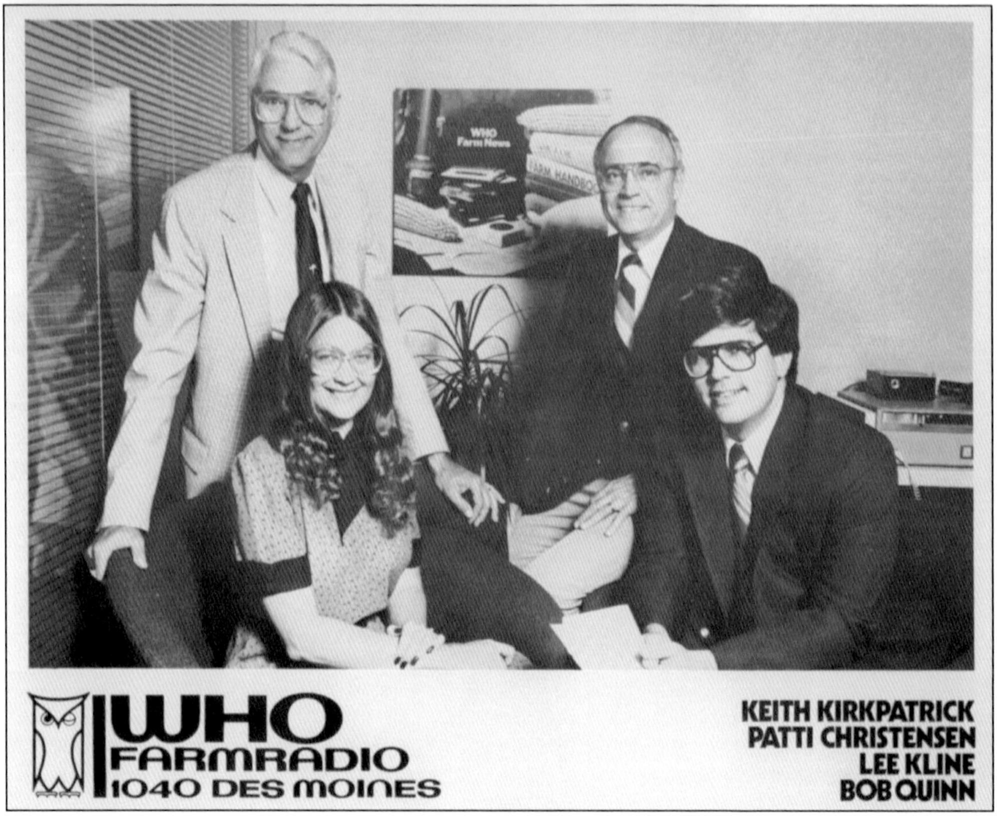

The WHO Radio farm department staff poses for a 1983 promotional photograph. From left to right are Keith Kirkpatrick, Patti Christensen, Lee Kline, and Bob Quinn.

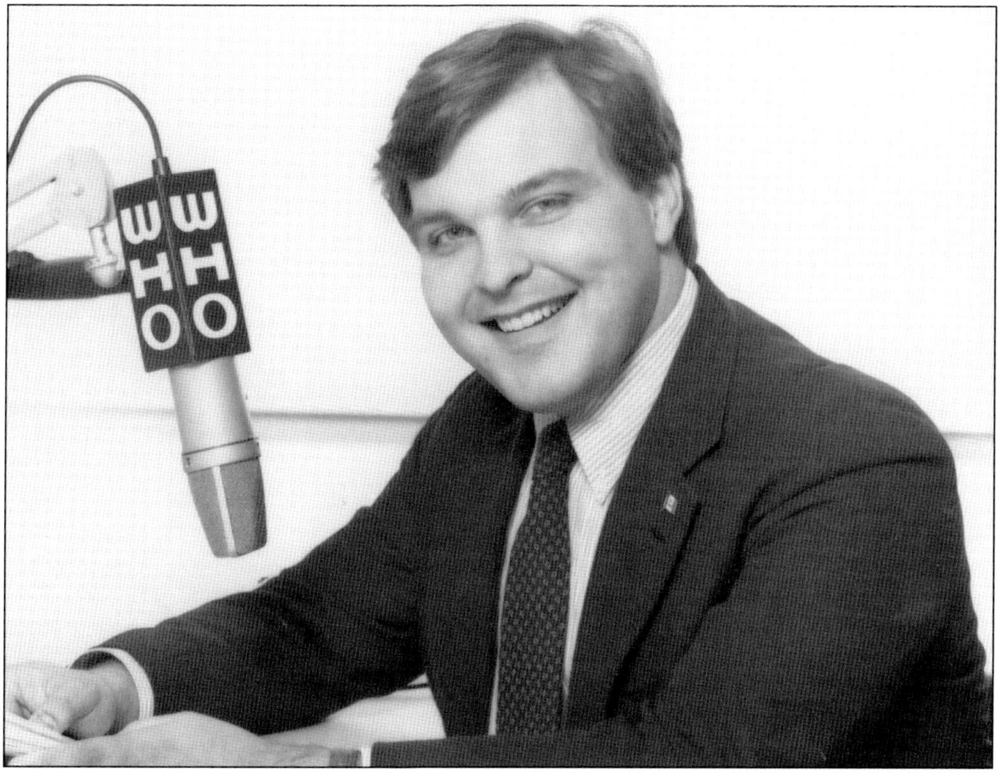

Today, they cohost the *Big Show* (see page 122), which originates from WHO Radio and is aired on other Clear Channel Communications stations throughout Iowa, but these photographs show Mark Pearson (above) and Bob Quinn (right) at earlier stages in their WHO Radio careers.

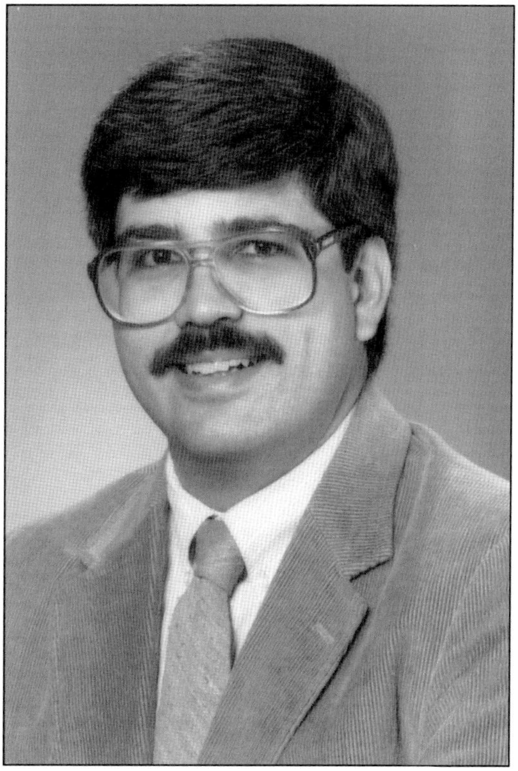

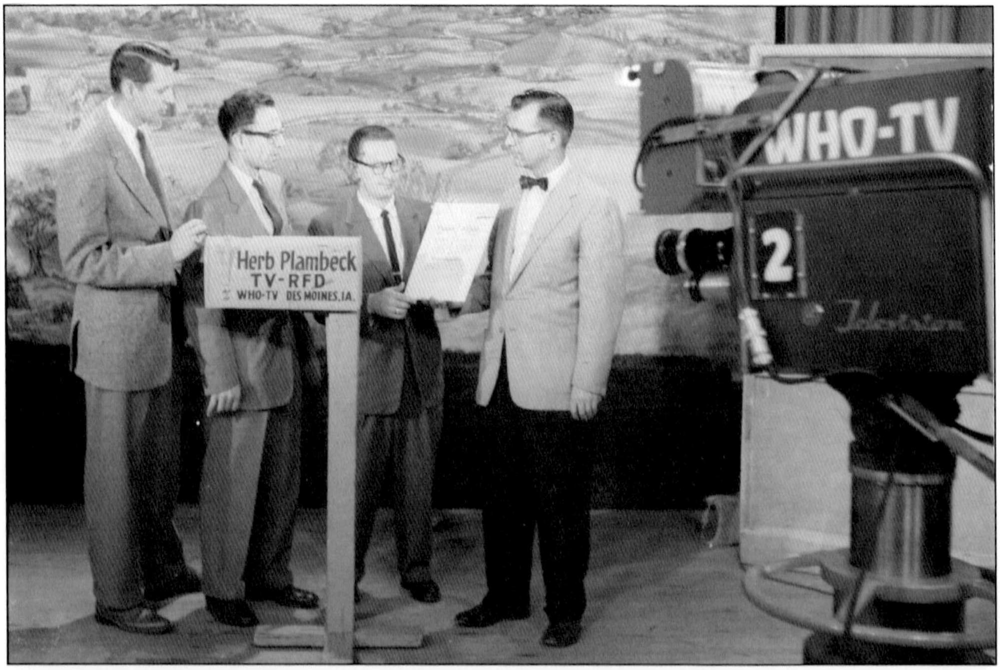

The WHO farm department expanded its service with a half-hour, midday program called *TV-RFD*, which ran on WHO-TV 13 for three years in the mid-1950s. While the program served the new television audience, it put great strain on WHO's farm news staff, because they were also doing WHO's established midday radio farm programs at the time. Staff members were often seen racing from the second-floor radio studios down the stairs to the first-floor television studios and back to cover the shifts during the busy noon hour. At times, celebrities visited the *TV-RFD* set, as seen below when Gene Autry paid Herb Plambeck an on-air visit.

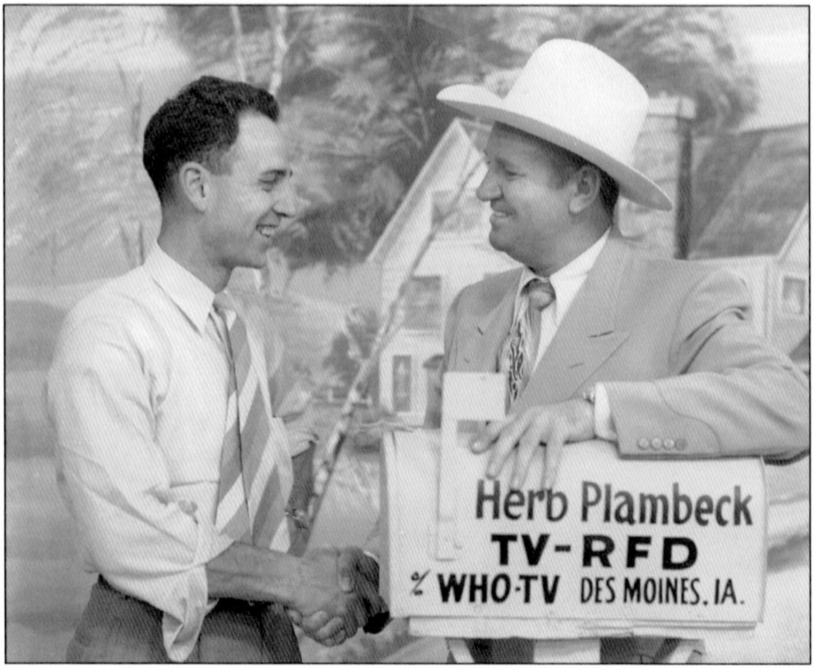

Five

From Sunset Corners to the Living Room

Many in today's world may think the concept of talent shows that seek the next great singing star is a creation of television. But in the pre-television era, radio was full of live performances, often with local talent trying to reach a broader audience.

The radio barn-dance concept sprang up at a number of stations around the country in the 1920s, but it did not take long for Iowa to have its own barn dance, which would be one of the nation's longest running and most well known.

The *Iowa Barn Dance Frolic* started as a half-hour program on WOC Radio in Davenport in 1931. The next year, when the Central Broadcasting Company gained ownership of both WOC and WHO, the program was moved to Des Moines, along with the rest of the WOC staff, and was greatly expanded.

First at the 1,500-seat President Theatre, and later at the 4,500-seat Shrine Auditorium, the *Iowa Barn Dance Frolic* aired before a live audience for more than two hours each Saturday night. By the late 1940s, station officials estimated that a half-million people had traveled to Des Moines to witness the live barn-dance broadcasts.

The program was built around the fictional town of Sunset Corners, and the performers assumed roles as members of the community. In an effort to broaden the appeal of the program in the 1938 season, the name of the program was changed to the *Sunset Corners Frolic*. But it was quickly changed back to the more familiar moniker, the *Barn Dance Frolic*, having already been so well established in the audience's mind.

WHO Radio received nearly 300,000 pieces of mail about the show from Iowa-based listeners in 1935 alone. That year, *Barn Dance* mail was received from each of the 48 states and from 13 countries.

Favorites such as Lem and Martha, Yodeling Cowboy Jerry Smith, Mountain Pete and his Mountaineers, and the Williams Brothers quartet were heard not only on the Saturday night *Barn Dance* broadcasts but on regular weekday programs on the station as well.

When WHO-TV signed on in 1954, the *Barn Dance Frolic* was broadcast on both radio and television and moved to Palmer Broadcasting's new studios at 1100 Locust Street where it ended its long run a few years later.

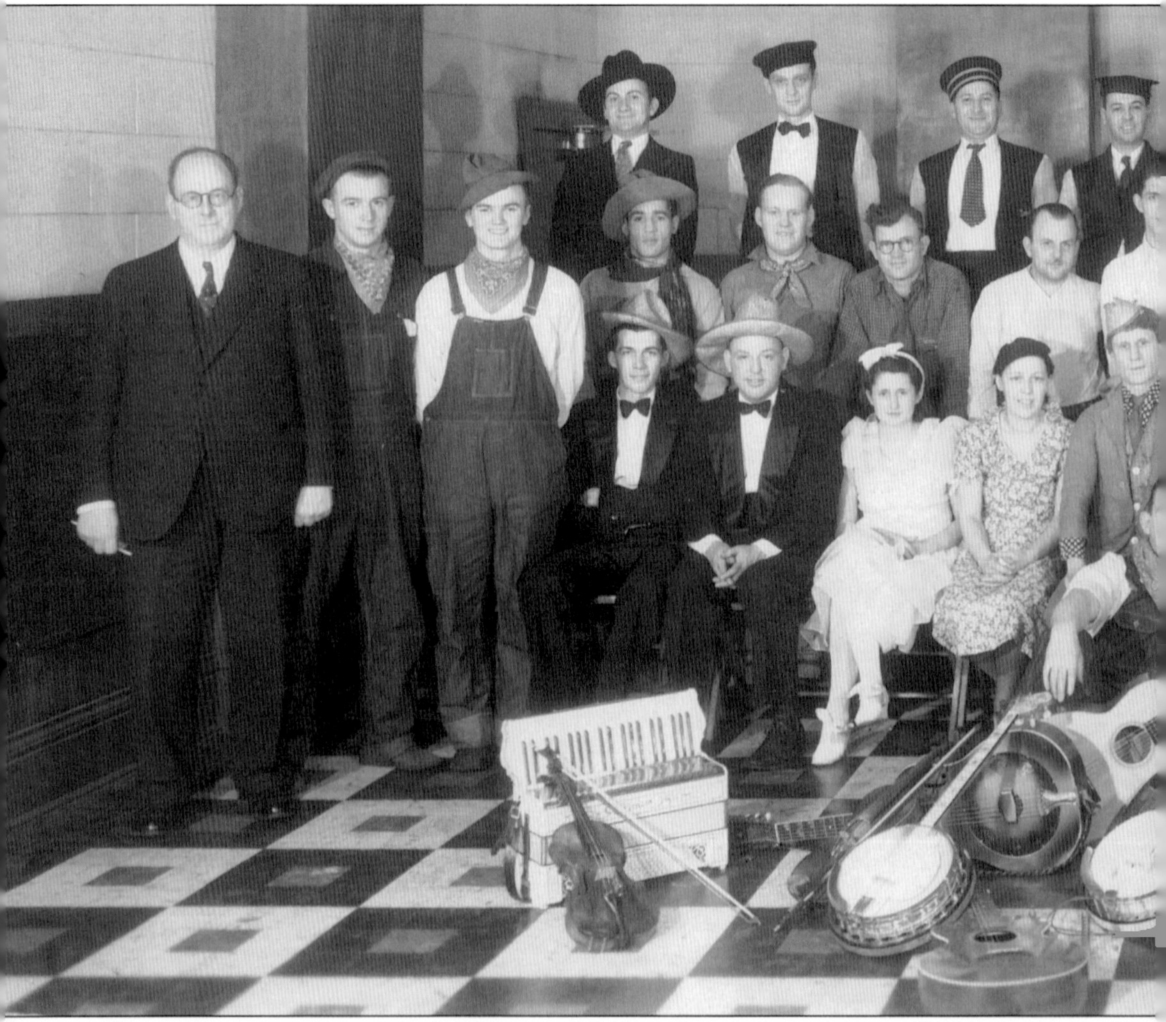

This cast photograph is from the 1933 season of the *Barn Dance Frolic*, the last with the combined WOC/WHO call letters. Station manager Joe Maland's experience with Chicago radio barn dances was essential to the success of the Iowa effort, as was the work of Peter MacArthur. MacArthur came to radio in 1921 after two years in musical comedies and operettas. He was

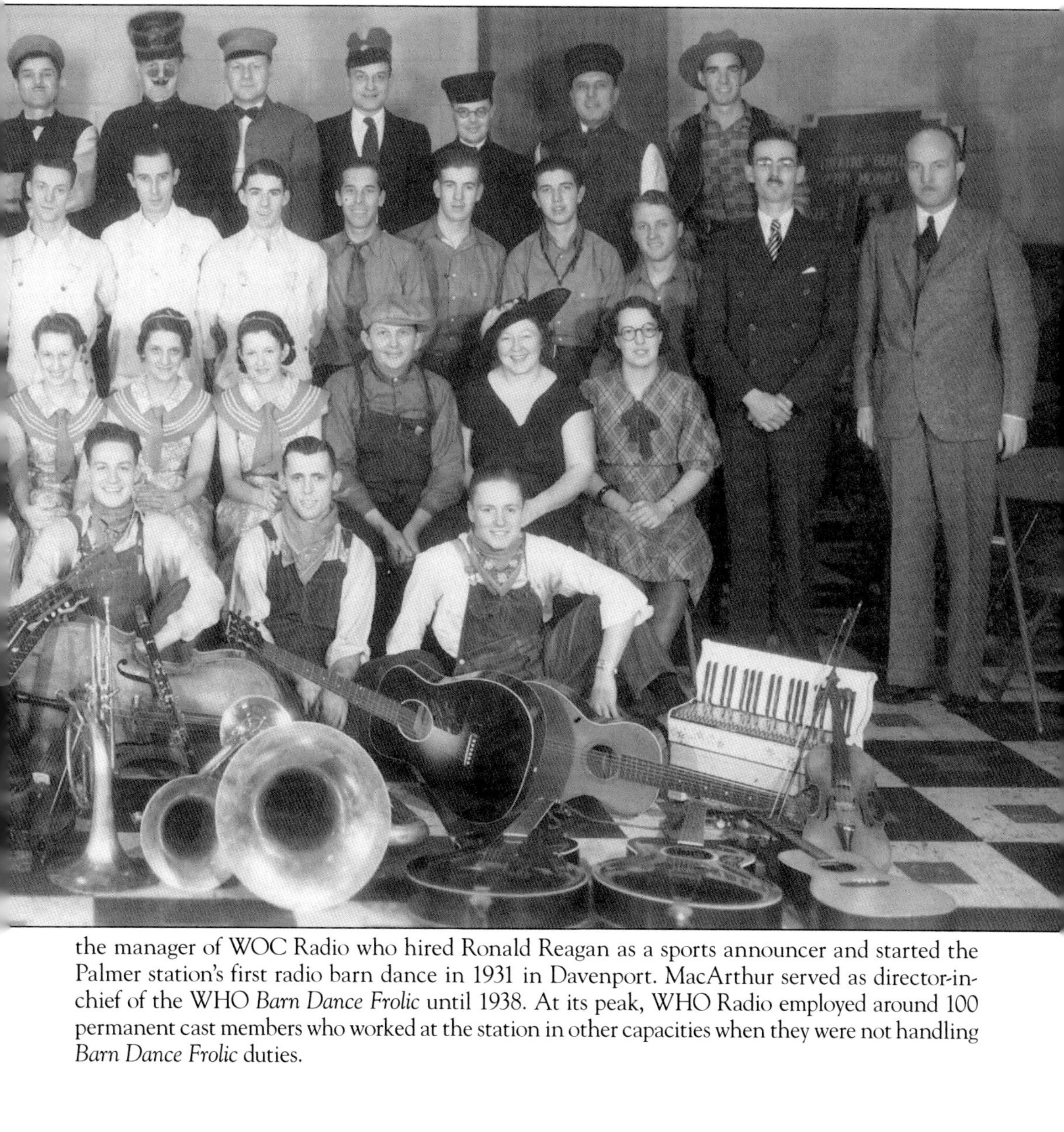

the manager of WOC Radio who hired Ronald Reagan as a sports announcer and started the Palmer station's first radio barn dance in 1931 in Davenport. MacArthur served as director-in-chief of the WHO *Barn Dance Frolic* until 1938. At its peak, WHO Radio employed around 100 permanent cast members who worked at the station in other capacities when they were not handling *Barn Dance Frolic* duties.

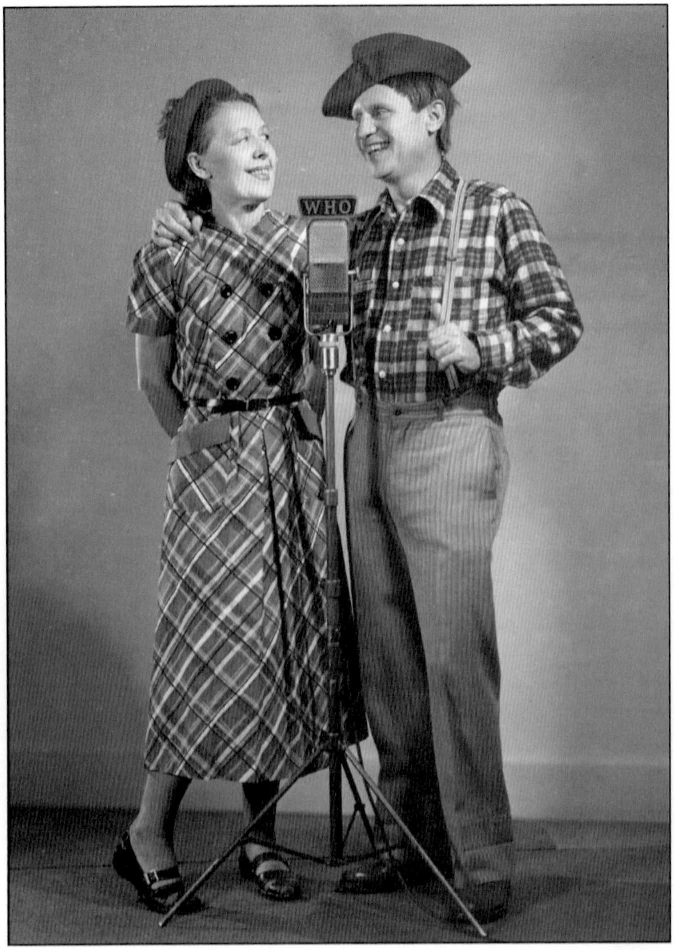

Performers Tom and Ann Lewis were better known to WHO Radio audiences as Lem and Martha. Both were in musical comedy, vaudeville, and dramatic stock before coming to WHO Radio in 1933. The character Lem Turner served as host of WHO's *Barn Dance Frolic* segments for many years, and Lem and Martha hosted a weekday morning program on WHO Radio in addition to their *Barn Dance* duties. A station promotional piece notes, "Their clever bantering, their rollicking comedy, [and] their musical versatility maintains them as Barn Dance Frolic headliners." Listeners could even send away for their own copy of *Lem Turner's Favorite Jokes*—although some claimed that those same jokes were used week after week on the *Barn Dance*, the audiences did not seem to mind.

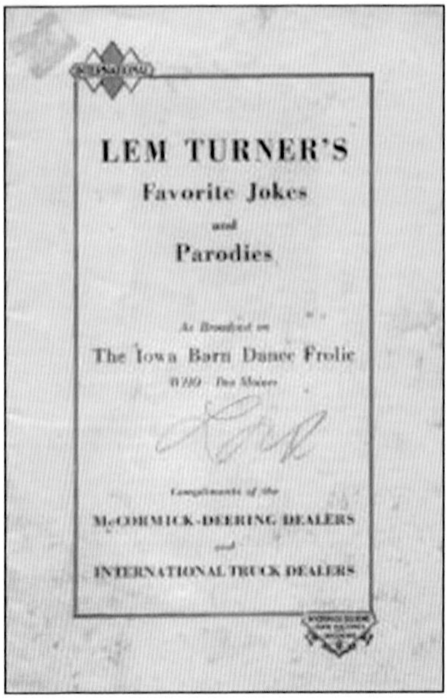

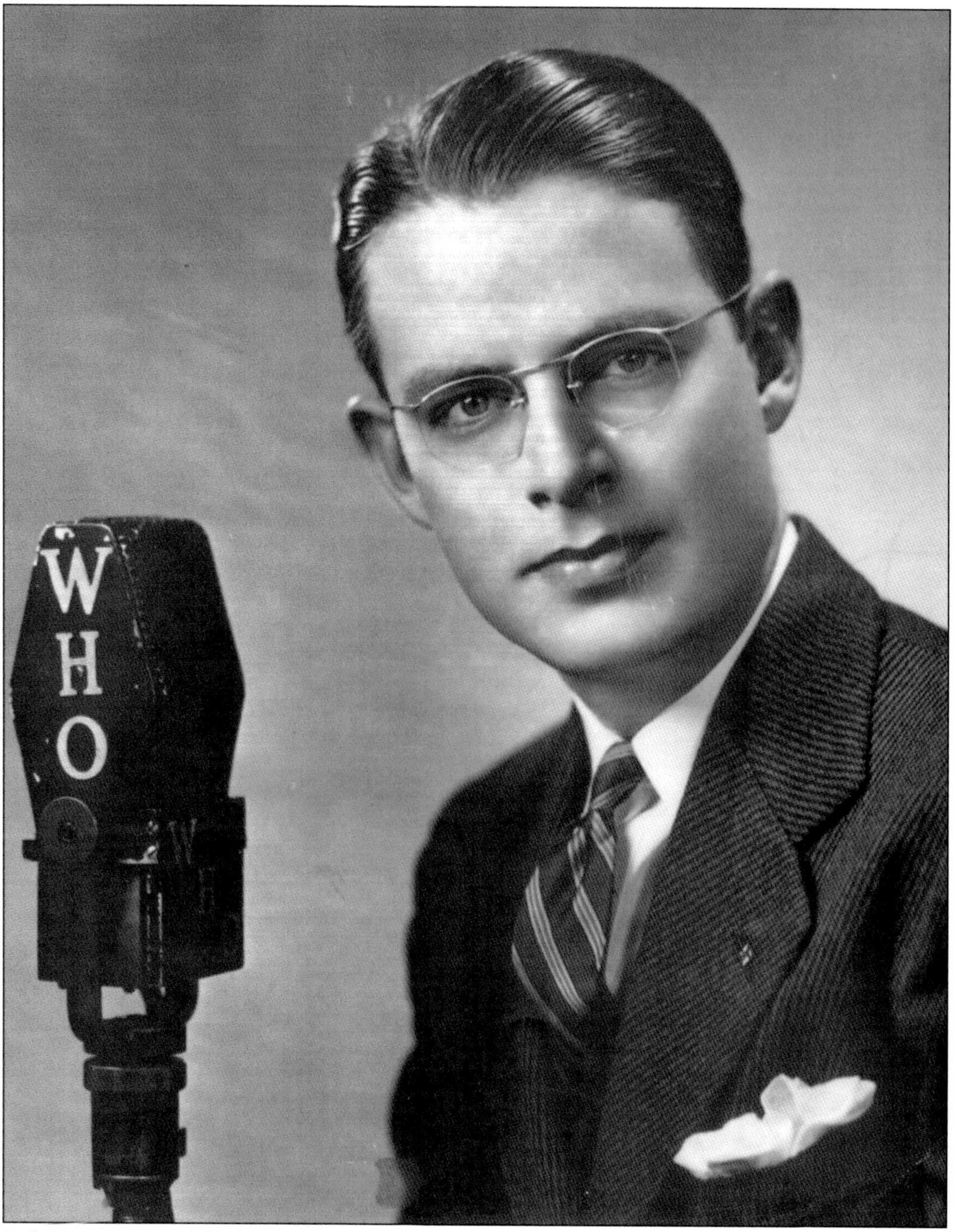

Jack Kerrigan was billed as WHO's singing announcer and was featured on several programs as lead soloist. Kerrigan produced the *Musical Pirates* program on Saturdays and wrote and produced the daily *Melody Madhouse* comedy-variety feature for more than a decade. Kerrigan recalled that one of his *Barn Dance* duties was to lift "Little Andy" Williams up on a box so he would be tall enough to reach the microphone when the Williams Brothers were called to perform. Kerrigan later became program director for both WHO Radio and WHO-TV.

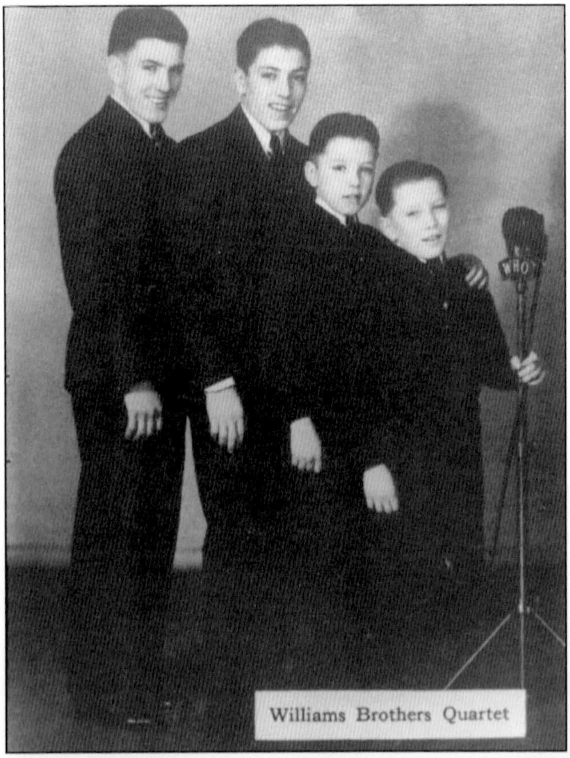

Likely the most famous alumni of the WHO's *Iowa Barn Dance Frolic* were the singing Williams brothers, seen at left. They are, from left to right, Bob, Don, Dick, and Andy. The quartet sang on WHO for three years before leaving for greater fame in Chicago. The youngest brother, Andy, would go on to international fame as a recording artist and television show host. In the photograph below, members of the *Barn Dance Frolic* cast gather with the Williams Brothers of Wall Lake. Sunset Corners residents Mayor Tillie Boggs and Pappy Cliff (played by Shari Morning and Cliff Carl) are seated in the center behind the Williams brothers.

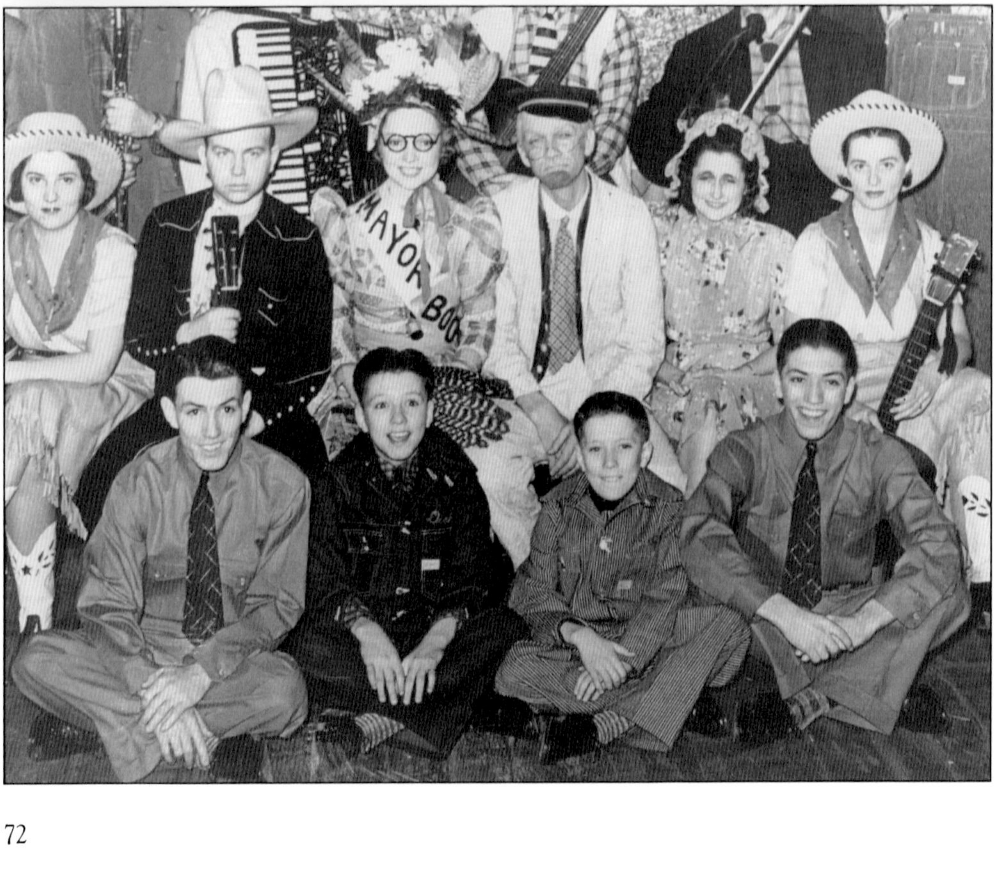

Longtime favorites in the early days of the *Barn Dance Frolic* were Mountain Pete and his Mountaineers. A barn-dance souvenir program describes them as "skilled musicians . . . these chaps play and sing concert music, ballads, rhumbas, American folk tunes, and swing."

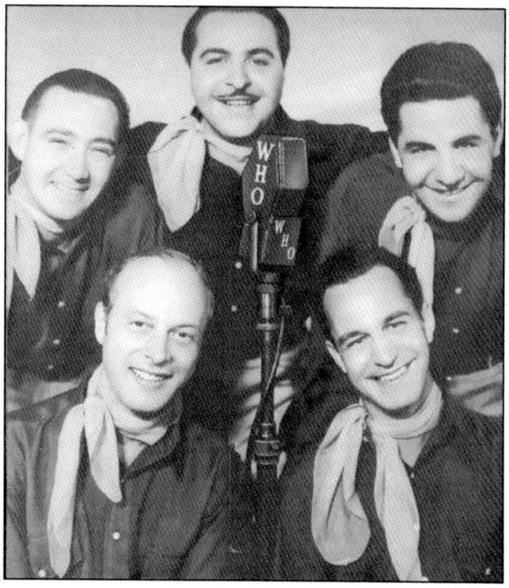

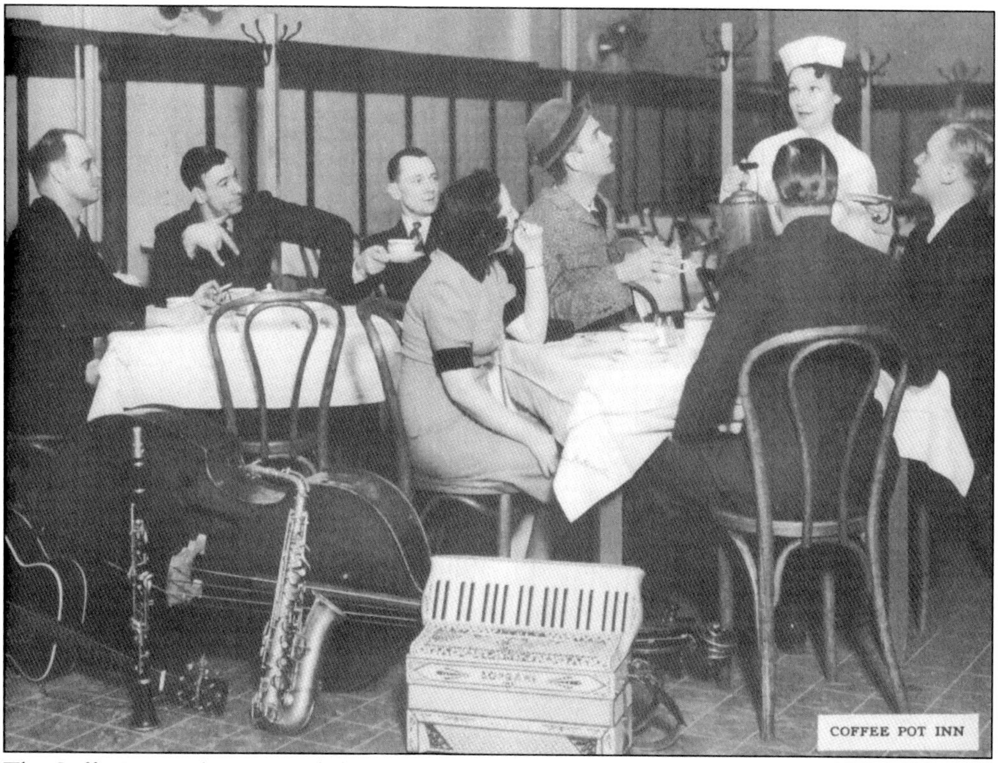

The *Coffee Pot Inn* show was a "hilarious quarter hour, broadcast six mornings a week." Originating in the studios of WHO and featuring *Barn Dance Frolic* performers, it was also aired on Corn Belt Wireless stations. In the spring of 1936, WHO inaugurated the Corn Belt Wireless, an experimental plan for rebroadcasting radio programs during the daytime without the use of telephone lines. Programs were exchanged from one control point, such as WHO, directly over the air to other stations within WHO's signal range and then retransmitted on those other stations. Kay Neal was the singing star, Hazel and Filbert McNutt provided comedy, and the Four Aces furnished instrumental numbers for the *Coffee Pot Inn*.

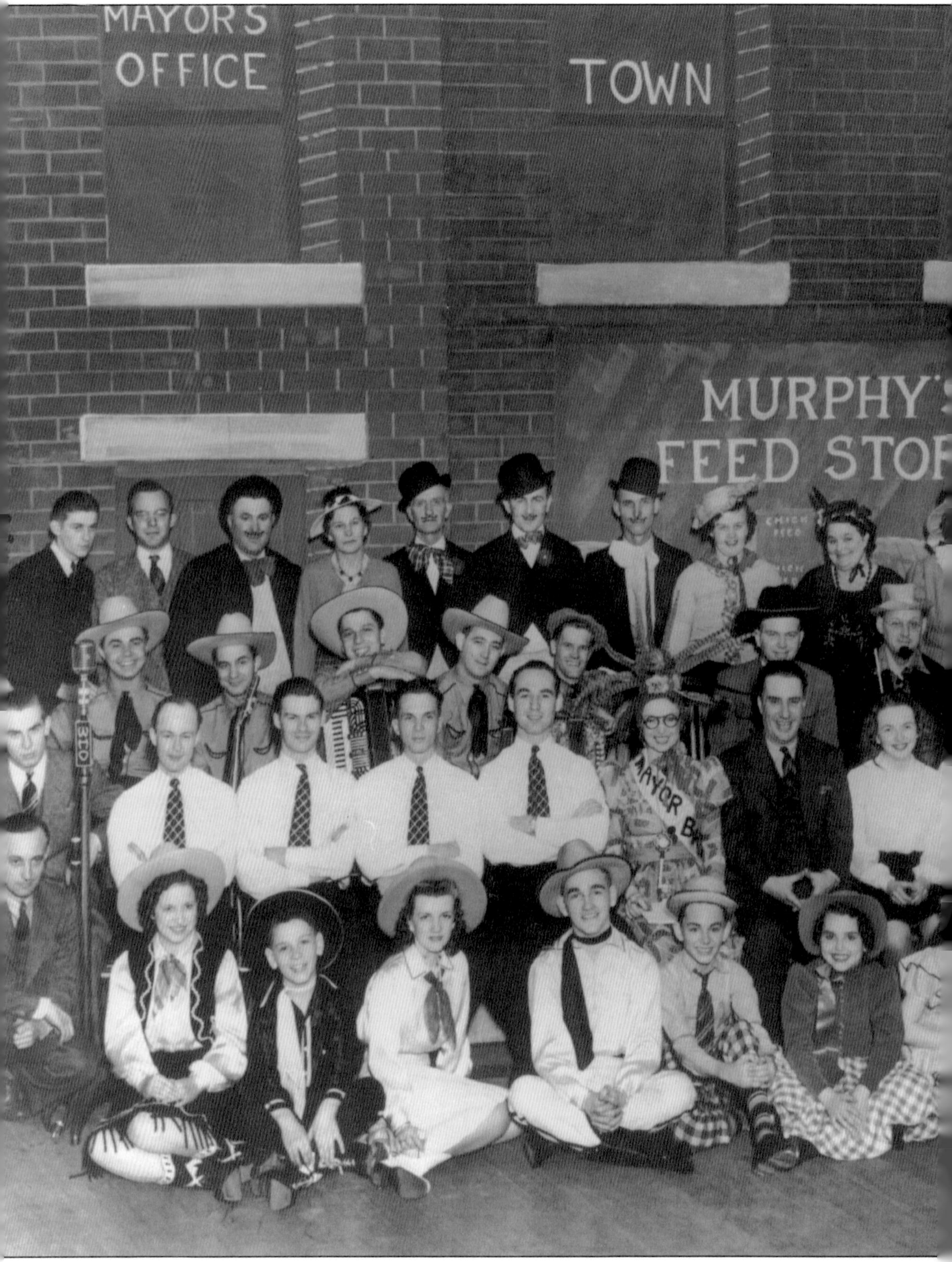
MAYOR'S
OFFICE
TOWN
MURPHY'S
FEED STOR
WTO
MAYOR

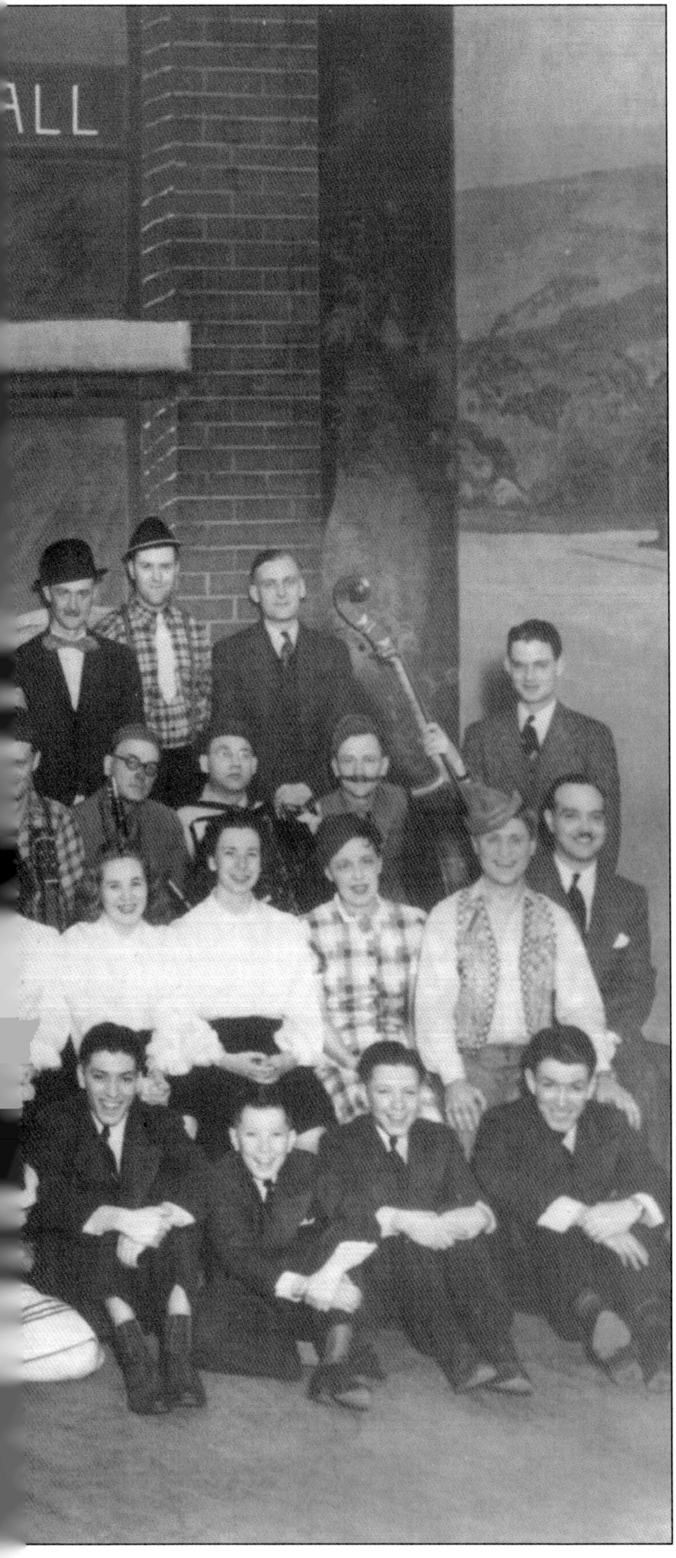

"It is much more than a 'barn dance,' it is a weekly exemplification of the best in American folk music plus a goodly assortment of modern airs with occasional flights into semi-classical melodies," a 1939 station promotional booklet claimed. "The wide favor with which the *Iowa Bran Dance Frolic* is received is attributed in large degree to the idea of giving people what they really want to hear, rather than trying to make them like whatever stations happen to broadcast. The depth and breadth of American people's affection for American Folk Music cannot be approximated in anyone's mind. It is a vast and enduring and very real love for the music that was dear to their parents and their parents' parents before them." Seated in the center (second row, with the suit) of this 1939 cast photograph is Stan Widney, who succeeded Peter MacArthur as the show's producer and served as a primary announcer and host for the program.

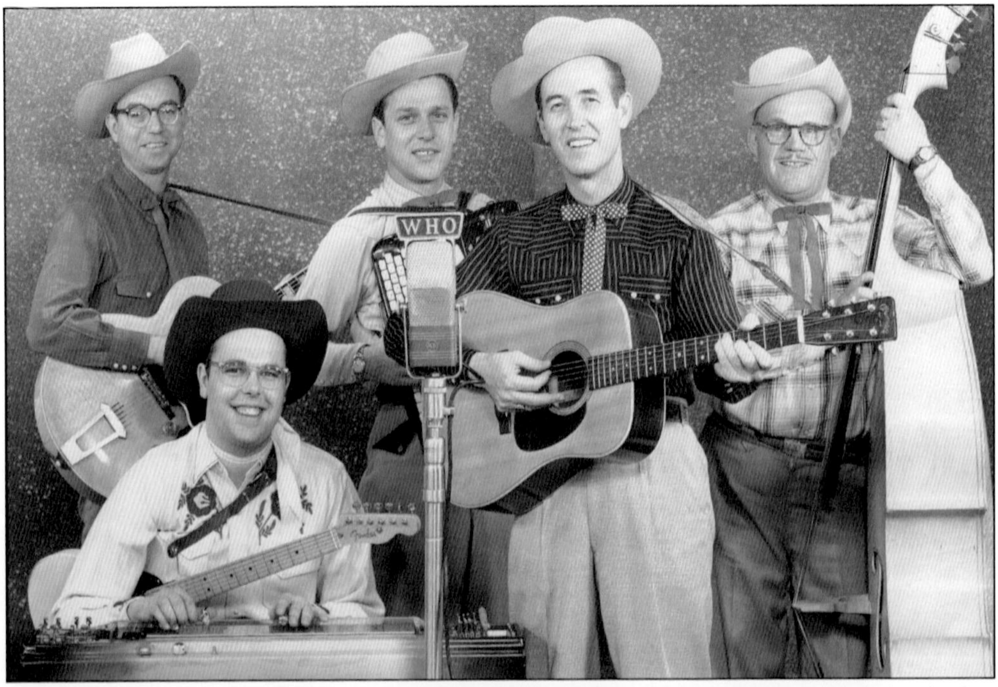

The Buckaroos were a well-known group on the *Barn Dance Frolic*. The group took a higher profile when Paul "Slim" Hayes, seen in the center with his guitar, left a Chicago radio barn dance and joined the group in 1940. For most of the 1940s, the group appeared weekday afternoons at 4:45 p.m.; by the early 1950s, the Buckaroos were on the air Monday through Saturday at 8:15 a.m. and again at 11:30 a.m. on weekdays just before the NBC broadcast of *Perry Mason*. Slim Hayes himself made the transition to television, hosting a children's show called the *Lucky 13 Ranch* from 1954 to 1962, at which time he returned to WHO Radio and hosted a country music program. Hayes died at age 80 in 1997.

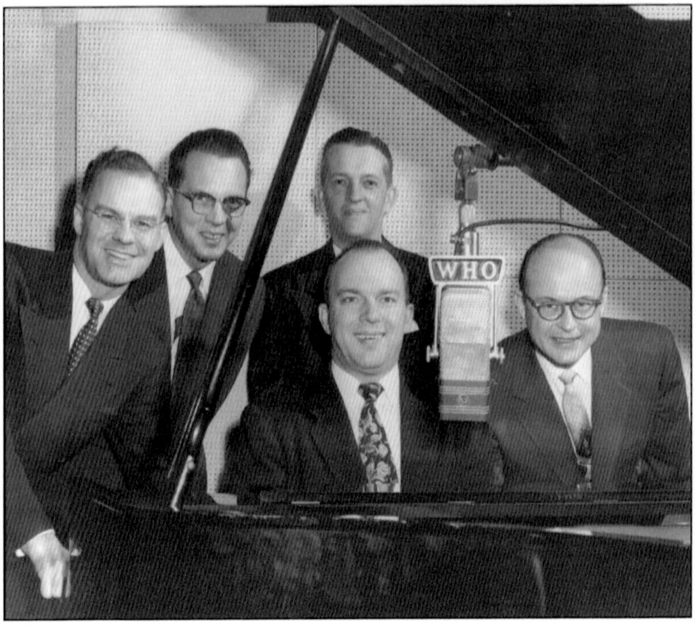

The Songfellows were a popular male quartet who performed contemporary songs in key time slots on the WHO Radio schedule. Accompanied by pianist Bill Austin, the group performed for years on Mondays, Wednesdays, and Fridays at 12:45 p.m. after the midday newscast anchored by Jack Shelley. The Songfellows were featured on NBC and eastern stations for six years before joining WHO and the *Iowa Barn Dance Frolic* in the mid-1930s. They appeared on WHO until 1958.

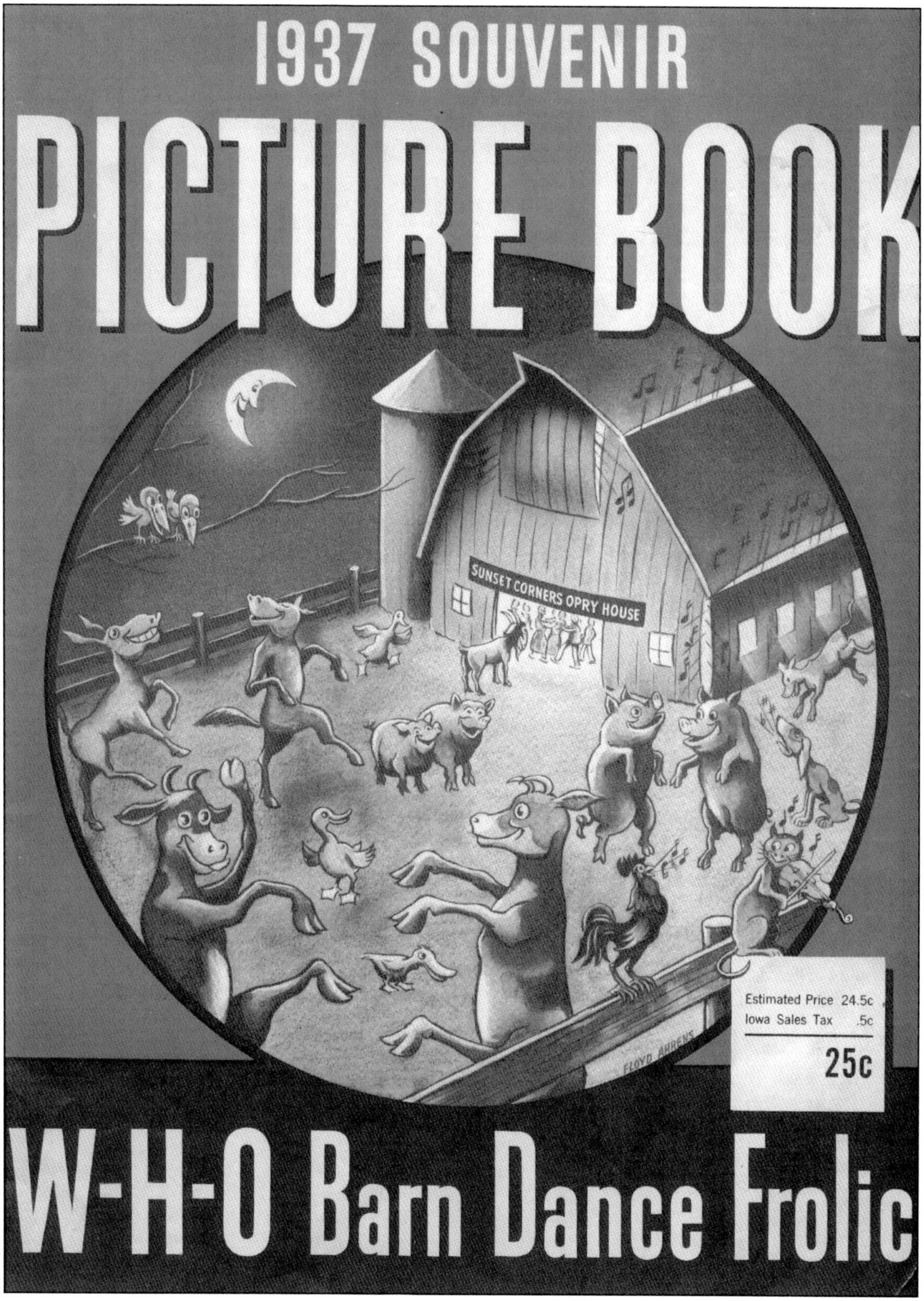

In response to audience demand, starting in 1936 and continuing until the war years, WHO Radio published a special souvenir picture book sold to those who attended the *Iowa Barn Dance Frolic* performances. The book included photographs and biographies of not only WHO Radio performers and management, but also those of performers heard on WHO from the NBC radio network. WHO became an NBC Red Network affiliate in 1927.

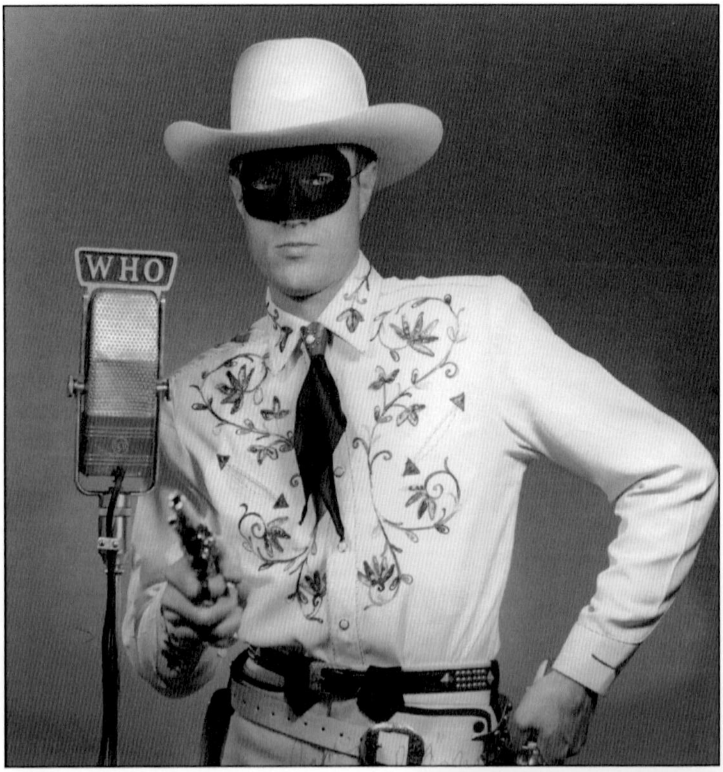

That masked man with the revolver is not the Lone Ranger—it is actually Duane Ellett, who joined the WHO Radio staff in 1947 following his graduation from Drake University. An accomplished musician, Ellett was part of the *Barn Dance* cast in addition to his work as a station announcer. This photograph was taken a few years before Ellett's partnership with a puppet named Floppy.

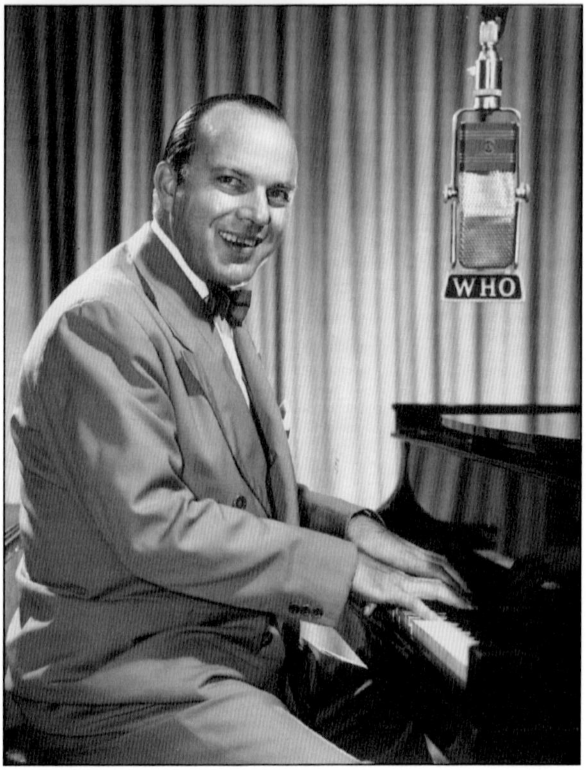

Bill Austin was the pianist and musical arranger for the Songfellows, who performed on WHO Radio daily in addition to their Saturday night *Barn Dance* appearances. Even into the early 1960s, Austin was featured playing the piano and organ on WHO radio and television programs.

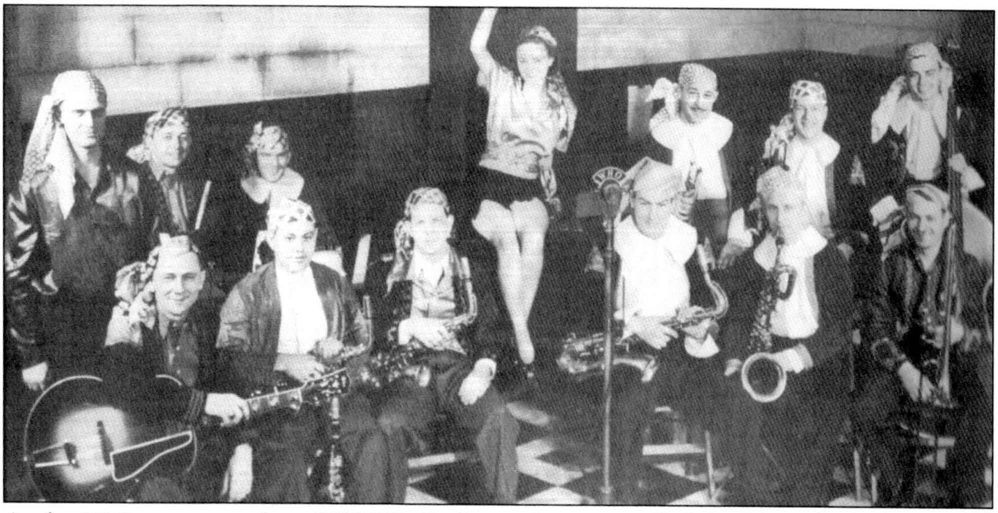

As the 1930s came to a close, WHO Radio featured a group called the Musical Pirates, directed by Don Hovey and designed to "bring you delightful late evening entertainment from 11:00 p.m. to midnight each Saturday," following the conclusion of the *Barn Dance* broadcast.

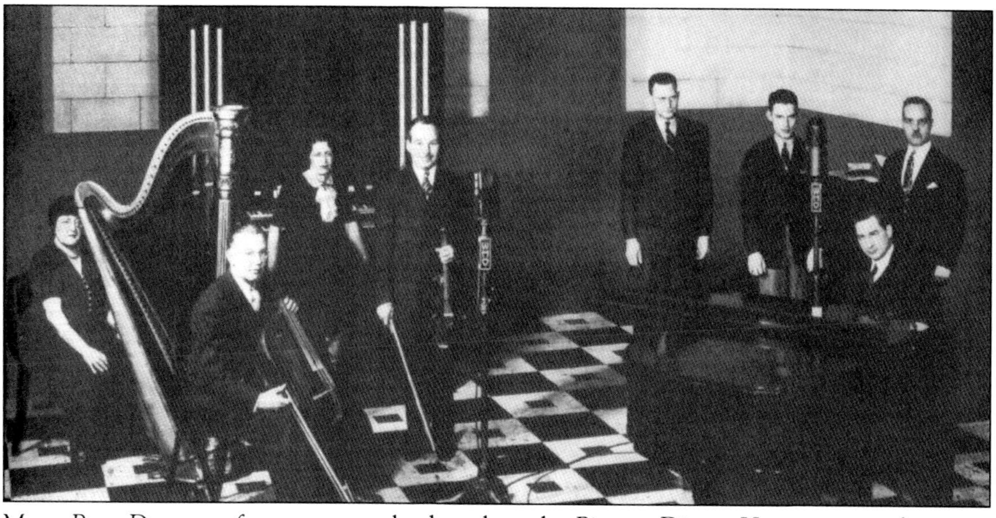

Many *Barn Dance* performers were also heard on the *Pioneer Dinner Hour* program featuring decidedly different musical fare. Pictured from left to right are Garnette Arrick, Ernie Mitchell, Lenore Mudge Stull, Roy Shaw, Dick M. Vawter (the Old Pioneer), soloist Jack Kerrigan, Harold Fair, and Ernie Sanders.

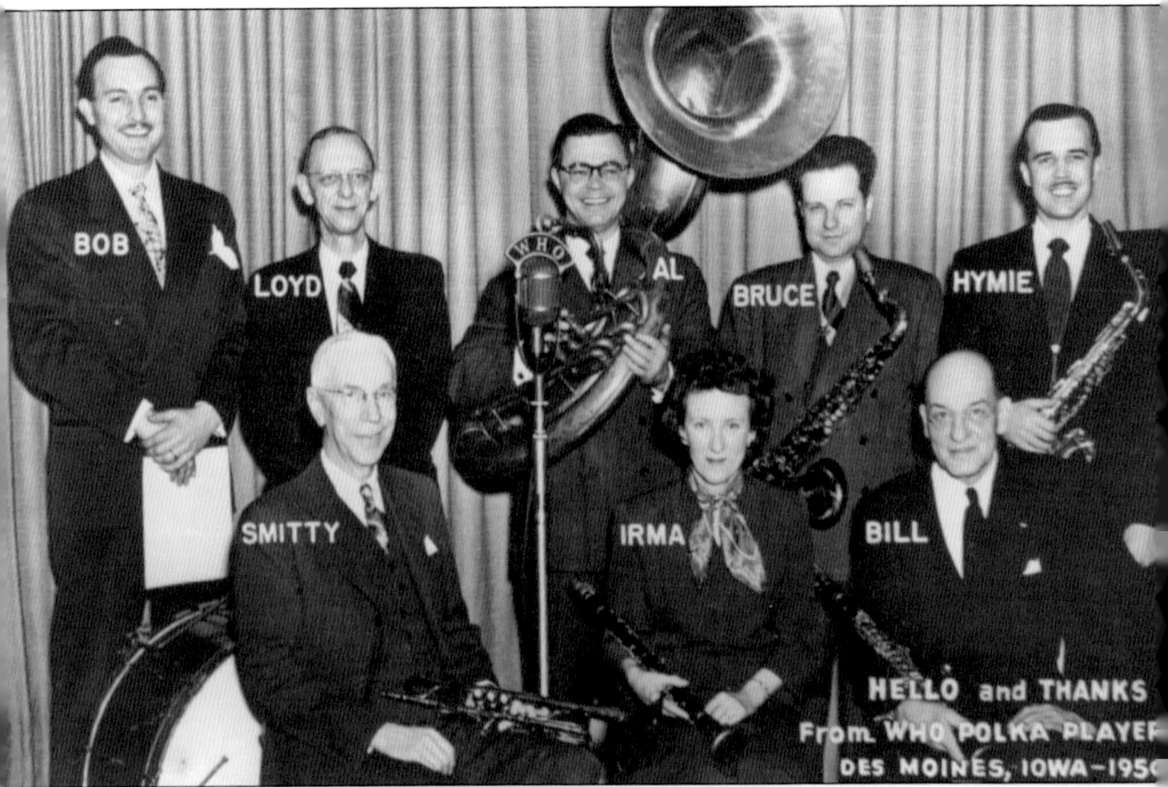

Often, listeners who wrote the station to offer praise for their favorite performers would receive a reply in the form of a postcard featuring a photograph of the group. The reply, "Hello and Thanks," was signed, "WHO Polka Players," in this 1950 postcard.

Six

A Friend in the Morning

Since the advent of television, more people listen to the radio in the early morning than at any other time of the day. Whether to find out the latest news, hear the day's weather forecast, or just be given a good reason to get out of bed, they rely on the voices coming through their home or car radios to help them start the day.

While today's radio formats are more narrow and niche oriented than in the past, morning radio's mission has been the same over time. And in a state like Iowa with more "early risers," that mission starts even earlier.

The image of Iowa children waking up to see snowfall and huddling around the radio while the announcer reads off the list of school delays and cancellations is common. As the school of interest is read, the news is greeted by both cheers and groans (depending on whether the listener is a child or a parent and whether the news is that school is cancelled or will still be held).

Traditionally, radio's morning drive time has been defined as being from 6:00 a.m. to 10:00 a.m. In recent decades, that has slid back even earlier, now beginning at 5:00 a.m. But lively local programming in the predawn hours is not new. A 1952 station program guide shows that *Barn Dance* performer Lem Turner hosted *Lem Turner's Coffee Shop* with comedy and music at 4:00 a.m., followed by another half hour of live music performed by the Crack-O-Dawners.

The economics of radio today dictate that, at many stations, the only live voice heard is the one in the morning; many music-intensive stations employ technology to record and insert the voice of the announcer between songs in times of lower listenership or simply program music without the use of disc jockeys or announcers during the majority of the day.

At WHO Radio, the morning show tradition has been strong, whether it was Don Warren playing "Reveille" each morning, or in more recent years, allowing cows in the studio one day a week. For the past quarter century, one voice in the morning has been a constant presence, sharing the microphone with three different cohosts in what has consistently been Iowa's most-listened-to radio program.

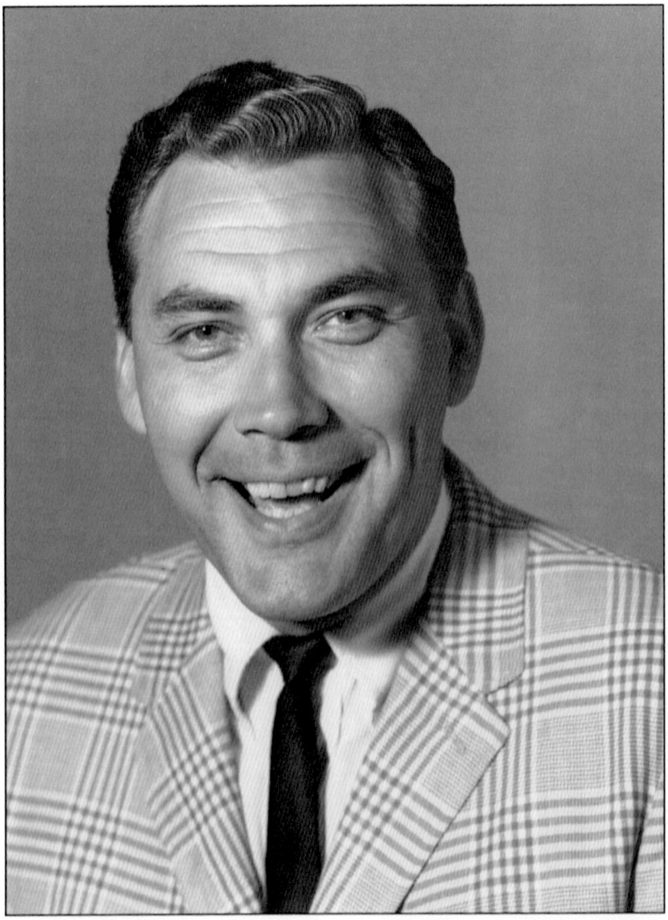

The gregarious Don Warren was a popular personality on WHO Radio from the late 1950s into the 1970s. He was known for his bright and lively demeanor on air, integrating popular music of the era with news and information—and for playing "Reveille" at the same time each morning to wake those listeners who were still slumbering. The *Don Warren Good Morning Show* aired six days a week, not uncommon for morning-drive-time personalities of the era. The versatile Warren also migrated to television, where he cohosted WHO-TV's midday cartoon program with Floppy for several years. Warren later moved to Cedar Rapids, where he delighted another generation of radio listeners, hosting the morning program on a country music station there for more than a decade.

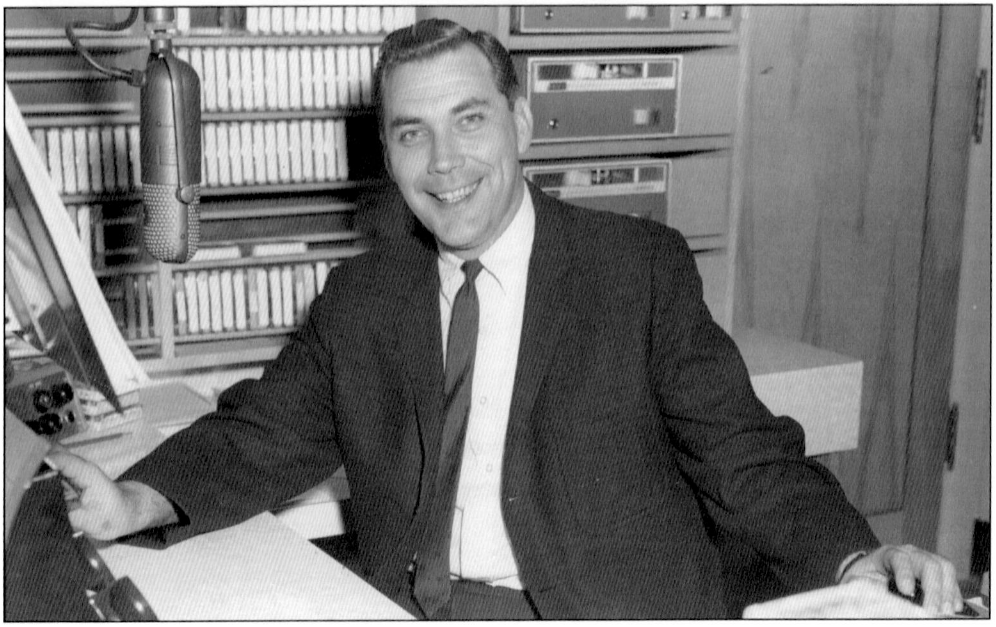

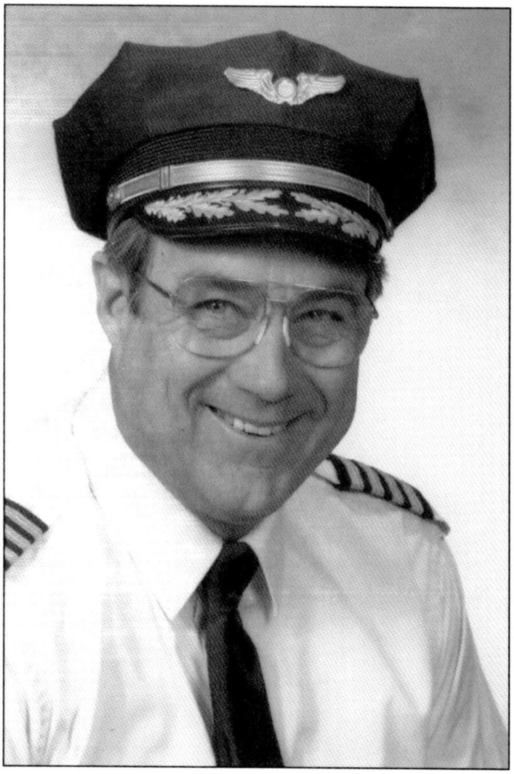

A hallmark of WHO Radio's programming for a quarter century was the daily traffic reports delivered from an airplane piloted by Captain Jack. For 24 years, Bill Dennis assumed the Captain Jack persona; there was another Captain Jack for a short time before Dennis began delivering the reports in 1977. Dennis became a diversified businessman, also operating Captain Jack's Christmas Tree Farm on 40 acres of land near Ankeny, and Captain Jack Communications, an Internet firm. Bill Dennis is pictured as Captain Jack at the controls of his plane in 1977 (below) and 1994 (right). He retired from delivering the daily morning and afternoon traffic reports in 2001.

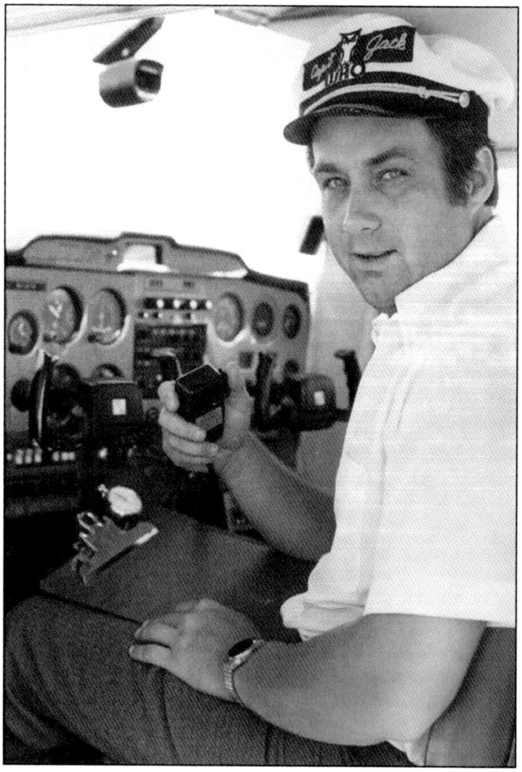

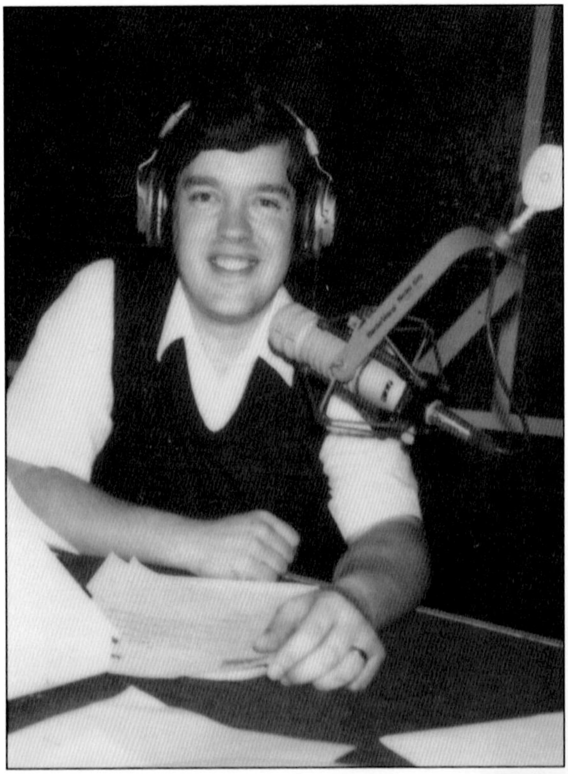

Van Harden has been a fixture on Des Moines radio for more than 35 years. A native of Adel, Harden first started at a Perry radio station while a student at Drake University. After a radio job in Oklahoma, Harden returned to Des Moines and radio station KRNT in 1975, hosting midday and afternoon programs. He was hired to move across town to WHO Radio in December 1986 and took to the air for the first time there on January 5, 1987; he has cohosted the morning program ever since. Harden is seen during a 1987 broadcast soon after he started at WHO Radio. He was ahead of a national trend by suggesting to station personnel that they start the morning program an hour earlier than their competition, which led to WHO's show starting at 5:00 a.m. instead of the customary 6:00 a.m.; other stations quickly followed suit, edging the start time of their morning shows earlier and earlier to keep pace.

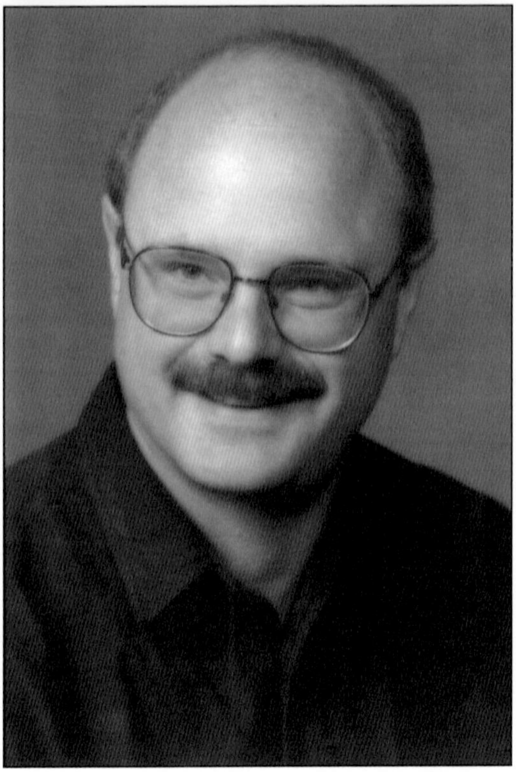

The voice of Steve Locker is familiar to WHO Radio's morning listeners as the man behind the controls during the weekday *Van and Bonnie* program and as the host of his own Saturday morning buy-sell-trade show, *Radio Tradio*, which mixes comedy with the listeners' desire to dispose of unneeded items. Dave Campbell hosted an earlier version of *Tradio* in the 1990s.

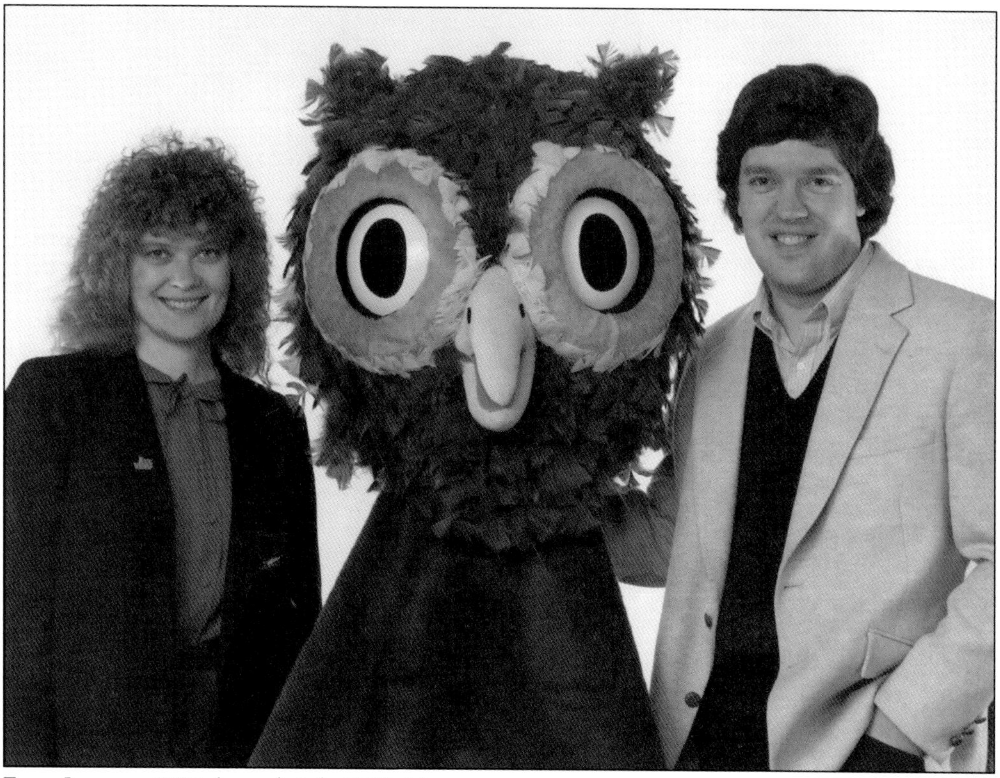

From January 1987 through July 1988, Van Harden cohosted the morning program with Patti Christensen, who was known to listeners through her work in the WHO Radio farm department. The WHO owl mascot made its first appearance in these promotional photographs, which date from November 1987. Despite strong audience acceptance, Christensen was not a fan of the early hours and personal appearances required by the job and returned to the farm department after a year and a half on the morning show.

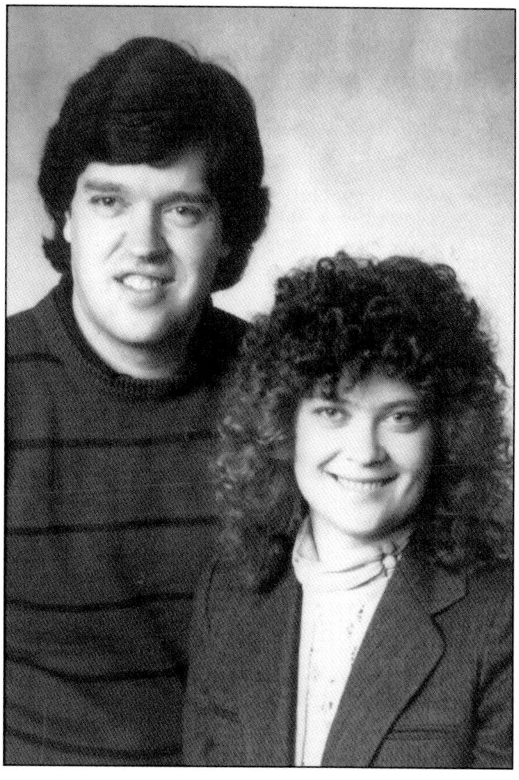

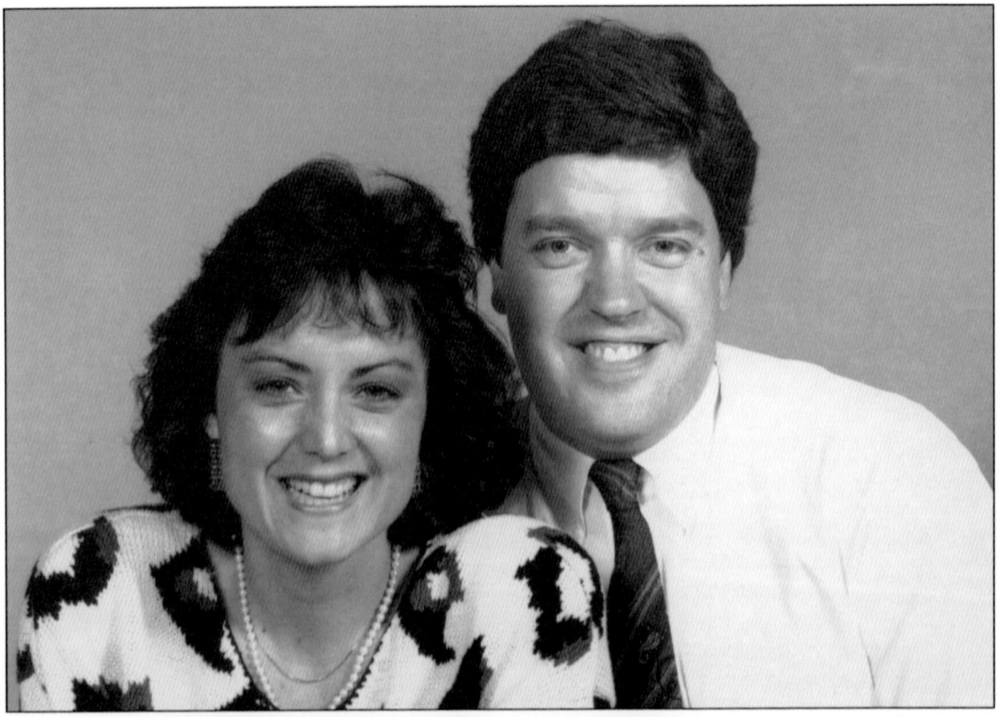

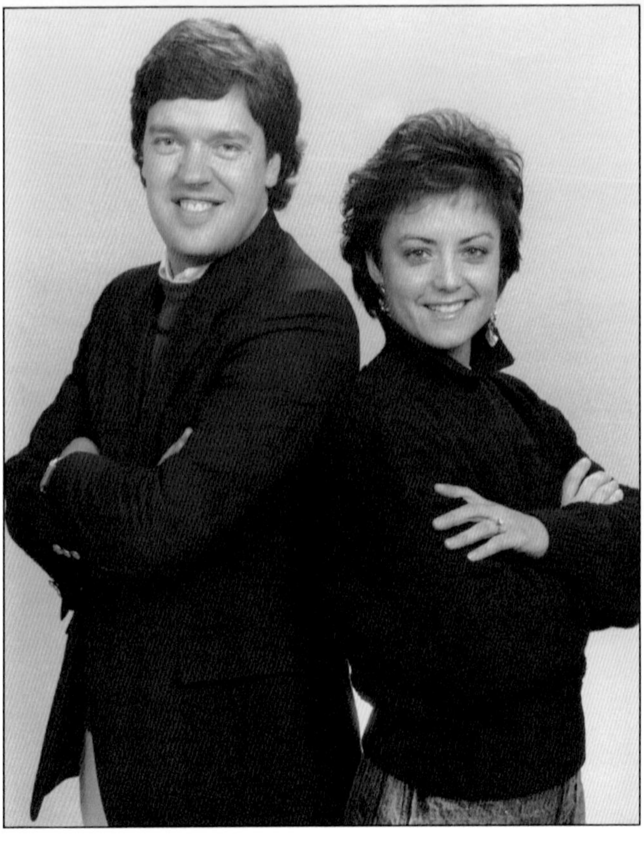

A seven-year partnership started in August 1988 when Connie Murad joined Van Harden for the newly named *Van and Connie* morning show. The publicity photographs shown are from 1991 (above) and 1994 (left). During their time together, the duo started the annual National Leisure Suit Convention events and grew WHO Radio's morning audience to the top ranking in the market. Murad left Des Moines for the Twin Cities in August 1995 for family reasons.

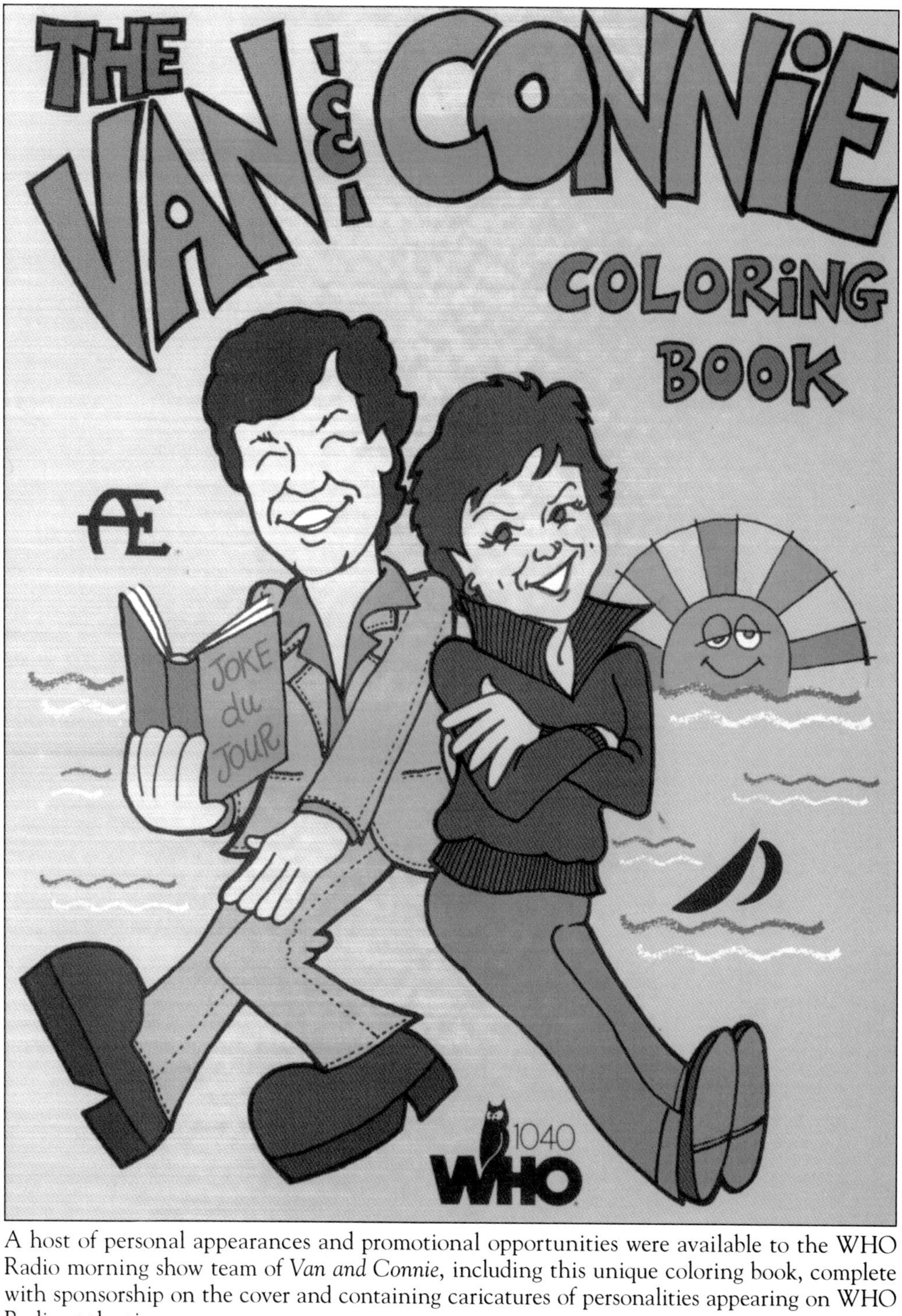

A host of personal appearances and promotional opportunities were available to the WHO Radio morning show team of *Van and Connie*, including this unique coloring book, complete with sponsorship on the cover and containing caricatures of personalities appearing on WHO Radio at the time.

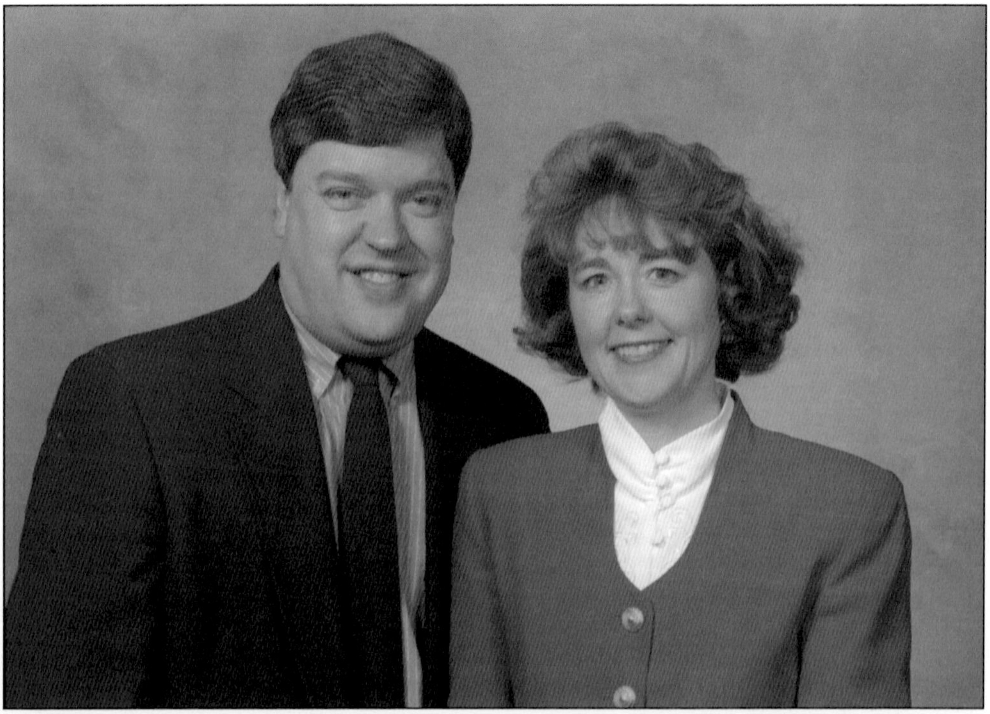

The WHO Radio morning show has been hosted by Van Harden and Bonnie Lucas since September 1995. The two had worked together previously off-air at KRNT Radio, and when the cohost position opened Harden contacted Lucas. The success of the duo led the Anderson Erickson Dairy to create an ice cream flavor named for them: the popular Van and Bon Bon ice cream, which was vanilla with chocolate bonbon candy mixed in. The ice cream was one of the company's big sellers from its creation in 1996, but it was discontinued in 2011 when AE Dairy eliminated its entire ice cream line.

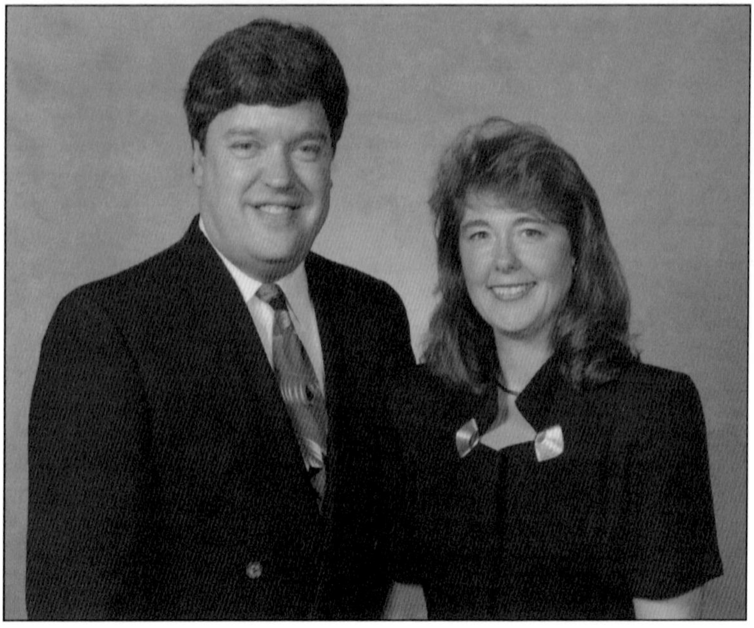

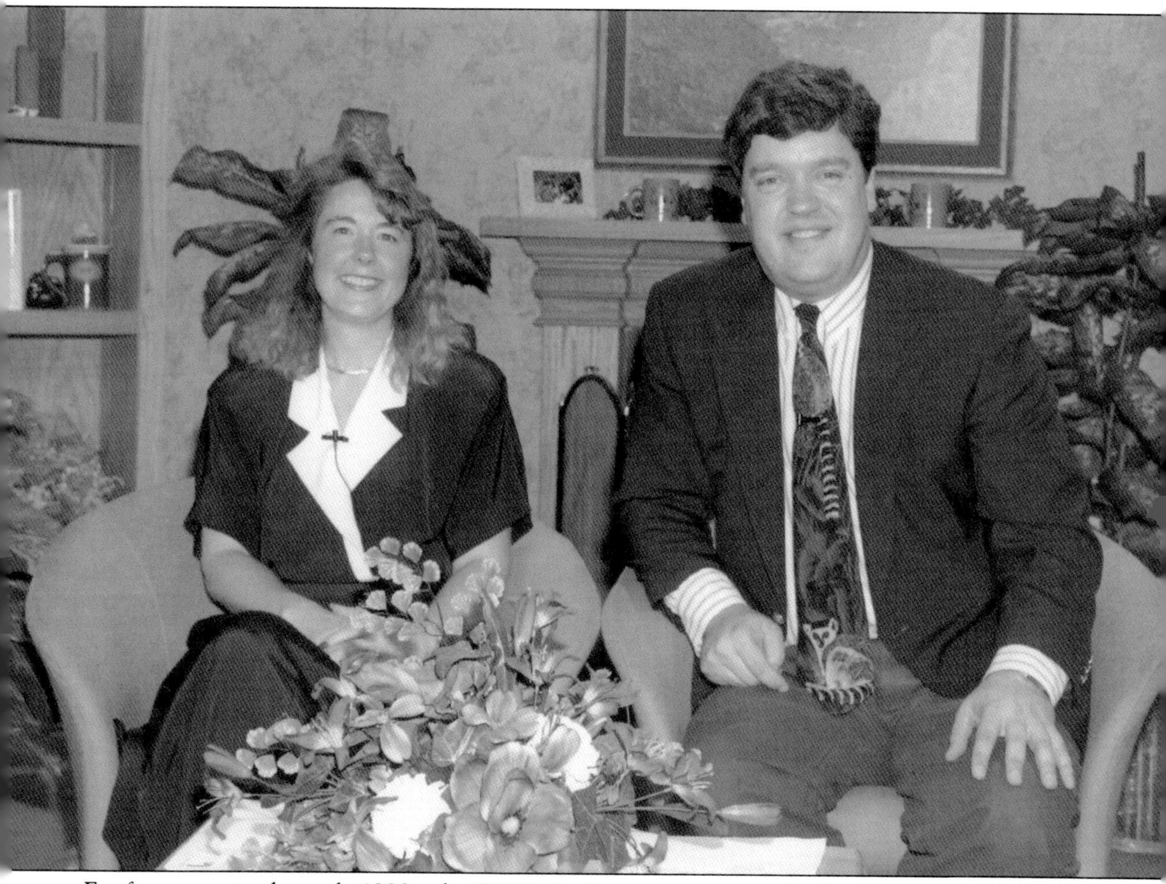

For four years in the early 1990s, the WHO Radio morning team also hosted a daily afternoon program on WHO-TV featuring interviews concerning community happenings and events. The program ended about the time the Palmer Broadcasting Company sold WHO-TV and the radio and television station were no longer under the same ownership.

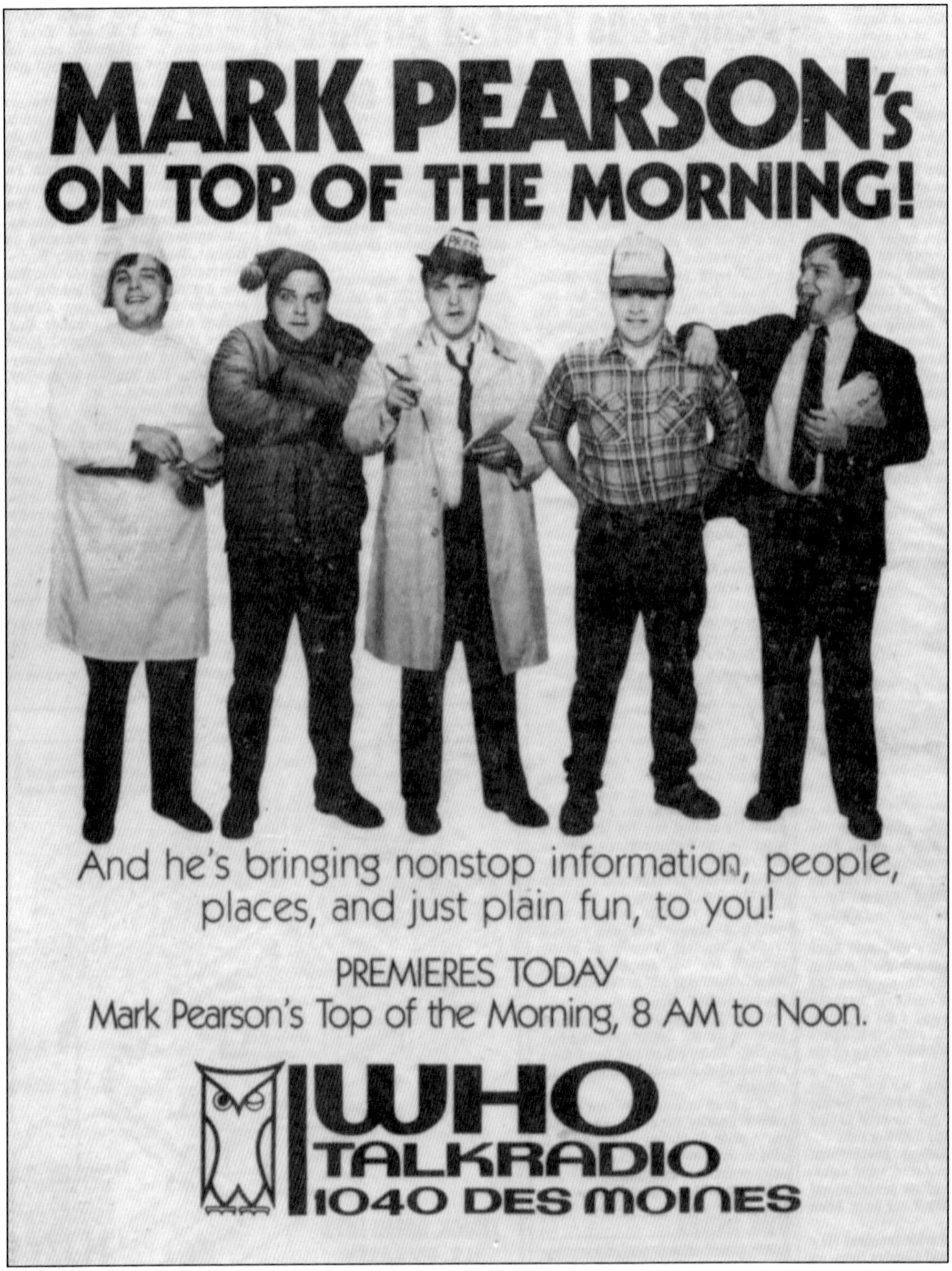

Starting in December 1983, farm broadcaster Mark Pearson was given a turn at hosting a morning program that promised slightly lighter fare. Since 1991, and in addition to his work in the WHO Radio farm department, Pearson has been host of the weekly public television program *Market to Market*, dubbed "the weekly journal of rural America."

Seven

Iowa's Open Forum

The human need to express one's opinion and be heard on a variety of topics is strong. Young people today spend much of their time interacting with one another through electronics. They feel a need to state their opinions and reach broad audiences through blogs, Twitter feeds, and Facebook posts.

That need has its foundation in radio call-in shows and interview programs. From topics ranging from the actions of state government to growing larger tomatoes, all subjects have had their place on the WHO Radio airwaves.

Listing the names of those who have moderated such on-air discussions will still generate a response from longtime listeners: Julie Gammack, Jim Frye, Susan Bray, Jan Mickelson, and dozens of others.

Whether they remember yesterday's *Phone Forum*, *WHO Talkradio*, and *Call Jim Zabel* or enjoy today's *Mickelson in the Morning*, generations of listeners can recite the station's studio line phone number—284-1040—by heart. And they are not shy about using it.

While many talk programs today feature hosts who are paid to say outlandish things and generate a response from the audience, the WHO Radio tradition has been to feature intelligent personalities who are unafraid to tackle important issues and are conversant on a variety of topics. They engage in conversation designed to stimulate thought. That is why getting a slot as a guest on one of these programs is coveted by politicians, authors, and community leaders: they know they will reach a thoughtful audience and receive a fair hearing with tough, but fair, questions from the hosts. And it is why a turn behind the WHO Radio microphone is required by any candidate who wants to earn the vote of citizens in the Iowa Caucuses every four years.

For those who rely on the radio as an electronic friend in the home or car, the conversation that is a hallmark of the format serves a comforting role as well.

And where else can listeners dispose of items they no longer want or need, if not for a program like *Radio Tradio*?

It is all part of the mix and part of why the interview and call-in program format has been a staple of American radio programming.

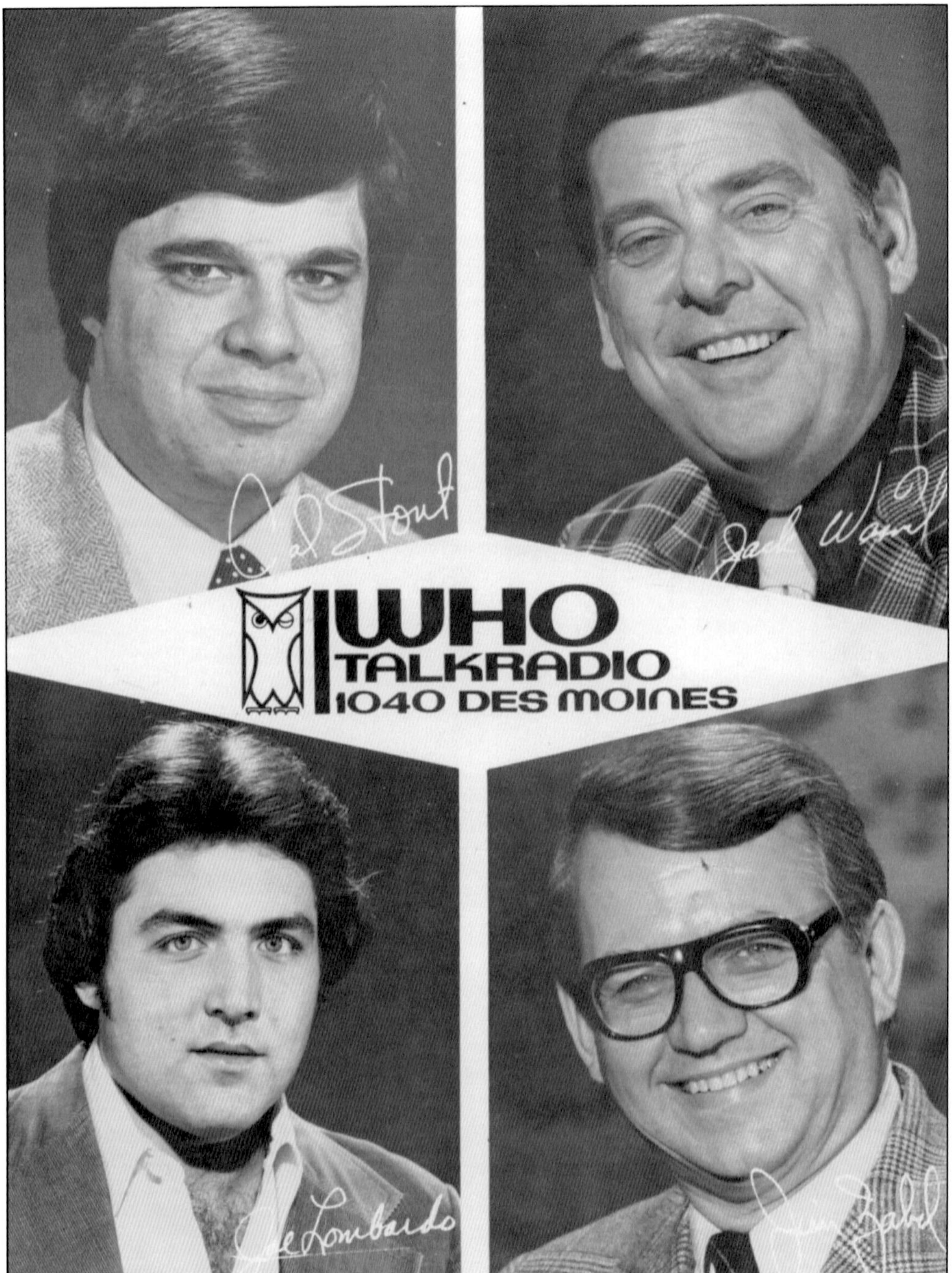

Promotional photographs, like this one featuring four hosts of *WHO Talkradio* programs, were handed out at events such as the Iowa State Fair in the early 1980s. Clockwise from the upper left are Cal Stout, Jack Warnell, Jim Zabel, and Joe Lombardo. Stout and Lombardo were familiar to audiences through their work at other Des Moines stations before coming to WHO Radio.

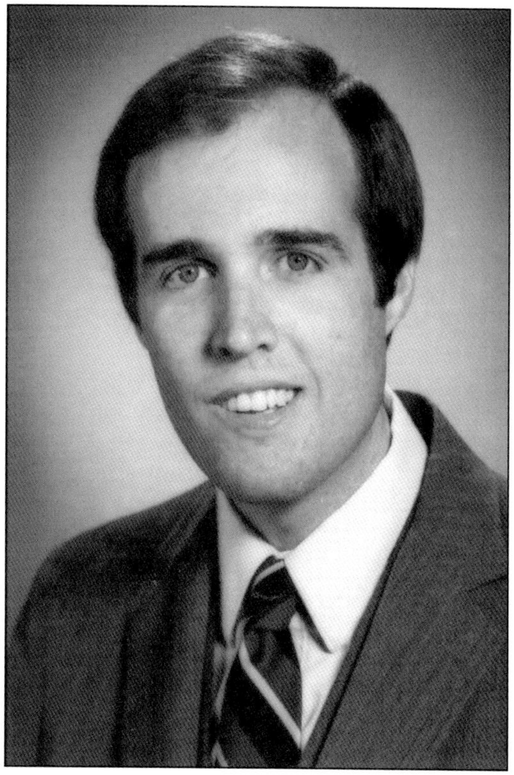

A number of broadcasters took a turn at the *WHO Talkradio* microphone during the 1970s and 1980s, including Jon London (right) and Jim Frye (below, with an appropriate partner). After leaving WHO in the mid-1980s, Frye moved to KIOA in Des Moines when that station tried a talk format during the evening hours.

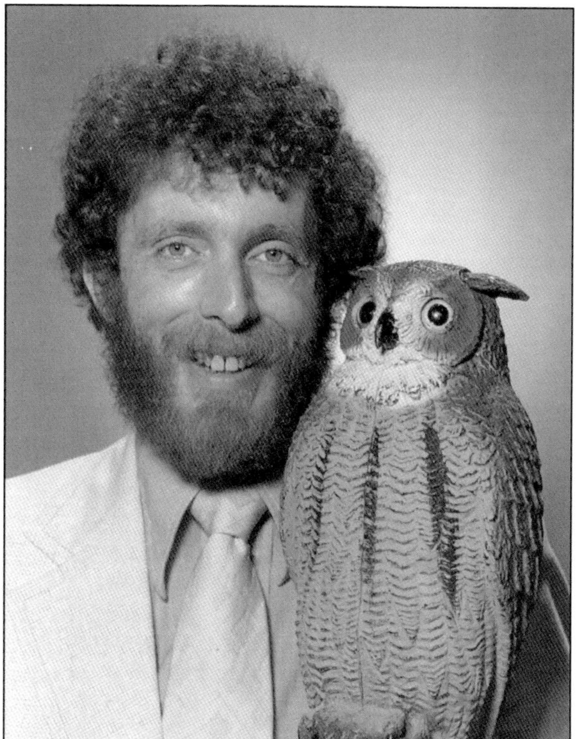

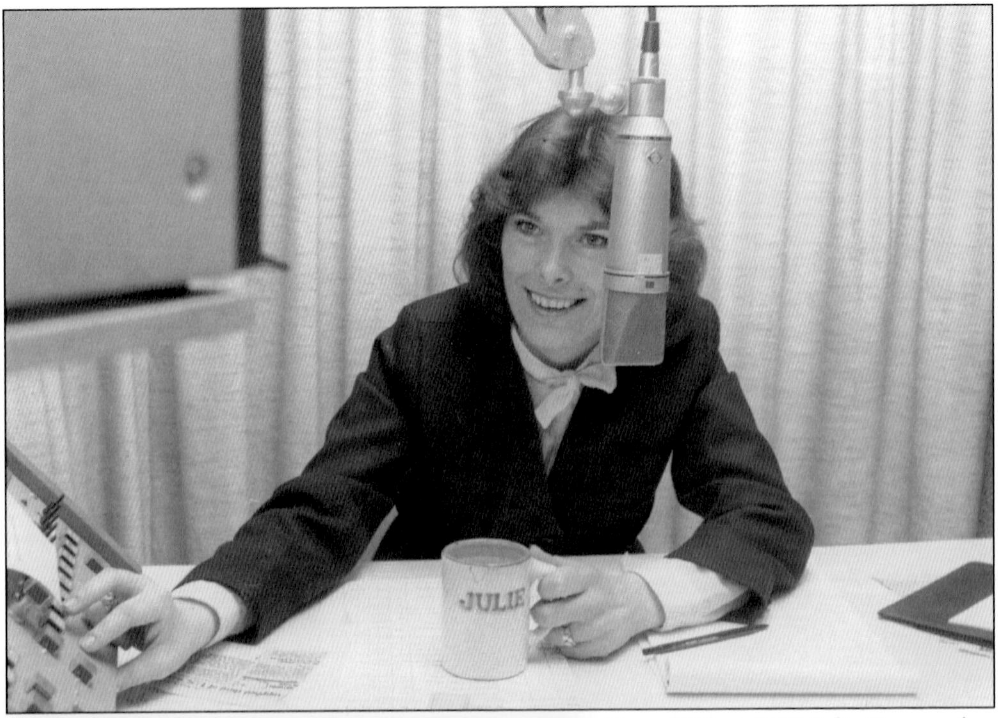

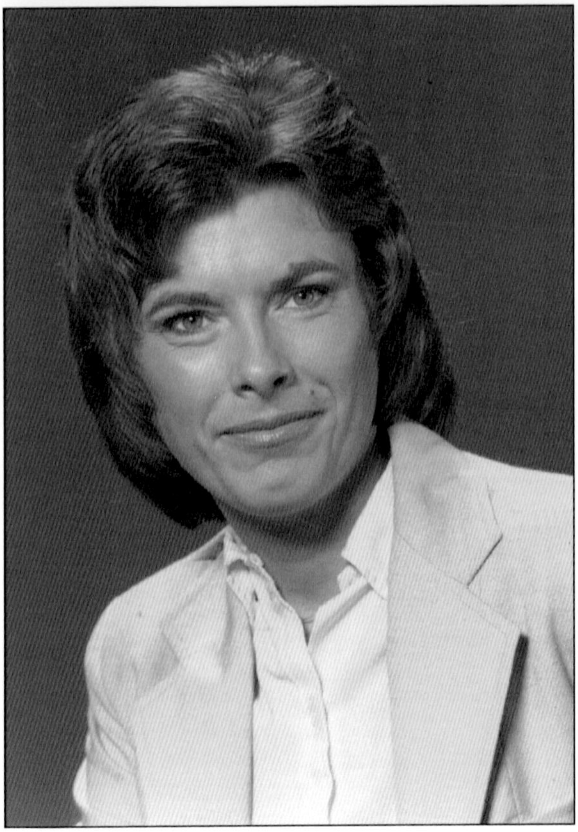

From 1982 to 1985, Julie Gammack hosted a morning talk program on WHO Radio, which was the top-rated program of that time period. A native of Des Moines, Gammack followed in her famous father's footsteps by also writing a daily column in the *Des Moines Register* for nearly a decade, starting in 1983.

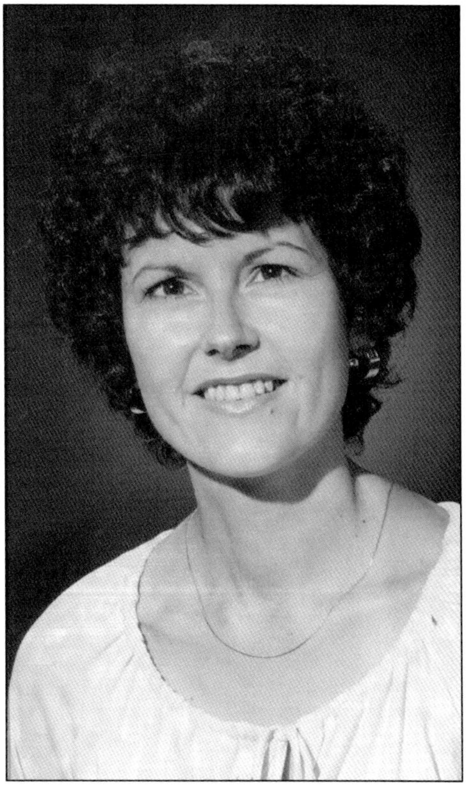

Susan Bray came to WHO Radio in February 1978 as the station's first female talk-show host. The native of Hay, Australia, hosted a three-hour program on Mondays through Saturdays from 8:30 a.m. to 11:30 a.m. Audience ratings showed that at its height, the program had approximately 200,000 listeners, correlating to roughly one-third of the Des Moines metro area.

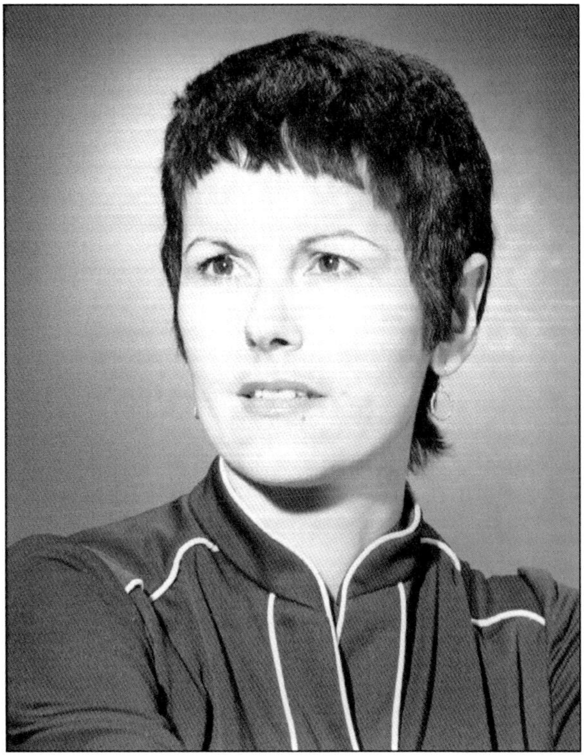

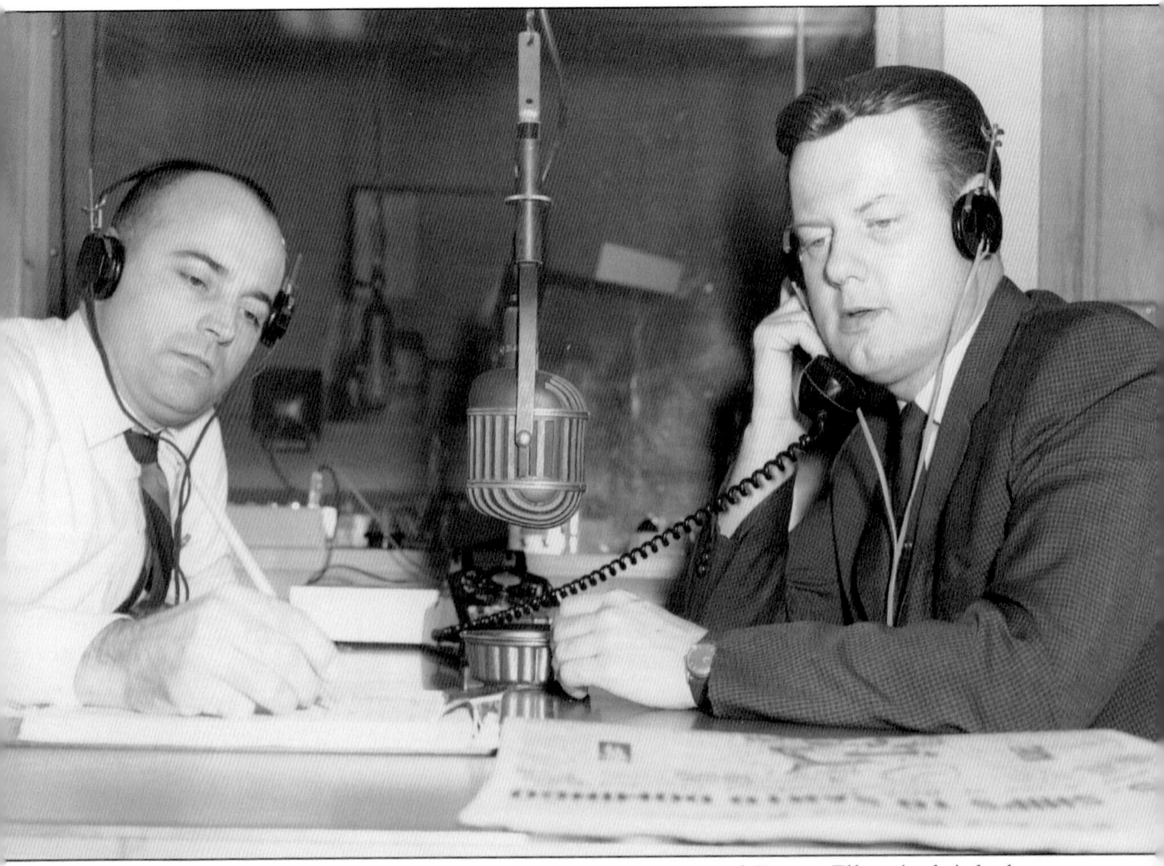

While Lee Kline (left) was best known for farm reporting and Duane Ellett (right) for being a children's television show host, the duo hosted editions of the *Phone Forum* program together for several years.

Bob Williams started in radio in 1933 and came to WHO in 1948 from a Fort Dodge station. A versatile personality, Williams hosted various talk programs on WHO Radio, including *Phone Forum* (at times with good friend Duane Ellett) and *Trade Central*, a forerunner of today's *Radio Tradio* program.

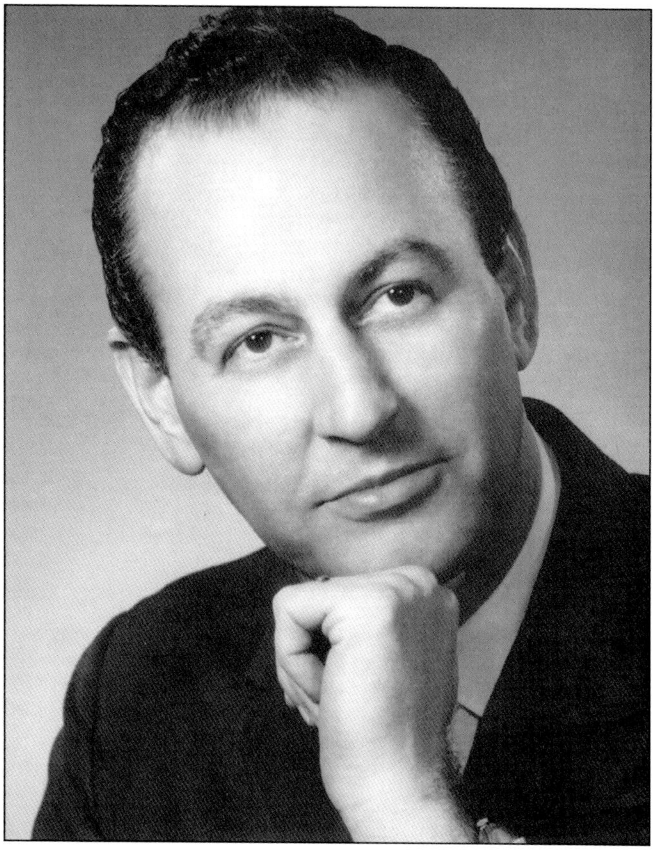

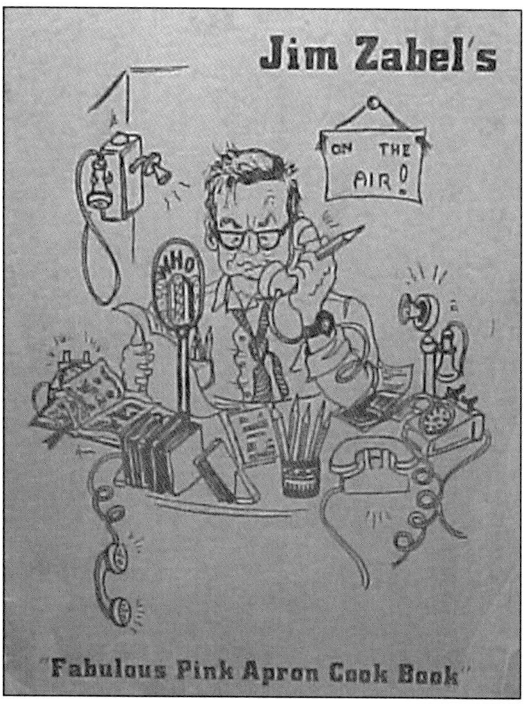

Call Jim Zabel was a favorite early afternoon talk program on WHO Radio for decades, starting in 1966. Listeners called in on a variety of topics, and because Zabel liked to cook, some called to share their favorite recipes. Just four years into the show, Zabel had accumulated more than 6,000 recipes, leading to the publication of the *Fabulous Pink Apron Cook Book* series.

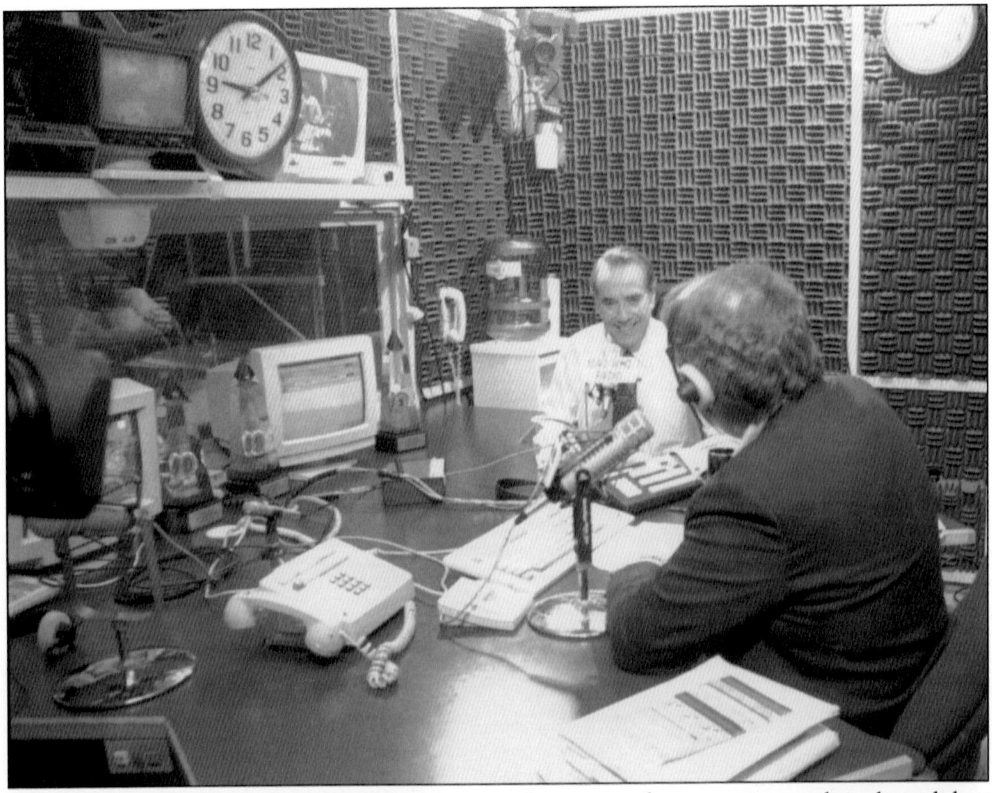

The WHO Radio microphone has become a mandatory stop for any serious political candidate regardless of political affiliation. In these photographs from the 1996 presidential campaign, leading to Iowa's first-in-the-nation caucuses, Bob Dole of Kansas (above) and Lamar Alexander of Tennessee (below) took turns at being questioned by morning talk-show host Jan Mickelson.

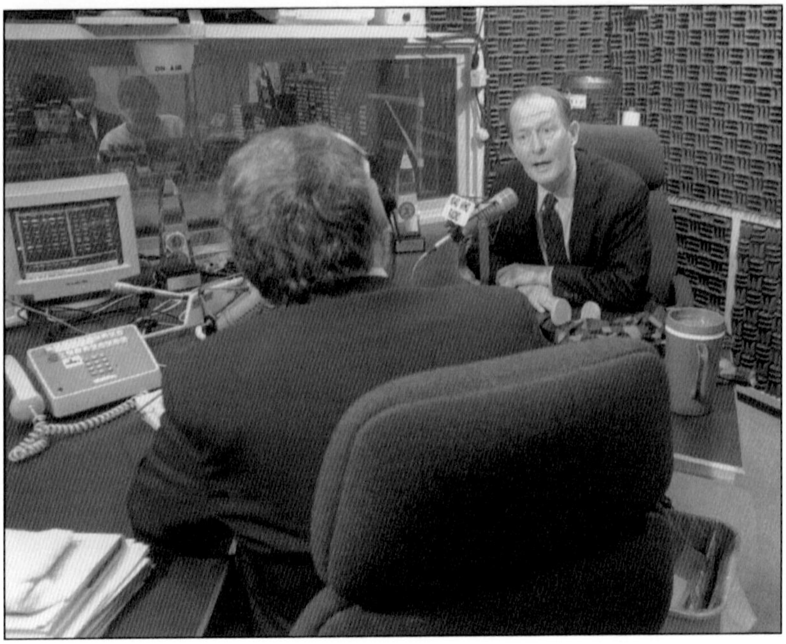

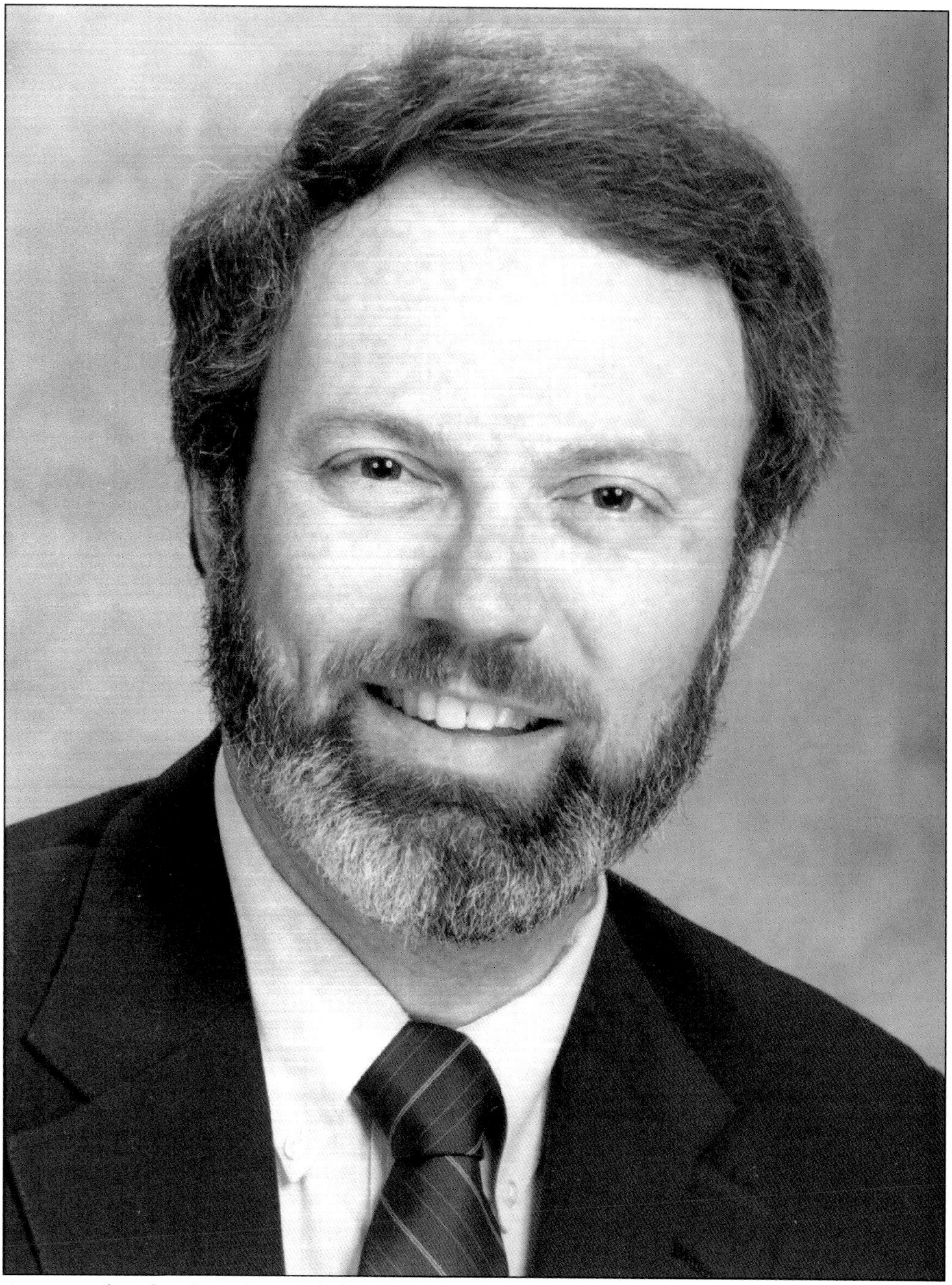

A native of Harlan, Iowa, Jan Mickelson has hosted WHO Radio's morning talk program since 1988. The *Mickelson in the Morning* program has established itself as one of the nation's longest-running local topical programs, airing daily from 9:00 a.m. to 11:30 a.m. For a time in the early part of the 2000s, the program was literally a statewide conversation simulcast on Iowa's two largest stations: WHO Radio and its Clear Channel Communications sibling WMT Radio in Cedar Rapids. An early adopter of new technology, Mickelson has made his program available for download from the WHO Radio website for many years, long before it was popular elsewhere.

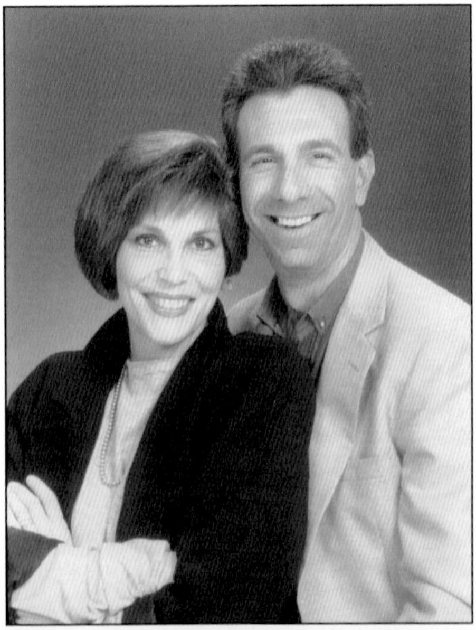

Dave Wingert and Melanie Workhoven hosted an afternoon-drive information and conversation program during the middle and late 1980s. The popularity of the syndicated Rush Limbaugh program, which premiered in 1988, shifted the focus of WHO Radio's programming during that part of the day, and the show hosted by Wingert and Workhoven was shortened and eventually replaced by the news-oriented *Drive Time Des Moines* program. Wingert and Workhoven continued to work in Des Moines radio after their time hosting the late afternoon WHO Radio program.

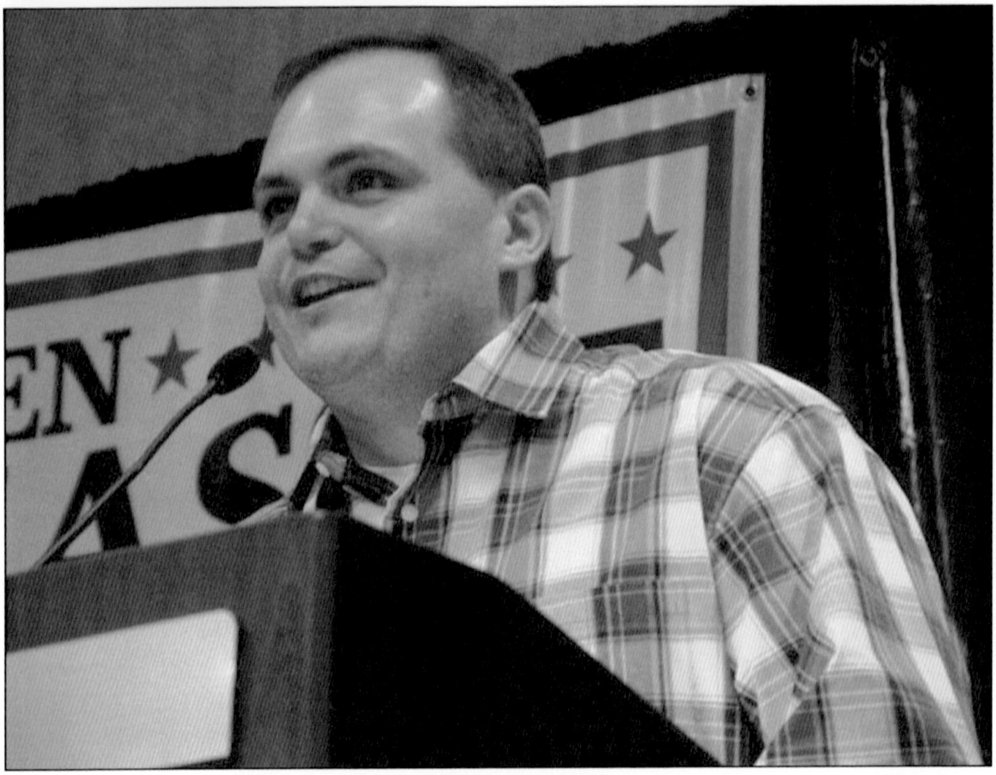

WHO Radio was a charter subscriber of the national Rush Limbaugh program in 1988. In an effort to build upon the audience for political conversation established by Limbaugh's afternoon time slot, WHO Radio aired a weekday three-hour program featuring Steve Deace for four years, ending in early 2011. Deace was first known in Des Moines radio for his work on sports-oriented stations, including the Clear Channel Communications–owned KXNO, before moving to current-affairs talk radio.

Eight

Music for All Tastes

When new media forms develop, old media forms have to evolve. Newspapers had to change to adapt to the competition from radio, focusing more on in-depth stories and nuances, as audiences already had heard the headline via radio. Radio has had to change twice in the past half century: first, in the 1950s when television came along, and then in the 1980s with the emergence of FM.

Radio program schedules in the pre-television days looked much like today's TV schedules. Dramas, quiz shows, soap operas, and comedies were fixtures in the evening schedule and sometimes were stripped at the same time of day five or six days a week. Those shows migrated to television, often being aired on both mediums for a time before completely moving to the new visual medium.

That led to radio stations focusing more than ever on music. This change dovetailed with the emergence of rock-and-roll music as a popular genre, and historians note that each helped the other to survive. While many stations narrowed their focus to serve specialized audiences, stations with powerful signals like WHO Radio operated under a mandate to serve a broad audience. That meant satisfying a variety of musical tastes, often within the same broadcast day.

Later, AM radio spent a number of years in the 1970s and 1980s finding its way in light of the increasing popularity of FM stations, which could reproduce music with greater sound quality because of the nature of the FM signal and became the choice for those who favored listening to contemporary music. That is why today more AM stations employ a so-called voice format (such as talk, news, sports) rather than music, a trend that crystallized in the 1990s.

As this evolution took place over time, the station employed a variety of versatile, well-known personalities and formats—from programs of contemporary music to the big-band sound to a weekly program of hymns and gospel music, and, of course, the *Country Music USA* overnight program—before settling on the Newsradio 1040 WHO news and talk format of today.

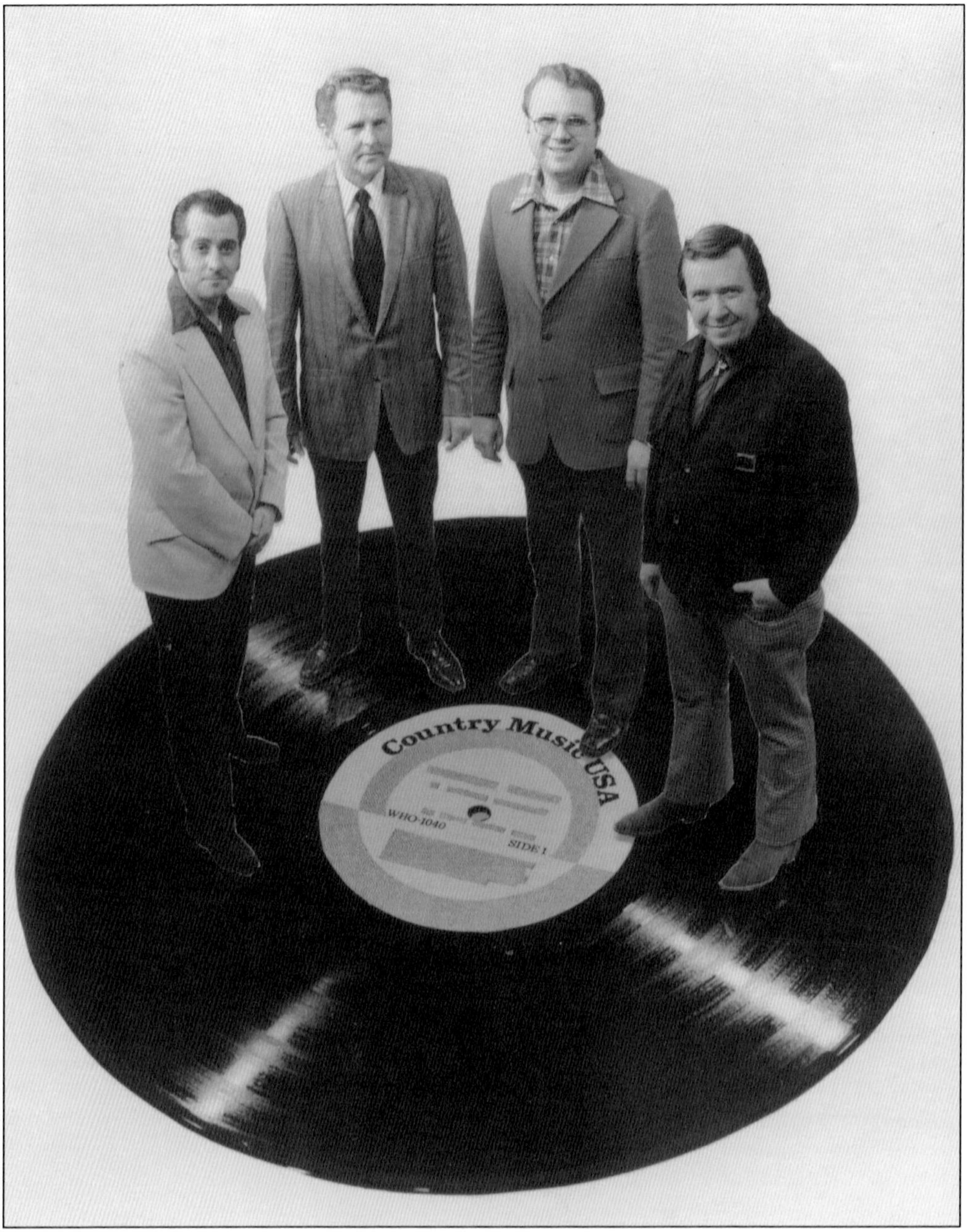

A promotional photograph spotlights the four hosts of *Country Music USA* on WHO Radio in the early 1970s. From left to right are Billy Cole, Max Bennington, Larry Heaberlin, and Dan Read.

Billy Cole joined the WHO Radio staff in 1972, replacing Mike Hoyer as the host of the station's signature overnight *Country Music USA* program. Cole came to WHO from WSM in Nashville, where he hosted the *Grand Old Opry Star Spotlight* radio program and served as announcer for the Saturday afternoon Opry matinees from the stage of the legendary Reimann Auditorium. He received the Country Music Association's DJ of the Year award in 1975 and was inducted into the Country Music Disc Jockey Hall of Fame in 2002. Cole died in 2007 at age 70.

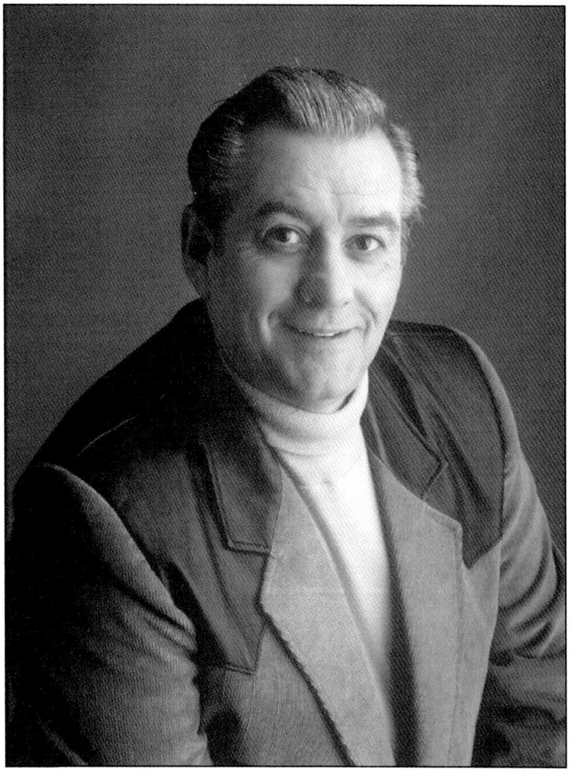

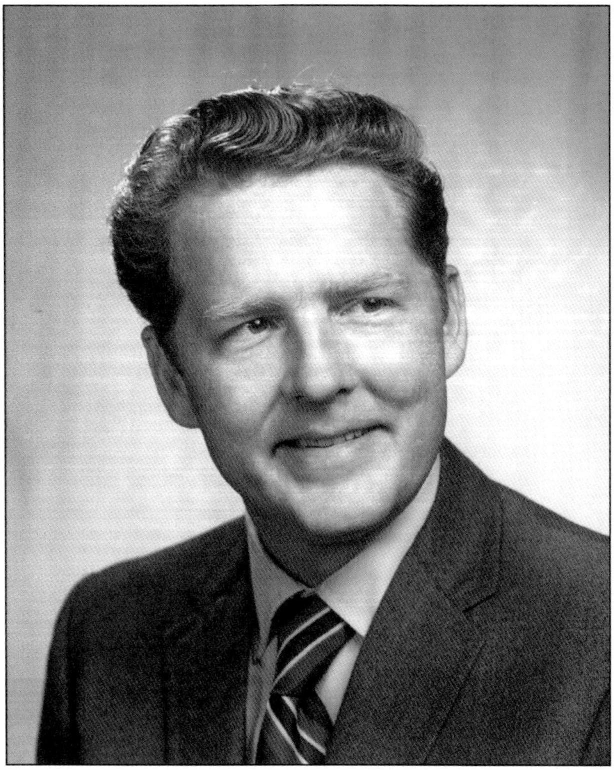

Max Bennington served WHO Radio in a variety of roles, memorably as one of the hosts of *Country Music USA*. He was a staff announcer at the station long after WHO discontinued the country music format in favor of other music genres.

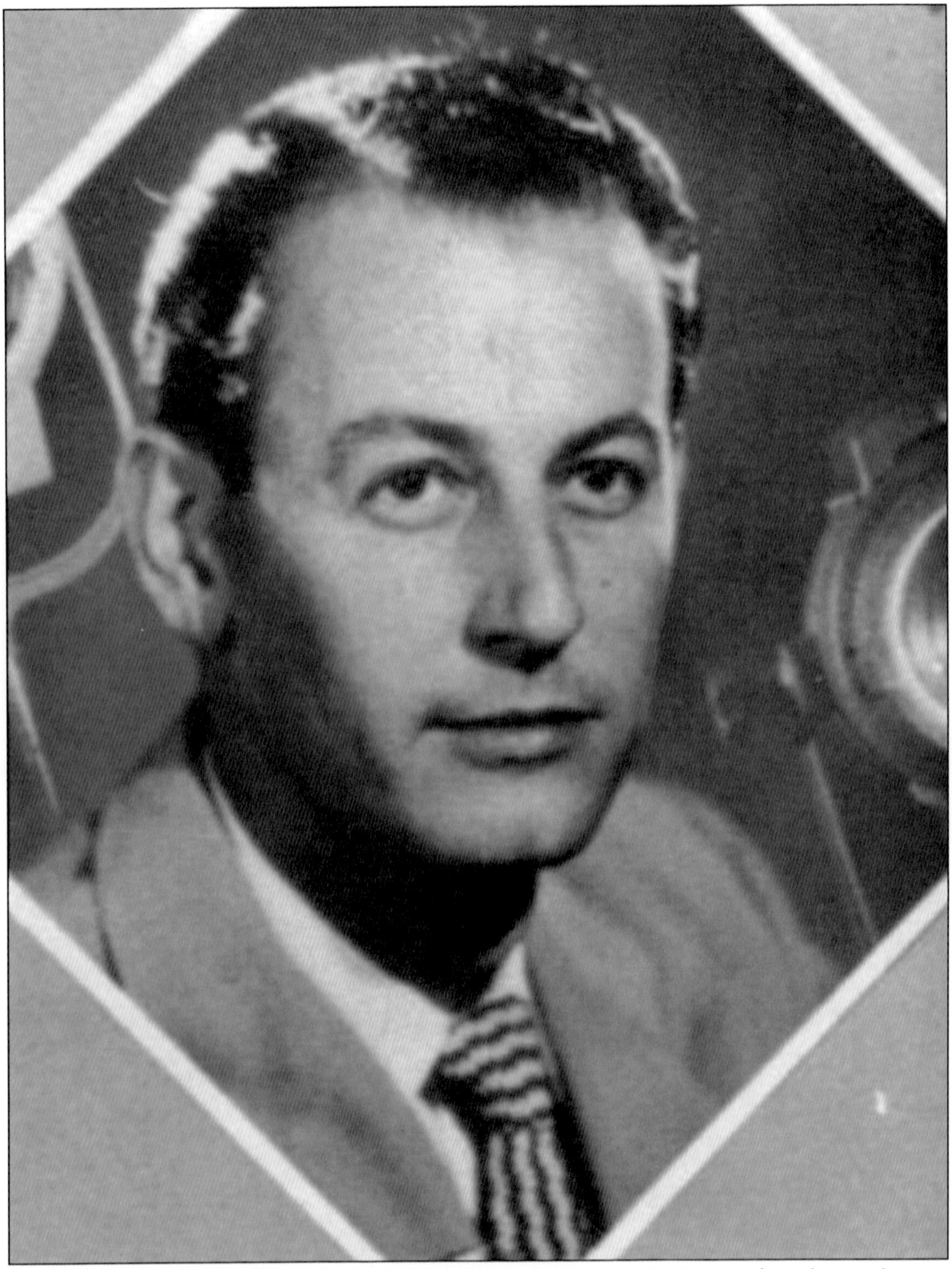

Bob Williams worked at WHO Radio for 37 years, starting in 1948. He was heard on radio as a staff announcer, music program host, master of ceremonies of the *Iowa Barn Dance Frolic*, and later as a talk-show host. In subsequent years, he hosted a weekly big-band music program on the station. When Palmer Broadcasting founded WHO-TV, Williams did duty there as well, hosting the weeknight late movie among other things.

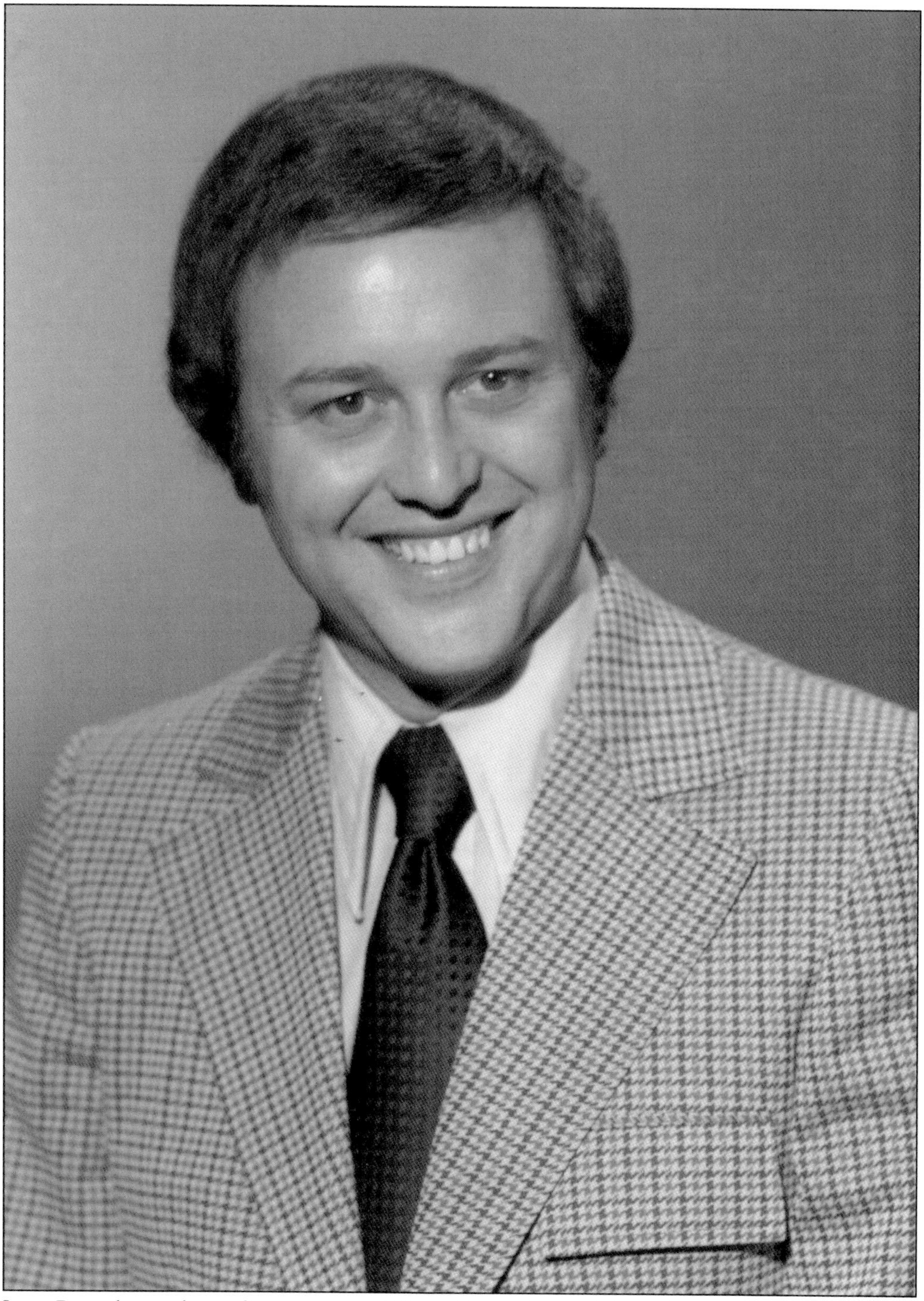

Jerry Reno began his radio career in 1959 and hosted a weekday, afternoon-drive-time music program on WHO Radio in the late 1960s and early 1970s. Reno was also a versatile talent, serving as WHO-TV's weathercaster for a decade, including time on Channel 13's *Eyewitness News*, where he shared the anchor desk with news anchors Jack Cafferty and Phil Thomas and sports director Jim Zabel in the mid-1970s.

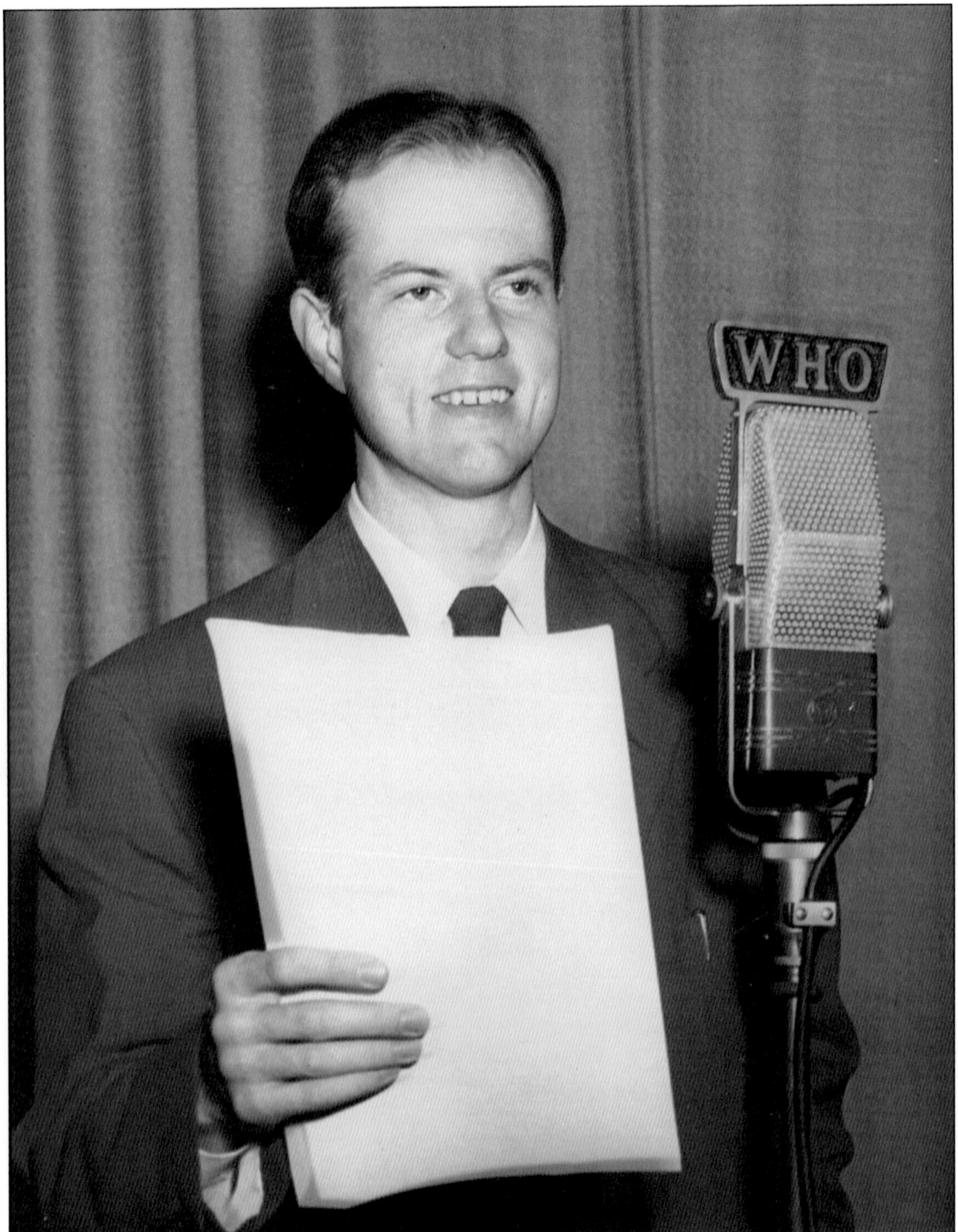

Duane Ellett, one of the WHO Music Men of the 1950s, is pictured in his role as a staff announcer for the station. The rarity of the photograph is that Ellett's right hand is visible; for 30 years, from 1957 until his death in 1987, Ellett was rarely seen in public without his puppet friend Floppy on his right hand, delighting thousands of children through television and personal appearances around Iowa, including yearly performances at the Iowa State Fair.

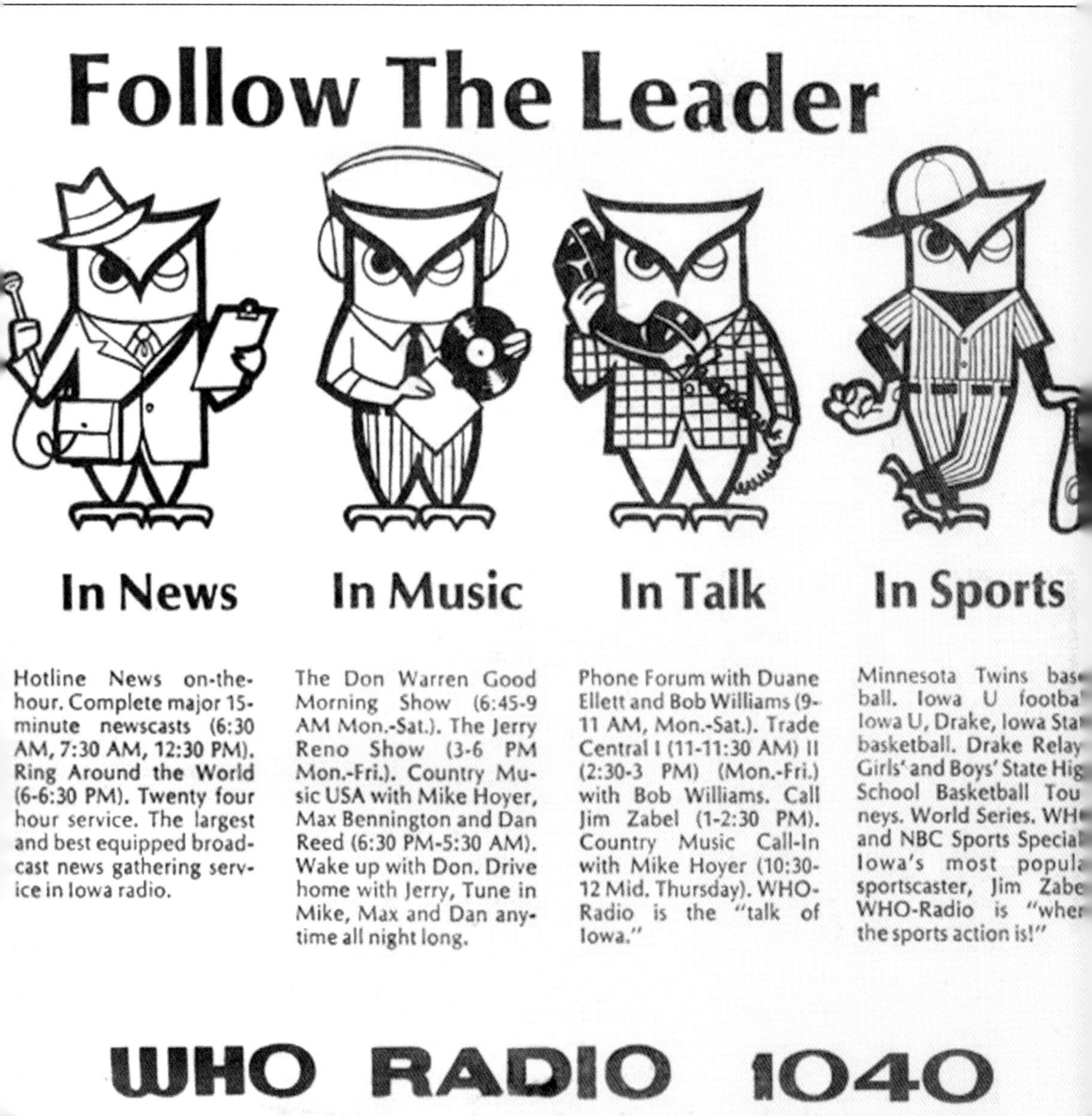

The WHO owl is personified in a variety of forms in this advertisement, which dates from 1969. In addition to promoting daily *WHO Hotline News* broadcasts and music programs such as the *Don Warren Good Morning Show* and the evening and overnight *Country Music USA*, the advertisement spotlights talk programs featuring Bob Williams, Duane Ellett, and Jim Zabel and sporting events featuring all the major Iowa universities as well as the Minnesota Twins major-league baseball team.

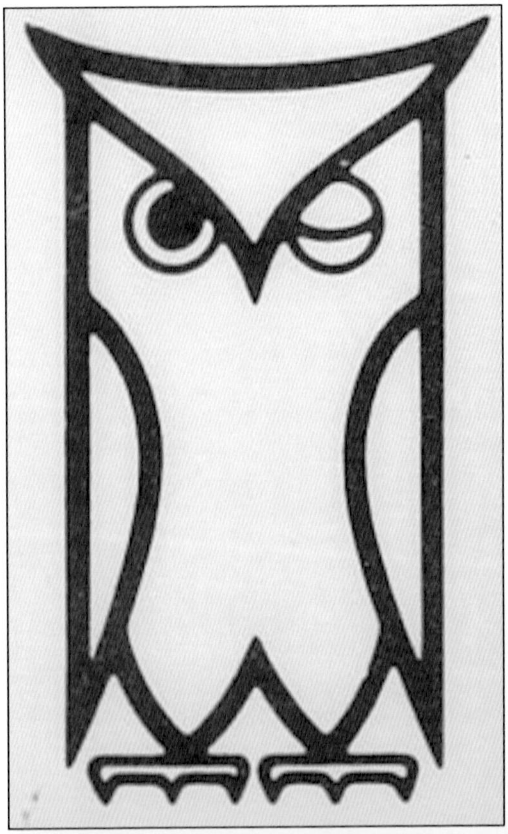

While the WHO owl logo has been around in one form or another for as long as the station has been on the air, the photograph at left depicts the logo that was used from the early 1960s into the 1980s. The logo was also used by WHO-TV 13 when the Palmer family owned both stations. In the 1980s, WHO Radio adopted the tagline, "The Spirit of Iowa," and discontinued use of the owl as part of a move to attract younger listeners. A stylized version of the owl soon returned to grace WHO promotional materials in the early 1990s (see page 127).

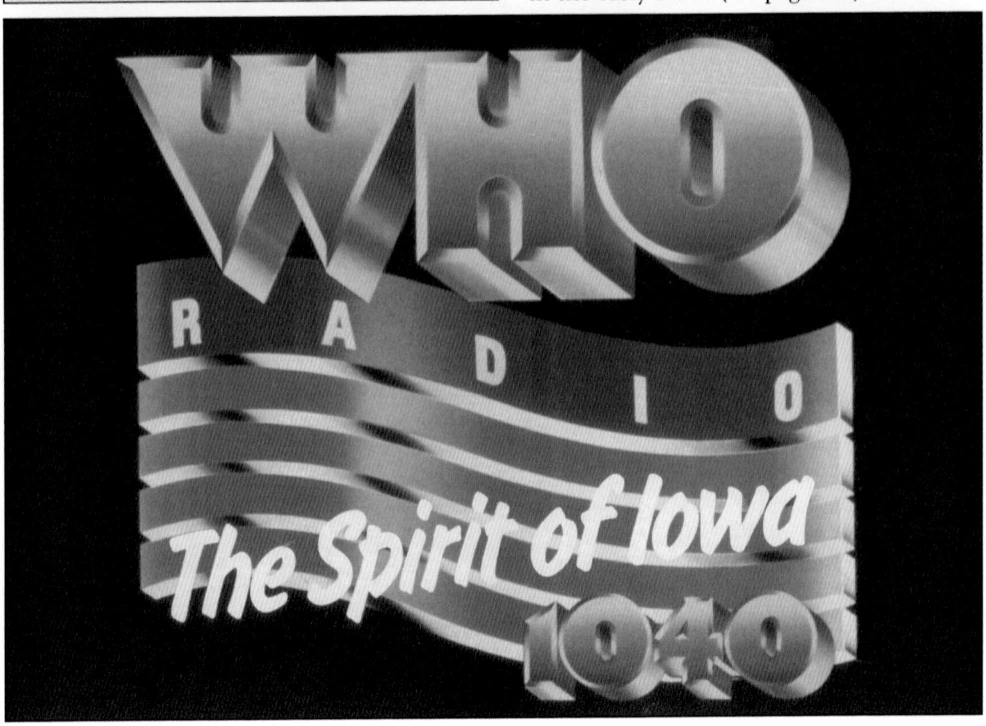

Nine

Providing a Community Service

Radio was an industry that proved the theory that technology evolves faster than the law's ability to control or regulate it. The earliest stations were often operated as experiments by physics and engineering professors at universities. Dozens of stations operated in America without any regulation at all into the 1920s when the first problems of signal overlap arose. Because radio waves travel through the electromagnetic spectrum, the federal government opted to regulate those waves by treating the spectrum as a natural resource, not owned by any individual but instead owned by all citizens. Government regulation would preserve the resource and make it available for the best use of all, much as government regulates the air and waterways to limit pollution.

The first legislation to comprehensively regulate the new medium of radio was the Radio Act of 1927, which placed authority in a new commission operating under the Commerce Department. The secretary of commerce at the time was Herbert Hoover, who soon would become Iowa's only native-born president.

In November 1929, the publication *Radio News* commented on the first two years of government licensing and regulation of radio by noting, "Without codified radio laws and in the almost total absence of judicial precedents, the Federal Radio Commission is blazing a new trail. While some of its rulings and decisions have fallen upon individuals with severe precision, the Commission's entire regard has been for the interest, convenience and necessity of the American public." That language—that broadcast license holders must operate in the public interest, convenience, and necessity—has been in the law from the start.

A 1938 promotional publication for advertisers notes how the station viewed its public-service responsibilities:

> When money is needed to meet special emergencies, WHO can be depended on to raise it. When the bitter winter of 1935–1936 threatened Iowa Wild Life with extinction, H.R. Gross, WHO's news editor, raised more than $10,000.00 in cash and supplies, and an undeterminable amount of man-power to meet the crisis. . . . The Veterans' Forum, a weekly service broadcast for disabled veterans, has drawn in excess of 80,000 letters asking for help and advice on adjusted compensation.
>
> The record goes on and on and on. But, it may be summed up in the statement that WHO is humbly grateful to be able to serve [and] is serenely proud of the record to date.

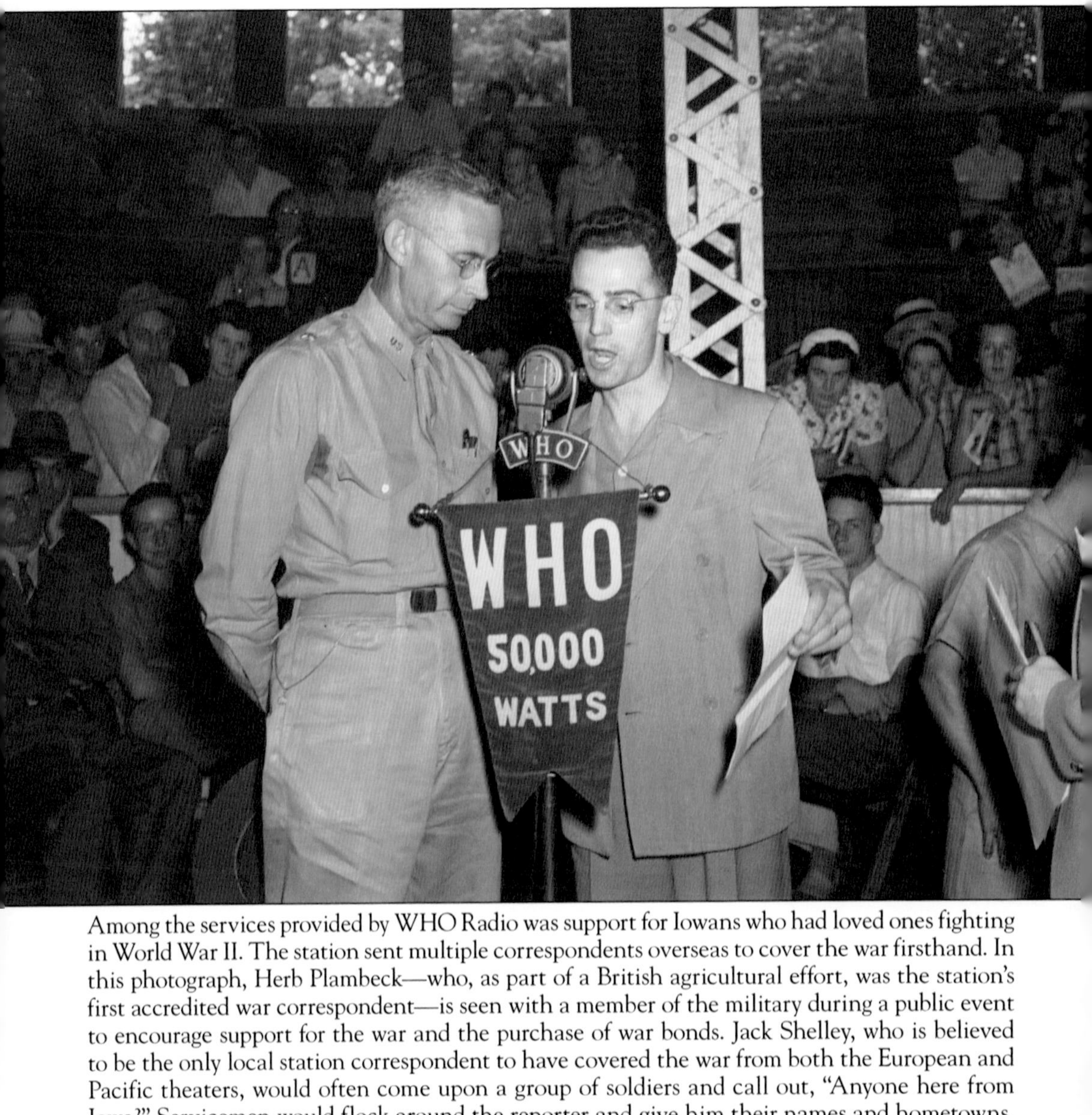

Among the services provided by WHO Radio was support for Iowans who had loved ones fighting in World War II. The station sent multiple correspondents overseas to cover the war firsthand. In this photograph, Herb Plambeck—who, as part of a British agricultural effort, was the station's first accredited war correspondent—is seen with a member of the military during a public event to encourage support for the war and the purchase of war bonds. Jack Shelley, who is believed to be the only local station correspondent to have covered the war from both the European and Pacific theaters, would often come upon a group of soldiers and call out, "Anyone here from Iowa?" Servicemen would flock around the reporter and give him their names and hometowns, whether from Iowa or surrounding Midwestern states. Those names and hometowns would be repeated by Shelley during his daily broadcasts back to Des Moines via shortwave radio, and they undoubtedly provided great relief to families back home, who crowded around their radios late at night on the chance the reporter might have seen their son, brother, or husband and could confirm his well-being.

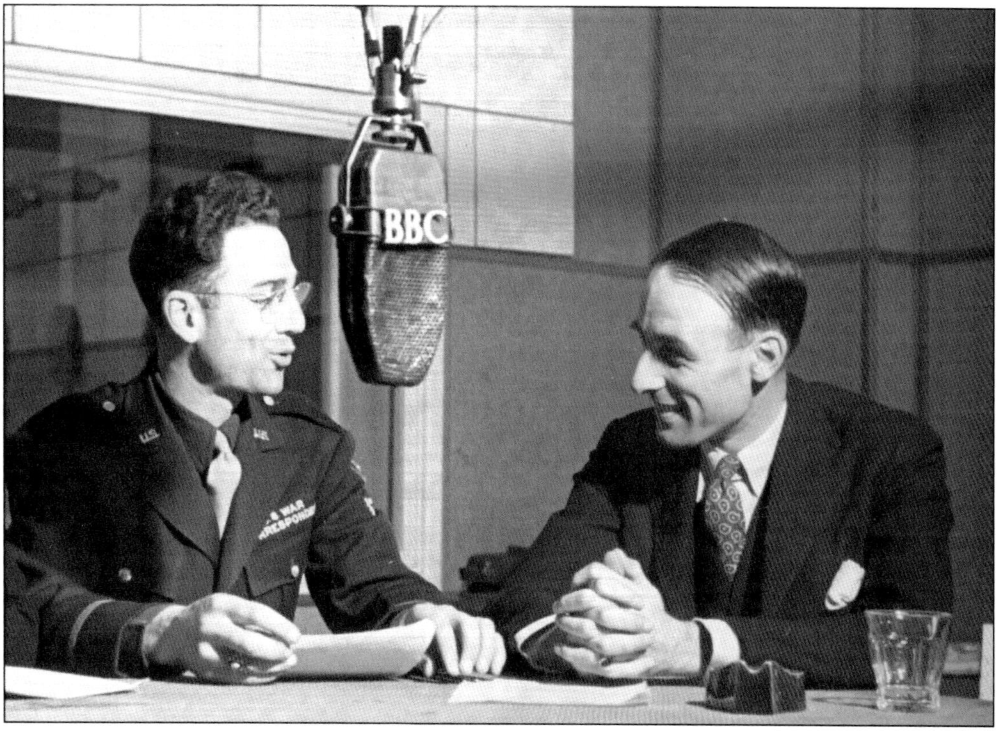

Herb Plambeck (above, left) did a number of broadcasts from England on BBC Radio and was in Germany at the time of V-E Day in 1945, leading to a special 30-minute Mother's Day program, where he recorded dozens of servicemen saying hello to their mothers. Jack Shelley garnered the first broadcast interviews of the crew that dropped the first atomic bombs on Japan. His Pacific theater reporting was based from a B-29 base in Guam, where he interviewed these servicemen (below) shortly before the Hiroshima and Nagasaki bombings. Both Plambeck and Shelley were known for their sharp writing and attention to detail, describing the scenes of war they saw in a manner that brought clear images to the minds of listeners.

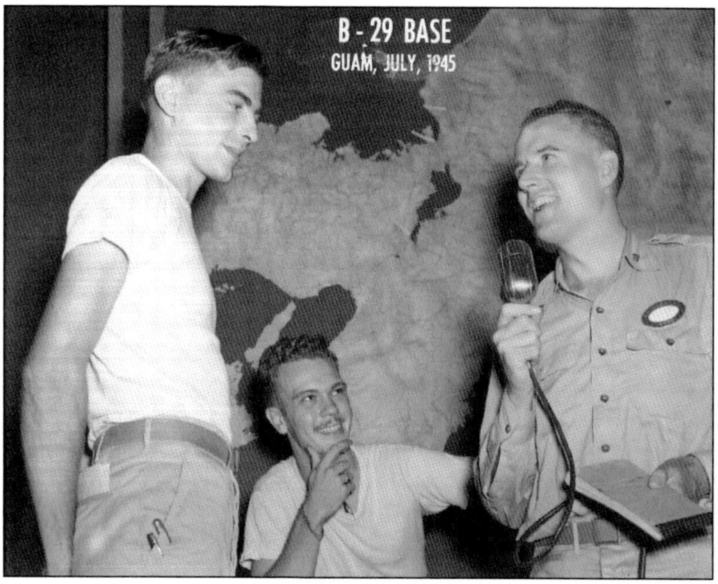

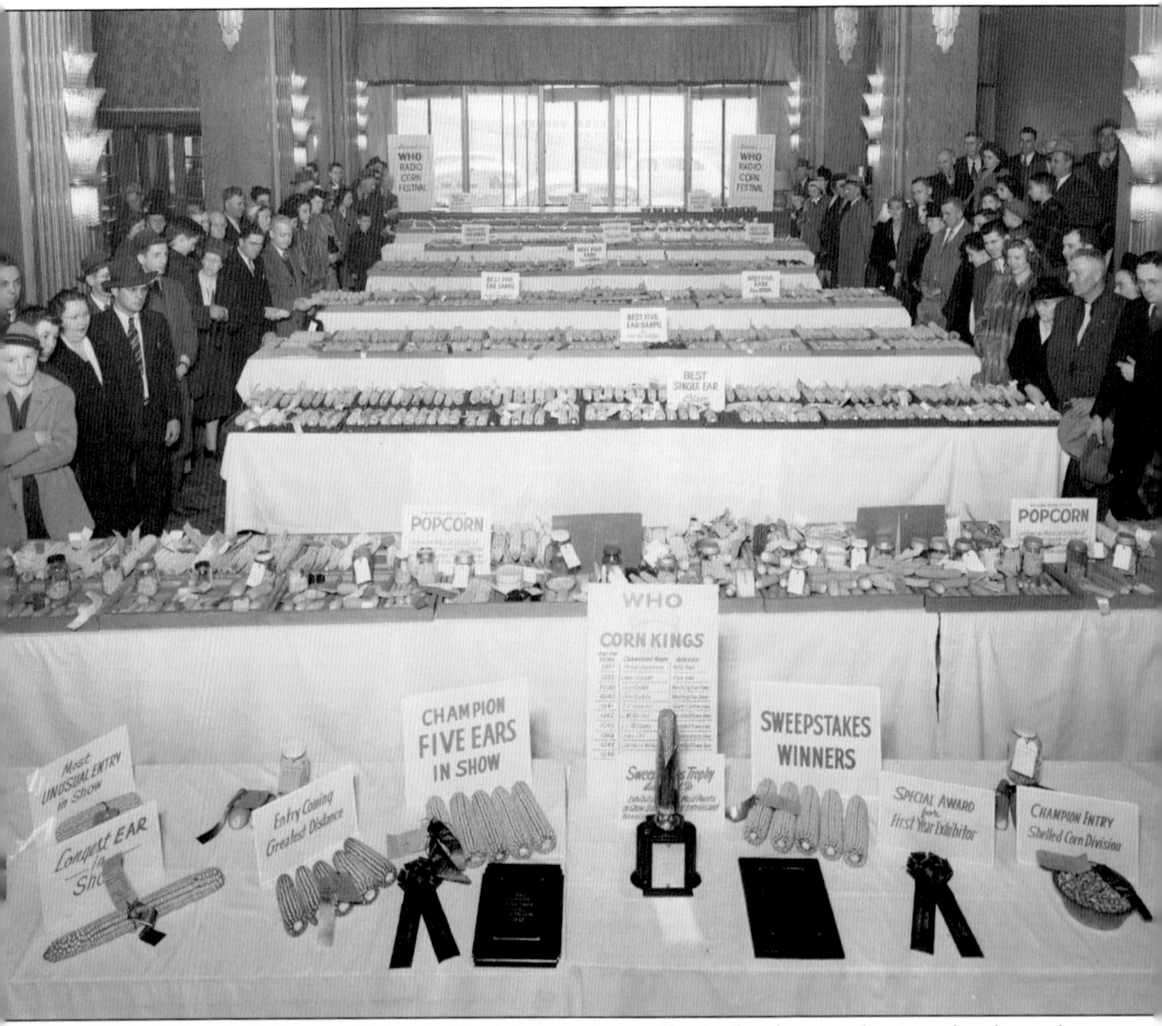

The studios at 914 Locust Street in Des Moines were well suited to large gatherings thanks to the ample studio space that was a hallmark of the pre-television days of radio. This photograph is from the WHO Radio Corn Festival in 1947, which attracted competitors from around the country, as well as a significant number of onlookers. The station's commitment to agriculture and supporting good farming practices has been recognized nationally by farming and conservation organizations.

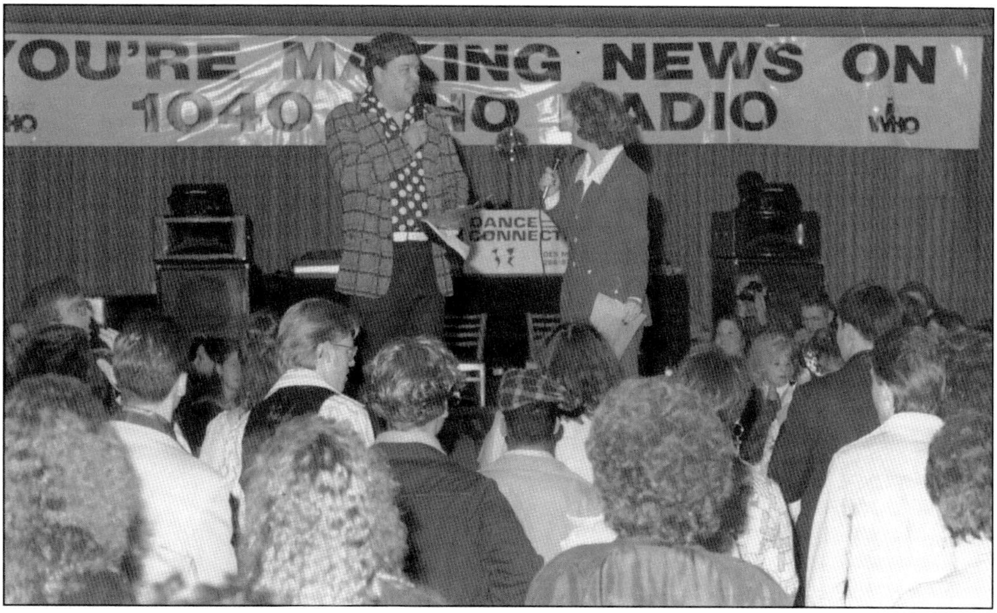

Sometimes community service takes on a less serious form. For about 10 years in the late 1980s and early 1990s, WHO Radio hosted the National Leisure Suit Convention at the Val Air Ballroom in Des Moines, encouraging listeners to search deep into their closets for their best disco-era clothing and relive the glory days of the 1970s; each year, some 3,000 persons did just that. These photographs, from the 1995 convention, show Van and Bonnie encouraging the crowd (above) and a quartet of WHO Radio staffers—from left to right, Bob Quinn, Jim Zabel, Jerry Reno, and meteorologist Gary Amble—reminding people why the fashion trend ended when it did.

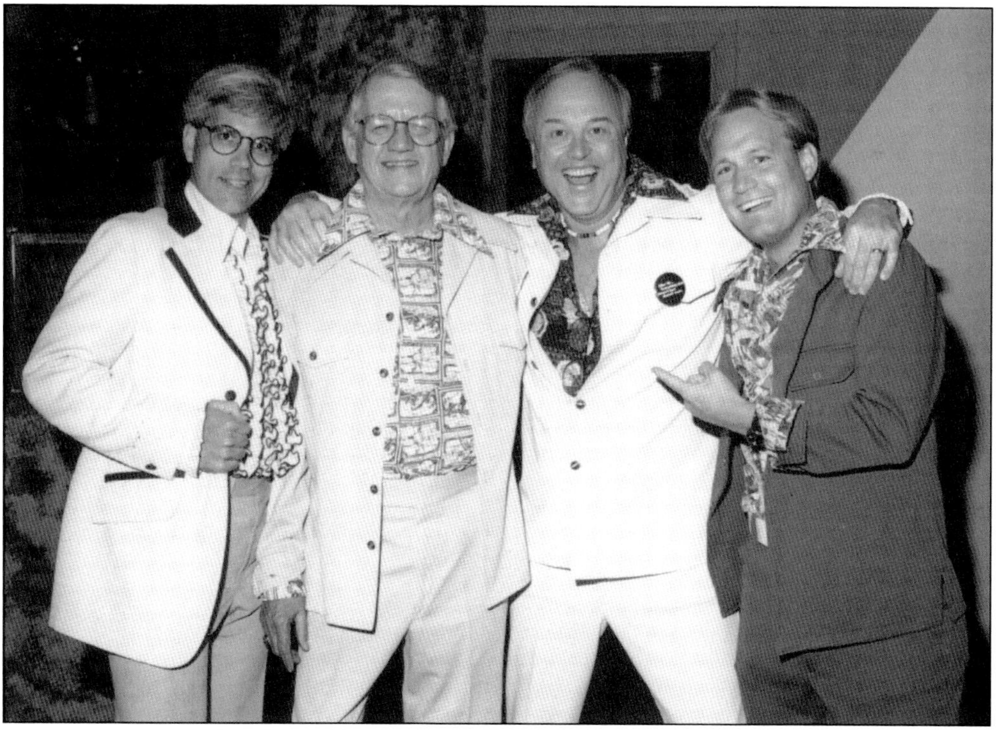

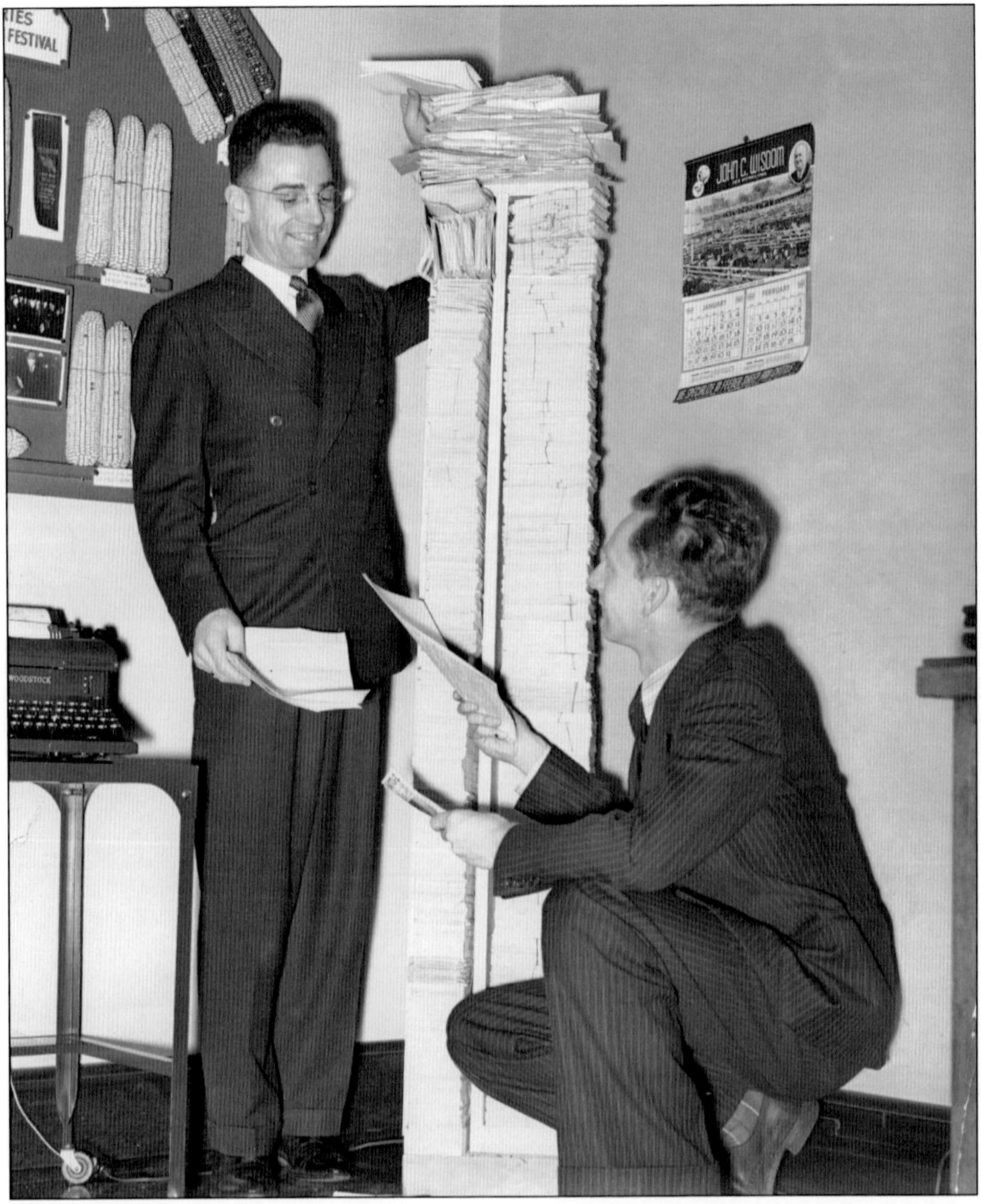

In the early 1940s, John Wisdom, owner of the Wisdom Livestock Company in Des Moines, became the 6:30 a.m. farm news sponsor on WHO Radio. On Christmas Eve 1943, rather than having an announcer read the normal message, Wisdom appeared on Herb Plambeck's broadcast in person and did a surprise commercial. He offered free illustrated, 12-inch-by-10-inch 1944 calendars to anyone who wrote WHO asking for one. Calendars were hard to find during the war, but Wisdom had been able to secure 5,000 of them. The only announcement of the calendar giveaway was that single commercial during the early-morning farm broadcast. On the first day of mail delivery after Christmas, a total of 4,255 calendar requests arrived. Within a week, the tally was 15,000. The final total topped 16,518, coming from 43 of the 48 states, five Canadian provinces, Mexico, and even England. Plambeck (left) is seen with an associate standing next to a stack of some of those letters with one of the popular Wisdom calendars hanging in the background.

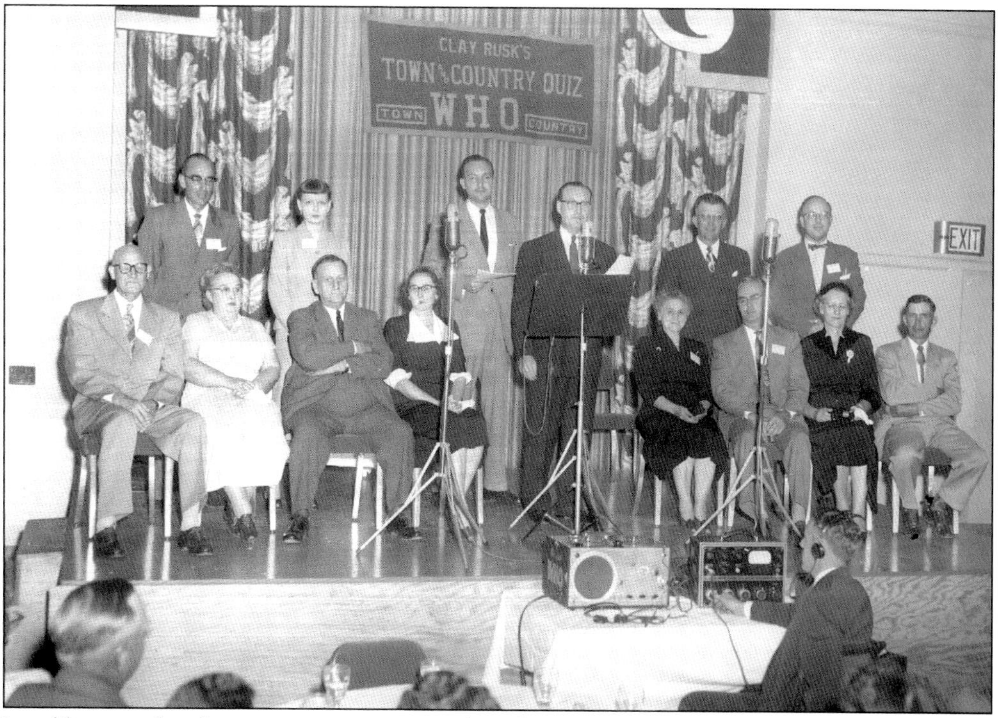

In addition to his duties as a newscaster and staff announcer for seven years in the late 1940s and early 1950s, Clay Rusk was quizmaster for the WHO *Town and Country Quiz*. Rusk would take the show to cities across Iowa as a fundraiser for local entities. An eight-page program for an October 8, 1952, edition of the quiz show in Bondurant was filled with advertising for area businesses and was sponsored by the local Future Farmers of America (FFA) chapter. Various local musical groups performed between segments of the quiz, which consisted of Rusk asking questions of two four-person teams, one representing "town" folks and the other made up of those from the "country." The show also featured local individuals who described the sponsoring FFA group and the town itself. Rusk took the *Town and Country Quiz* to some 325 communities in Iowa and surrounding states, typically to large crowds in local gymnasiums.

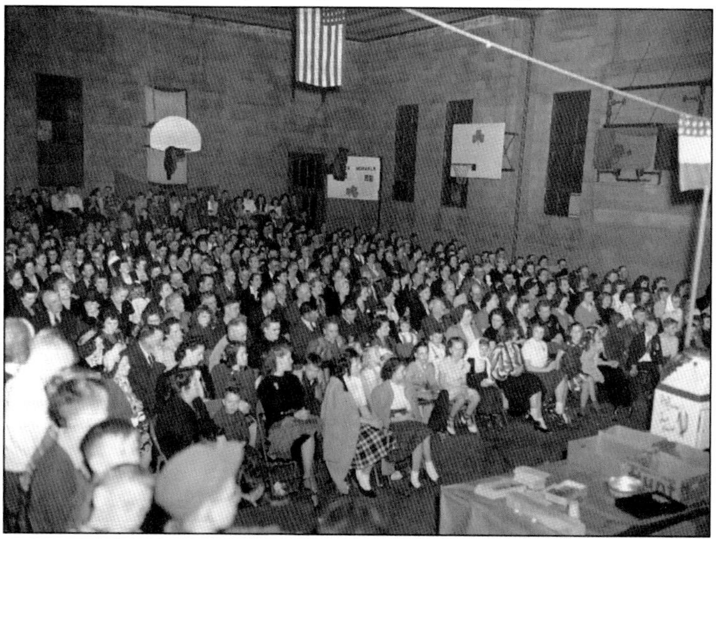

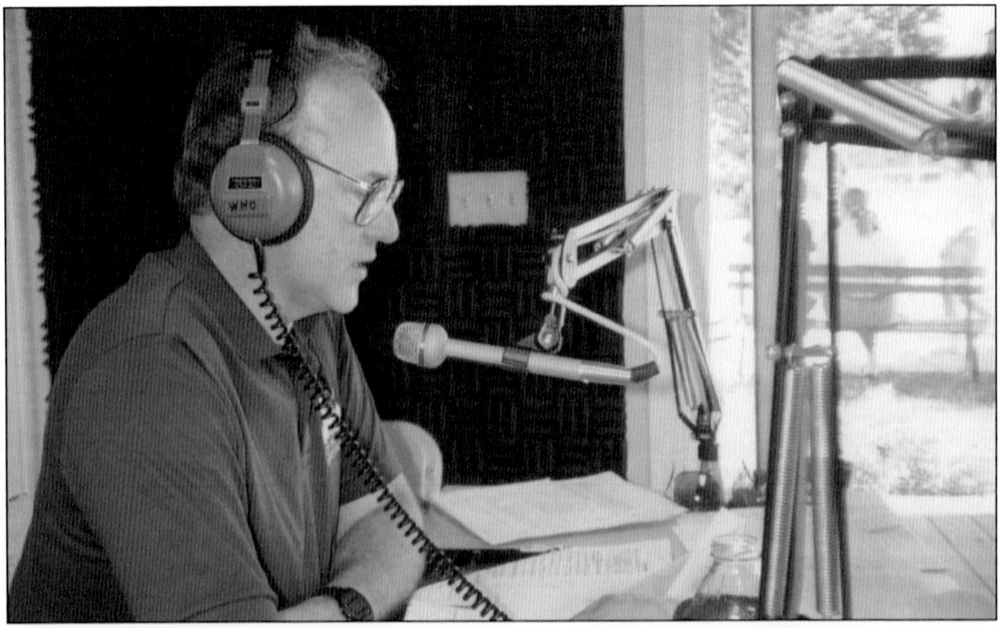

The WHO Crystal Studio has been a fixture at the Iowa State Fair since 1932, but it has taken on different forms over time. Fair attendees enjoy watching live broadcasts and meeting their favorite personalities. The current Crystal Studio is a permanent structure on the Grand Concourse and opened in 1987; it was remodeled in 2009. Jerry Reno is seen delivering news for *Drive Time Des Moines* during the 1989 Iowa State Fair.

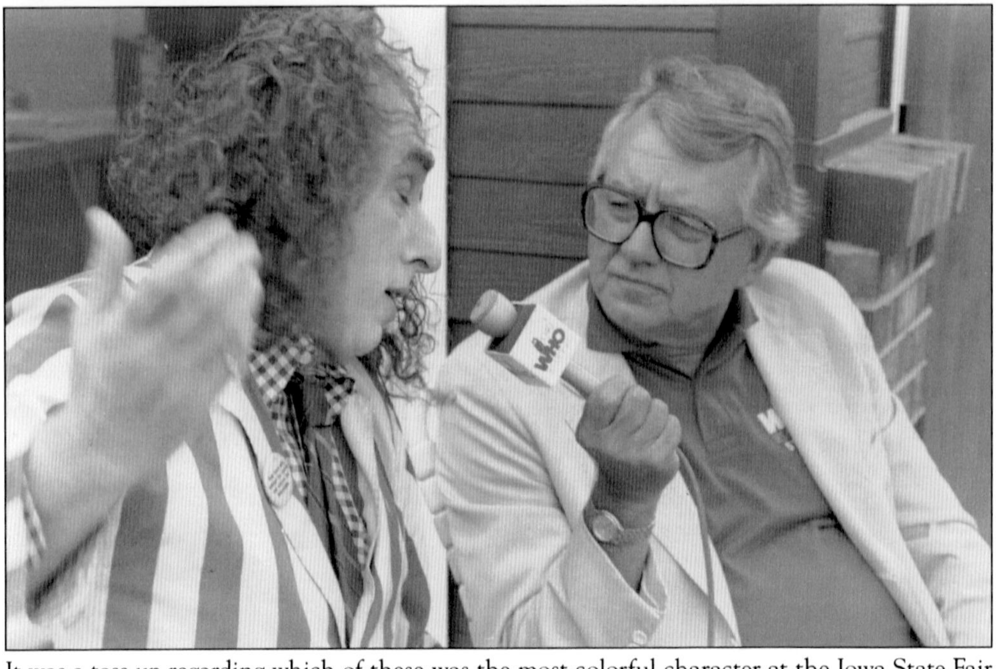

It was a toss-up regarding which of these was the most colorful character at the Iowa State Fair in 1989—novelty singer and performer Tiny Tim, who later in his career lived for a time in Des Moines, or WHO Radio personality Jim Zabel, who is seen interviewing Tiny Tim on the patio outside the WHO Crystal Studio.

In the days before cellular phones, more primitive communication methods were required to get information from one place to another. WHO Radio farm director Keith Kirkpatrick was one who used two-wheeled transportation—the so-called "WHO Pony Express"—to get from one end of the Iowa State Fairgrounds to the other in good time. Kirkpatrick is on his bicycle, with a tape recorder over one shoulder, in front of the grandstand.

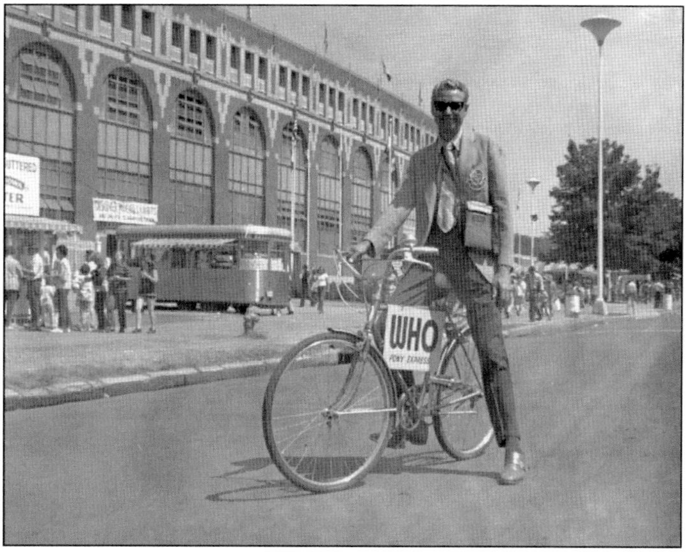

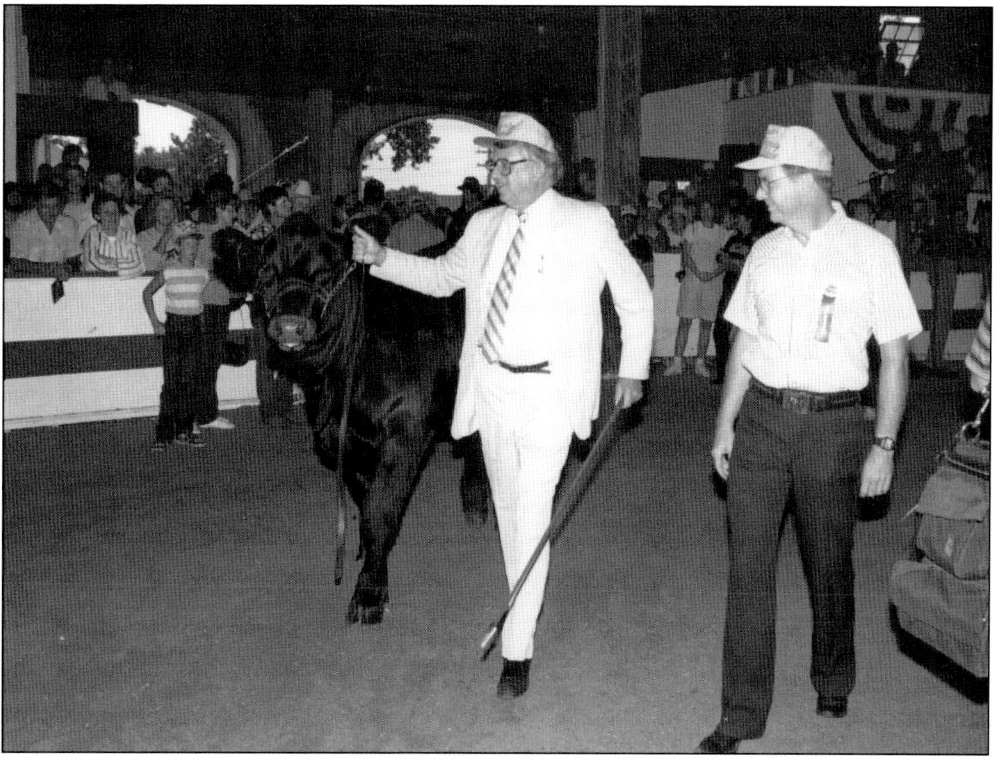

Since 1983, the Governor's Charity Steer Show has been a fixture at the Iowa State Fair to raise money for the Ronald McDonald Houses, aiding families with sick children. The event, sponsored by the Iowa Beef Industry Council and the Iowa Cattlemen's Association, has raised more than $1 million for the cause. Among the celebrities who have helped to promote the beef industry and raise money for charity at the event is WHO Radio's Jim Zabel, seen guiding a show contestant.

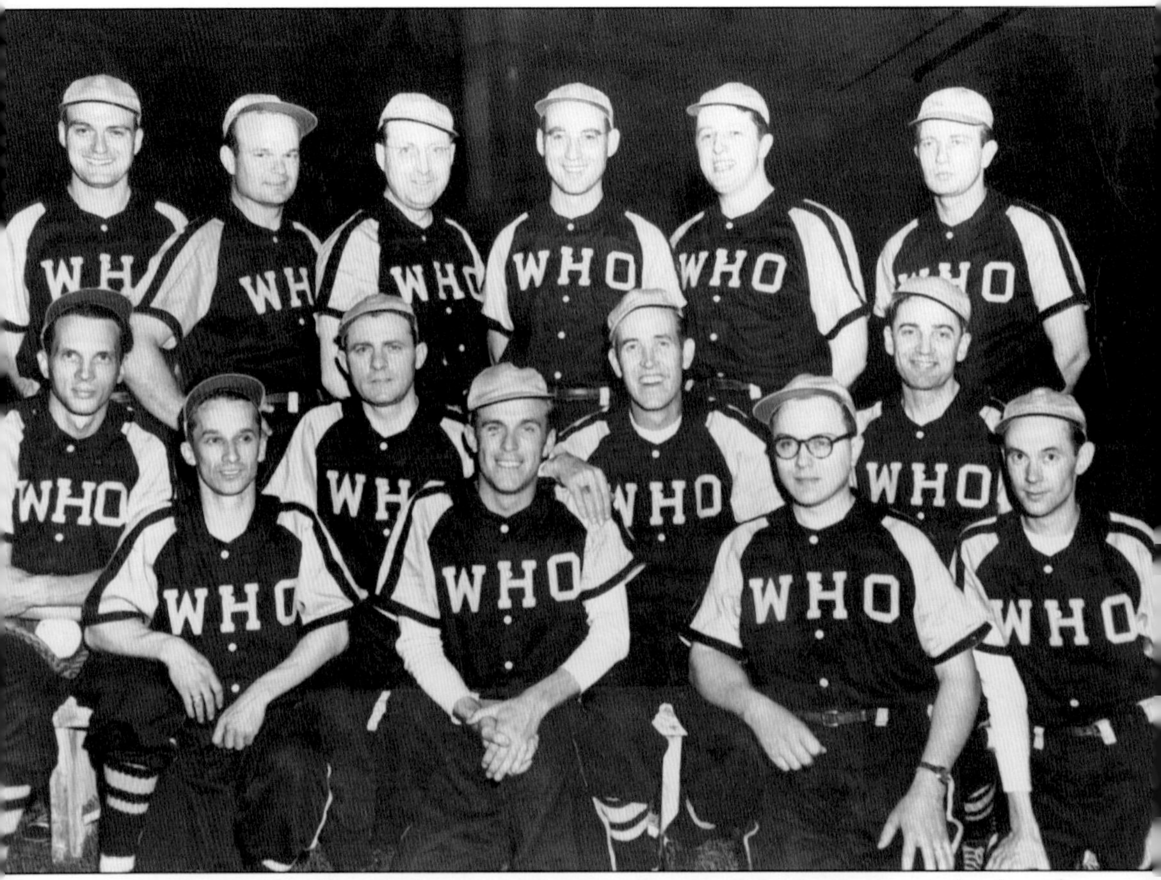

A common way for radio and television stations to connect with local communities has been for station personnel to form softball or basketball teams and travel throughout the region playing other local teams in fundraisers for various causes. This photograph from the mid-1950s shows a WHO softball team ready for action.

Ten

RADIO'S FUTURE

In an era of iPods® and smartphones, some are pessimistic about the future of radio. But in many respects, the future has never been brighter.

Even in the economic downturn of the current decade, radio shows signs of recovery when compared with other media. The Radio Advertising Bureau noted that radio posted its fifth straight quarter of advertising sales gains in the spring of 2011, especially in important categories such as automobiles, beverages, and insurance.

While music fans can select their own songs to listen to from their personal devices, nowhere besides radio can they find local personalities, information, and interaction. Radio plays a unique and significant role in reflecting the life of a community, as it has throughout its century of existence.

Even a station with the signal strength of WHO Radio reflects the life of its community. Des Moines is rated by the Arbitron firm as the 90th-largest radio market in America, and WHO Radio is consistently at the top of the ratings list. In the last five ratings periods alone, WHO Radio tops all stations in the 17-station market, leading its closest competitor by at least a full ratings point and often the only station with a double-digit share. Those ratings are limited to central Iowa. Enhancing the true numbers of citizens who spend part of their day with Newsradio 1040 is the fact that WHO consistently shows up in the ratings of other adjacent markets, outpacing many local stations in those markets.

But rather than resting on success, the station continues to evolve to meet the expectations of a changing audience. The WHO Radio signal reaches a global audience via the Internet, with online streaming from www.whoradio.com. Podcasts of many talk programs are available for downloading and listening at any time. Show hosts have blogs and personal web pages and are active on social media platforms, such as Facebook and Twitter. The WHO Radio website offers online-only contests and information for site visitors. Mobile applications for iPad® and Android® devices are now available.

At most stations, personalities come and go. In the case of WHO Radio, most stay for a career. Iowans know they can still rely on 1040 WHO to carry on in the tradition they grew up with, a comfort for many given all the uncertainties in the world today.

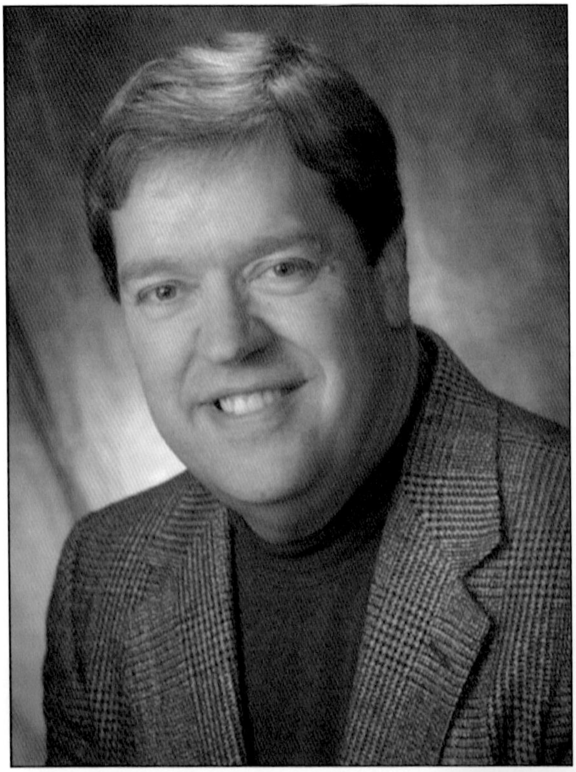

They may claim to just be "a couple of small town kids trying to make it in the big city," but WHO Radio's morning team of Van Harden and Bonnie Lucas consistently has the highest rated program on Iowa radio. Their weekday program actually begins at 4:59 a.m., and they count a surprising number of listeners who claim to be "4:59ers," folks who are there for the very start of each day's program.

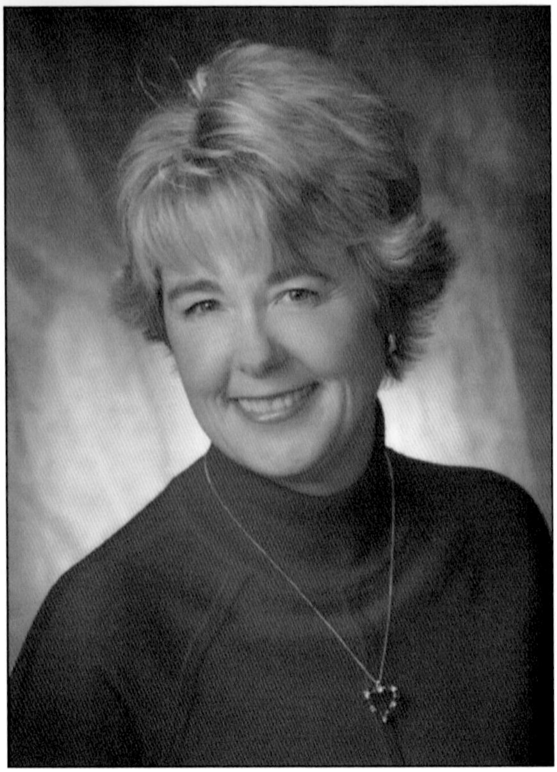

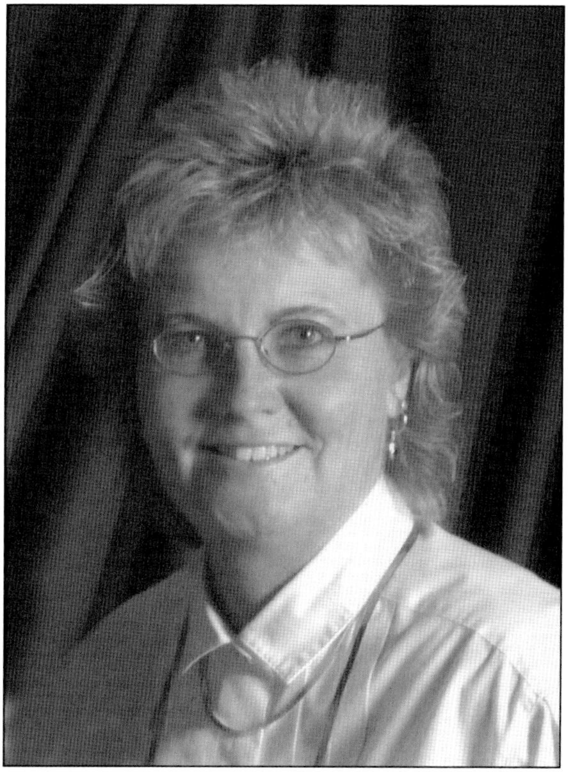

In addition to their regular duties Monday through Friday, WHO Radio operations manager Cheryl Pannier and weekday morning news anchor Dick Layman team up for the *Saturday Morning Live* program from 6:00 a.m. to 9:00 a.m. The self-proclaimed one-of-a-kind morning show is designed to start the weekend off on a lighthearted note.

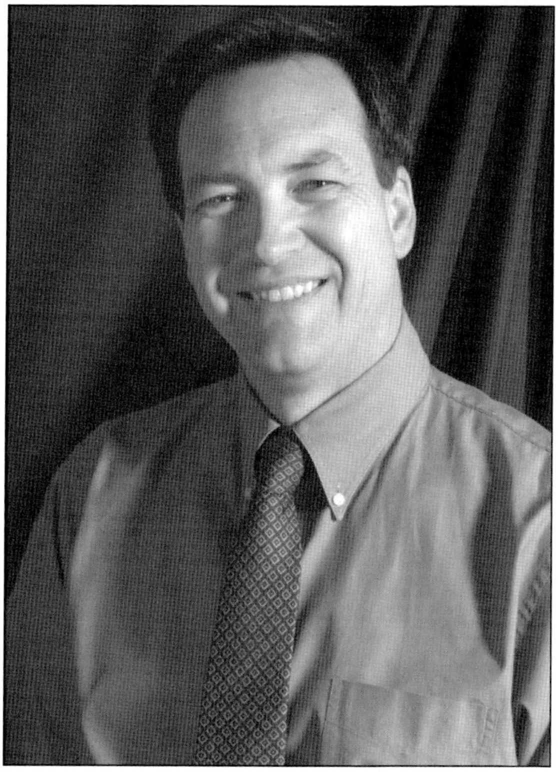

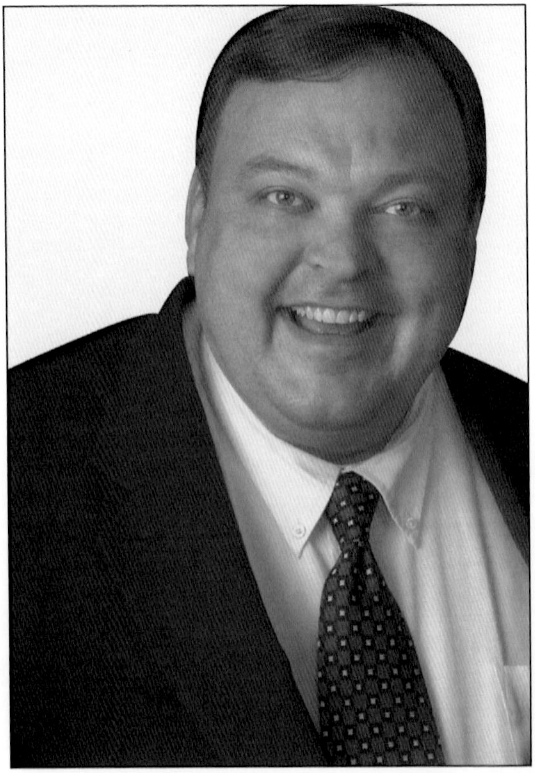

WHO Radio's farm department presents the *Big Show* weekdays from 11:30 a.m. to 1:00 p.m., featuring Mark Pearson (left) and Bob Quinn (below). The program is carried on a number of other Iowa radio stations as well. Since 1996, WHO Radio has sponsored the Great Iowa Tractor Ride, the success of which has spawned a second fall tractor ride as well. Quinn also delivers a series of morning farm reports, including market updates and agribusiness news.

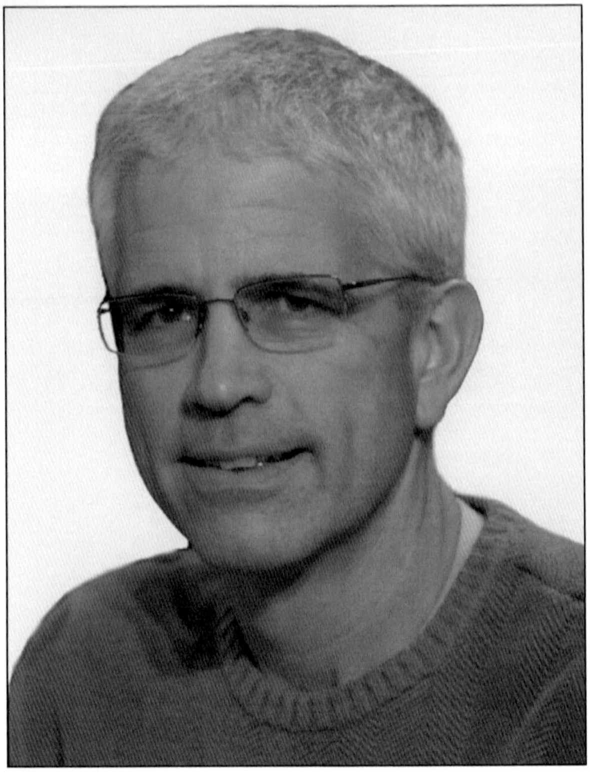

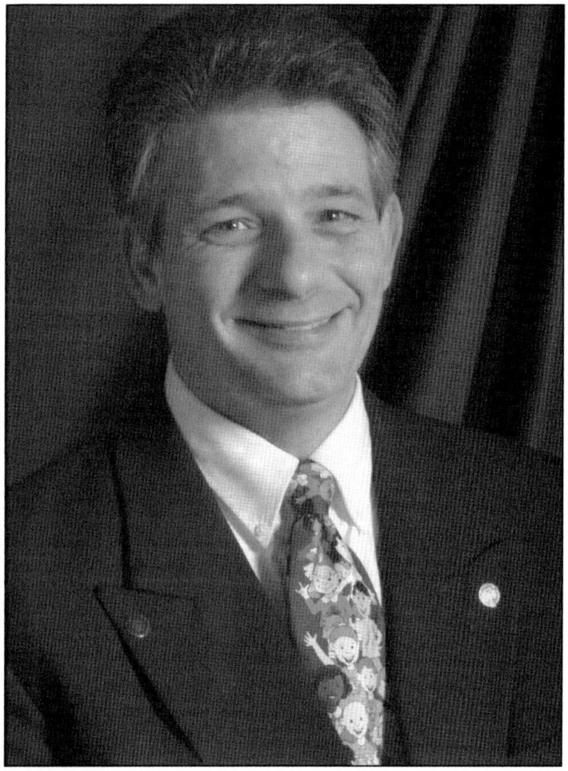

The legendary WHO Radio news department is led by news director Jim Boyd and anchor-reporter Sue Danielson. Boyd was awarded the Jack Shelley Award for lifetime achievement from the Iowa Broadcast News Association in 2001 and was formerly news director at WMT Radio in Cedar Rapids, another legendary station. Danielson is an award-winning reporter who cohosted the news-oriented *Drive Time Des Moines* afternoon program for nearly 20 years.

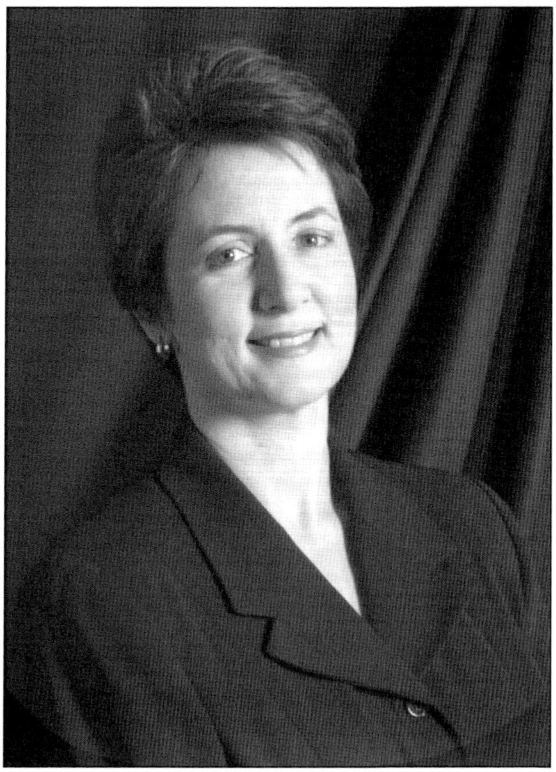

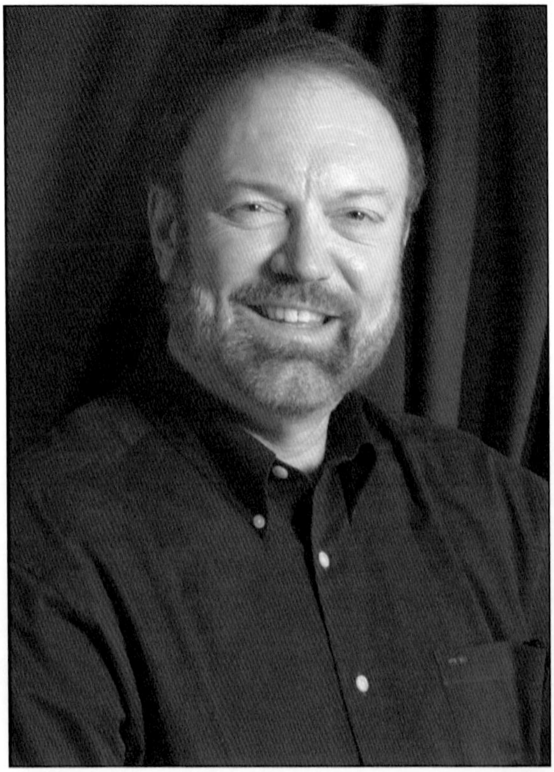

The tradition of local talk radio continues today with the popular program hosted by Jan Mickelson (left) weekday mornings from 9:00 a.m. to 11:30 a.m. and newcomer Simon Conway's (below) three-hour afternoon program from 4:00 p.m. to 7:00 p.m. Mickelson has been on the WHO Radio airwaves since 1988, while Conway started his program in 2011.

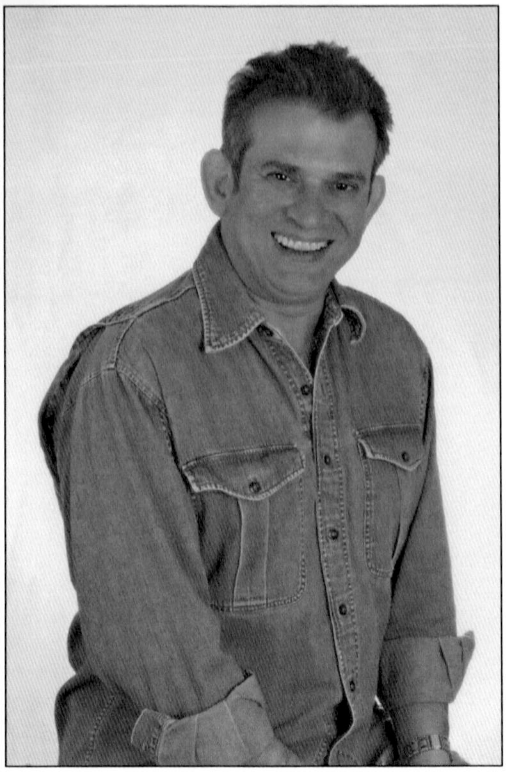

Joel McCrea serves as vice president and market manager for the Clear Channel Communications–owned properties in central Iowa. This includes WHO Radio and two other AM stations and four FM stations licensed to Des Moines and Ames. McCrea recently completed a term as president of the Iowa Broadcasters Association, the state's organization of owners and managers.

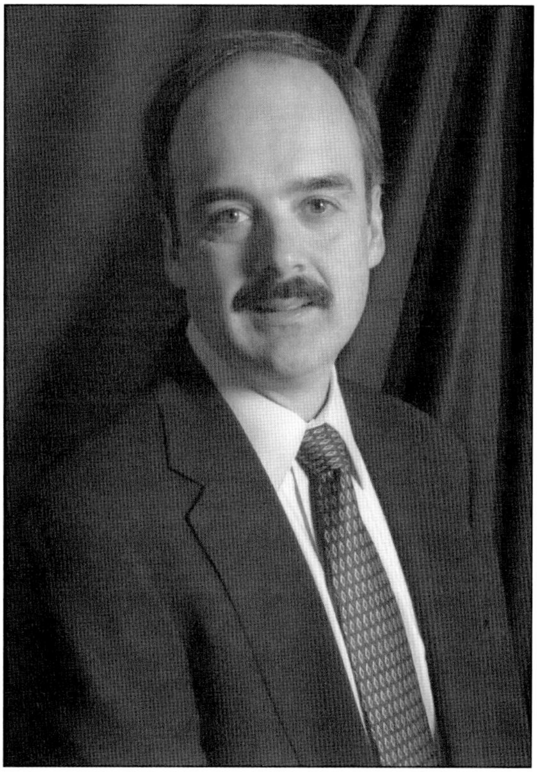

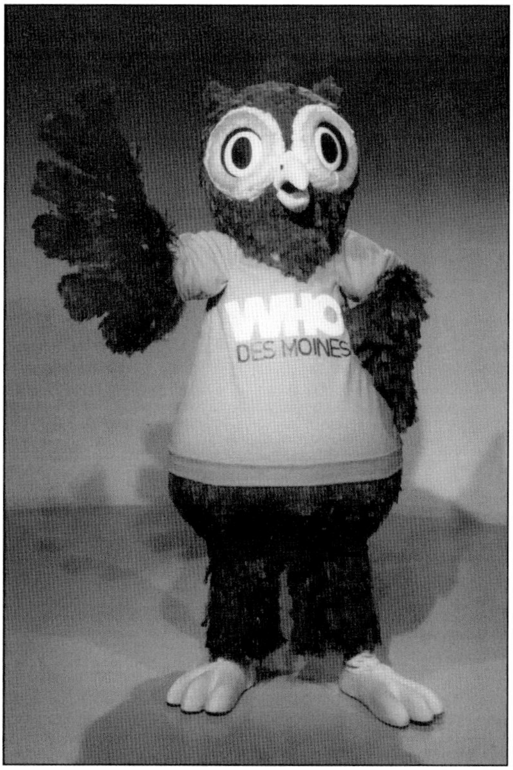

The WHO Radio Owl was personified in the 1980s and 1990s and frequently made personal appearances in a six-foot-tall owl suit, complete with bright red T-shirt.

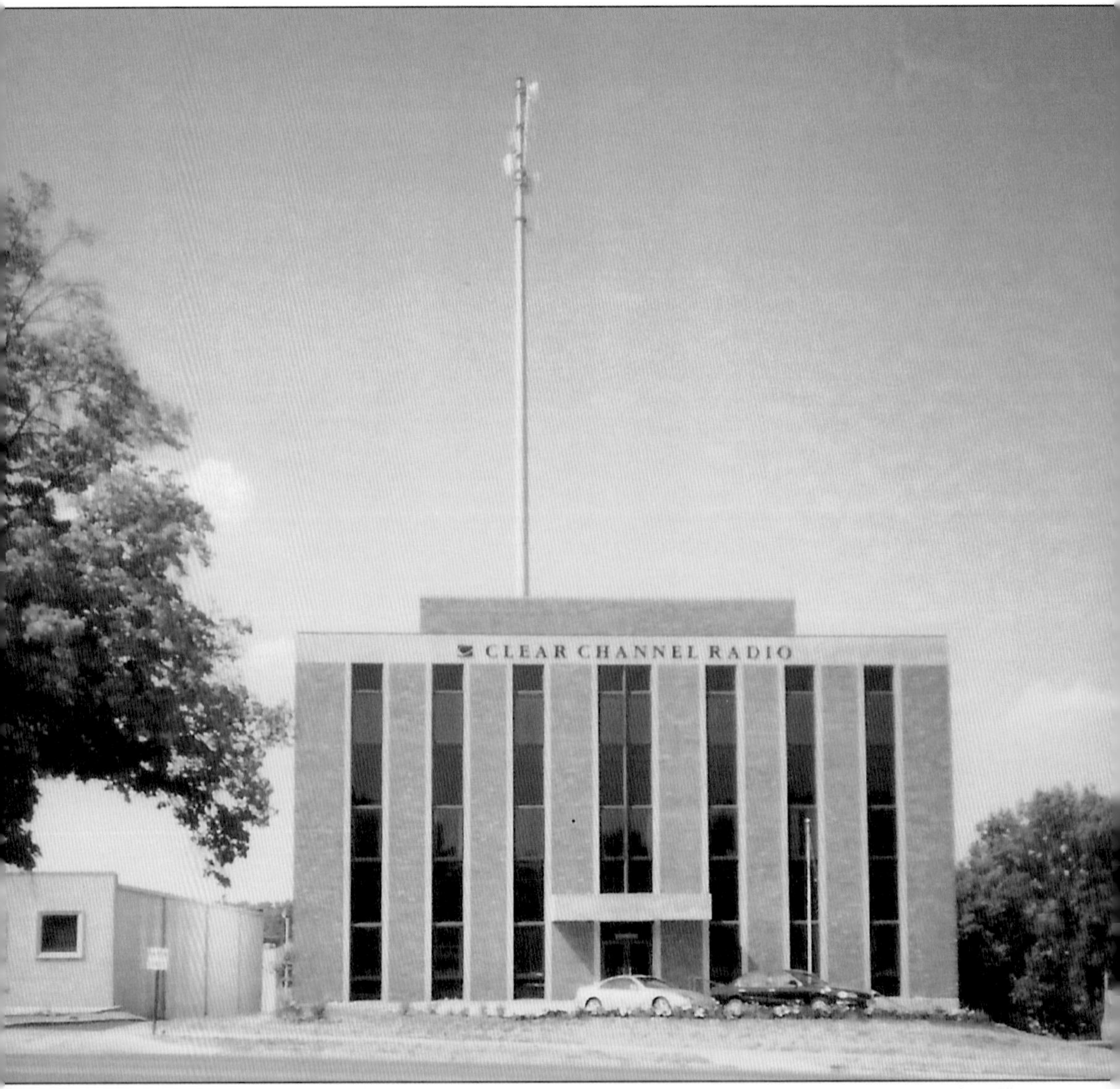

After two decades housed with WHO television in facilities at 1801 Grand Avenue, the Clear Channel Communications radio stations were moved in the spring of 2005 to a custom-built location just up the street at 2141 Grand Avenue. The building provides ample space for growth and the expansion into other modes of communication, including the Internet technology required to operate radio stations today.

WHO

NEWSRADIO 1040

A 1939 station publication described how a radio program gets from the broadcasting studio to a listener's home. In part, it describes the output as when "your radio set separates the carrier wave and the electrical impulse, throws out the carrier wave, and sends the electrical impulse to the loud speaker of your set. That makes the loud speaker vibrate just as the inside of the microphone vibrated. This makes sound waves in the air, and when the sound waves reach your ear drums you hear the same sound that started way back in the studio." That is a fairly clinical description of the process, but the real connection between the signal sent by the station and the audience that receives it is a personal one. If the station is devoted to serving the public through the programming it presents, the bond created between a listener and his or her favorite radio station or personalities can be strong. In its nine decades of service to the people of Iowa and the nation, WHO Radio has created one of the strongest station-listener bonds in history—and given the audience ratings and response, there is no sign of that bond changing anytime soon.